Student Book Clubs:
Improving Literature Instruction in Middle and High School

Student Book Clubs:
Improving Literature Instruction in Middle and High School

Mark Faust

Jennifer Cockrill

Cheryl Hancock

Holly Isserstedt

Christopher-Gordon Publishers, Inc.
Norwood, Massachusetts

Copyright Acknowledgments

Christopher~Gordon Publishers, Inc.
Bridging Theory and Practice

1502 Providence Highway, Suite #12
Norwood, Massachusetts 02062

800-934-8322
781-762-5577
www.Christopher-Gordon.com

Printed in the United State of America
10 9 8 7 6 5 4 3 2 1   07 06 05

ISBN: 1-929024-82-7
Library of Congress Catalogue Number: 2004110623

Table of Contents

Introduction

> "If three or four persons agree to read the same book, and each bring his own remarks upon it, at the same set hours appointed for conversation, and they communicate mutually their sentiments on the subject, and debate about it in a friendly manner, this practice will render reading of any author more abundantly beneficial to every one of them."
>
> —Ian Watts, *The Improvement of the Mind* (1811)

A book club, as we understand and use the phrase, is an umbrella concept that covers a wide variety of experiences and contexts of reading. Whenever two or more people voluntarily convene on a regular basis for the purpose of talking about their reading, we think it is fair to say they are creating a book club. In the early stages of writing this book, the four of us came to a realization that each of us has a long history of sharing books one-to-one with family members and others, yet until very recently none of us would have thought to call what we were doing a book club. Nonetheless, we are proposing that these experiences—and parallel experiences described by other adults we have met during the past several years—serve as a powerful starting point for explaining what we mean when we say that book clubs, whether they take place in academic settings or elsewhere, have the potential to enhance reading as a social event without negating the personal space that, for many people, is an essential aspect of what has led them to choose lives that include reading.

Almost without exception, adults who are avid readers can trace their love for books back to early experiences of being read to as children. That special connection with at least one other human being made possible through a shared experience with a book forms a lasting impression that many people remember throughout their lives. For some, that memory remains dormant during their school-age years to be rekindled later in life by the realization that private, intensely personal experiences with reading are not necessarily compromised when shared with others, that is, provided those others are motivated by an ethic of care. One of the striking things we have noticed while participating in book clubs with other adults is the way people talk about rediscovering the heartfelt enthusiasm they felt for reading as a child.

Sadly, many adults point to a loss of enthusiasm for reading as a direct consequence of school-based literature instruction. This book addresses that concern head on through our approach to using student book clubs based on an honest appraisal of how and why we as adults read literature in our personal lives combined with an equally honest appraisal of the potential value of schooling with respect to the goal of helping students not just to become life-long readers but to become adults who use reading to make a difference in their lives.

Give him a few minutes and Mark will gladly describe the transformative power of reading books on spirituality and parenting as well as the occasional work of fiction with his wife. The same could be said about Jennifer who similarly shares an active reading life with her husband. Cheryl and two of her colleagues frequently discuss books they have read in common and share ideas for further reading. In addition, as a parent of two young children, much of her reading revolves around their interests. Holly is a passionate, omnivorous reader of contemporary fiction and will strike up a conversation with just about anyone who shows an interest in a recently published book. None of these experiences would qualify as a book club in a strict sense, but we would argue that all of them open up a space for active listening, exploratory talk, and self-formation that are the hallmark of what can happen when groups of adults choose to read books together whether or not they call what they are doing a book club. Like the adults interviewed by Appleyard (1991) and others (e.g., Atwell-Vasey,1998; Long, 2003; and Sumara 1996) we would describe our reading as "pragmatic" in the sense that we seek experiences with books that make a difference in our lives by helping us engage, immediately and concretely, with ourselves, others, and the world at large.

Part 1 of this book (Teachers as Readers) includes an opening chapter that explains why we are not ashamed to identify ourselves as "amateur" readers and introduces us as individuals who see a connection between our teaching practice and reading we choose to do in the context of our personal lives. Among the various influences on our lives as readers, the experience of reading with others stands out. In fact it was a book club experience that brought the four of us together and initiated the conversations that ultimately led us to formulate our concept of a student book club. Jennifer, Cheryl, and Holly all enrolled in a university class Mark had designed to provide teachers with (1) a first-hand experience of what it is like to participate in a book club and (2) a context for considering the potential role of book clubs in middle and secondary school classrooms.

A second chapter, in which we situate ourselves as amateur readers/language arts teachers, follows up on our individual profiles as we elaborate on specific practices that for us are associated with reading experiences that are worth having. We invite you to join us in considering what it means to live a life that includes reading. We do not believe there is a language arts teacher anywhere who does not embrace the goal of helping his/her students become "life-long readers." At the same time, we think most teachers— beginning with ourselves—should devote more attention to this issue. Thus, we open our book by responding to provocative questions, such as: Why is becoming a life-long reader a worthwhile goal? How does someone become a life-long reader? What and how do life-long readers read? In what ways do typical secondary school curricula support and/or hinder a desire among teenagers to become life-long readers? In responding to these and other related questions, we situate ourselves as "amateur" readers who use what we know about language and literature to enhance the value of reading in our personal lives. As such, we distinguish what we do from those who explicitly pursue a scholarly or academic stance toward reading literature.

In Part 2 (Readers as Teachers) each of us takes a turn describing in detail the challenges we overcame in order to successfully engage students ranging in age from 14 to adult with book clubs across very different academic contexts. Though representing our different styles and perspectives, these four chapters are joined by a common desire to avoid a prescriptive, cookie-cutter approach as we illustrate and explain what distinguishes our idea of student book clubs from the more free-wheeling concept of literature circles advocated by Daniels (2002) and others. Typically, literature circles are framed as a supplemental approach to reading, offering students an additional alternative within the language arts curriculum (e.g., Chandler, 1997). Our definition of student book clubs is geared more toward recognizing students as readers within the confines of a mainstream literature curriculum. As such, our approach is based on a theoretical stance toward reading as an open-ended, exploratory process. We encourage practices that help students see the value of critical thinking in connection with their personal responses to literature albeit in classroom contexts.

Our various experiments with using student book clubs as a tool for promoting the habit of reading widely and thoughtfully among high school students have grown out of our personal reflections on life-long reading. Here, as well, we invite you to join us in considering provocative questions related to our classroom practice: How does a student book club work? What does a good one look/sound like? What are good ways to anticipate the challenges a teacher should expect to face when introducing the concept of a student book club to middle and high school students? How might student book clubs be constructed so as to correlate with overall curricular goals?

In addition to offering practical guidelines for making student book clubs work in classrooms, this book includes a theoretical rationale that accounts for their value as a learning tool. Part 3 (Readers/Teachers as Learners) contains two chapters. Chapter 7 connects our overarching stance toward reading as a process with new developments in reader-response theory and in particular with our interpretation of Louise Rosenblatt's theory of "literature as exploration." Reading Rosenblatt as we do makes it possible to align her work with powerful claims about language and literacy advanced by the philosophers, Mikhail Bakhtin and Jacques Derrida, both of whom are discussed at length in Chapter 7. Altogether, this body of theoretical work offers strong support for a revaluation of amateur or life-long reading, which we believe goes hand in hand with raising tough questions about the way literature instruction is practiced in middle and secondary schools. The book concludes with a summary chapter that pulls together the multiple strands introduced throughout and offers some final thoughts for teachers who are inspired to experiment with student book clubs with their own students.

This book also includes material facilitating various ways of reading and using our work. Each of us has created a file containing materials related to our different approaches to using a concept of student book clubs in structuring our classroom practice. Readers who find themselves gravitating toward one or another of these approaches can easily access the relevant materials for use in their own classrooms. We have designed this book so that the chapters in Part 2 can stand alone as individual descriptions of our classroom practice. This decision is based on an assumption that not all our prospective readers will be interested in the superstructure of concerns we use to frame our work. Having said that, our ideal reader is of course going to be one who desires something more than a cookbook approach to a currently fashionable methodology. Our best hope is that readers will choose to join us in contemplating the profound difference reading can make in a person's life and thus arrive at a powerful standpoint from which to situate the practice of using student book clubs with respect to their own personal understandings of what it means to live a life that includes reading.

Is There Anything New About the Concept of a Book Club for Students?

Oprah Winfrey certainly deserves the adulation she received for bringing book clubs to the attention of the mass media during the 1990s. How else can one account for the sudden appearance of "quality" literature on shelves in grocery stores and discount centers everywhere? This fact alone points to the existence of a large number of people nationwide who would consider Oprah's televised book discussion groups the inspiration behind their own renewed interest in reading (Creegan, 1997). But there are additional indications that something is afoot. Is it coincidental that ten years ago one would be hard-pressed to find a single session devoted to the topic of literature circles/book clubs at conventions sponsored by professional organizations such as the National Council of Teachers of English (NCTE), International Reading Association (IRA), and National Reading Conference (NRC) while today such venues are common? It might be an exaggeration to claim that literature circles/book clubs have replaced portfolio assessment as the latest fad among literacy educators, but it cannot be denied that there is widespread interest in this topic especially in the field of early childhood education. Moreover, a perusal of journals read by secondary school teachers clearly indicates that the rise of interest in this idea is not limited to those teaching in the primary grades. Burgeoning online support and sponsorship of book clubs for all ages provides a third source of evidence that the current popularity of shared reading experiences is a significant phenomenon. While the precise extent of Oprah's influence on these developments is debatable, one thing is clear: The recent proliferation of interest in literature circles/book clubs spanning academic and non-academic contexts gives the appearance that a new and exciting trend is shifting the contours of literary culture in America.

All this notwithstanding, there is ample evidence that Americans have been reading together in book groups of one form or another since the colonial period of our history. Furthermore, a historical look at the practice of reading through the ages reveals that the notion of reading as an essentially solitary activity is actually of quite recent origin (Manguel, 1996). It may well be, as David Laskin and Holly Hughes (1995) point out, that the current "book club buzz" represents "just the latest variation on a very old theme" (p. 1). They credit the Puritan religious leader Anne Hutchinson's celebrated book club that shook up the Massachusetts Bay Colony in 1634—and led to her banishment from that community—with being America's very first literary discussion group. Whether or not this claim is true, we know that many other— though perhaps less contentious—groups dotted the landscape of the colonial era and these paved the way for the flowering early in the nineteenth century of more high-profile groups led by such luminaries as Elizabeth Peabody and Margaret Fuller. An important observation to keep in mind about these groups (one will we discuss more fully later in this introduction) is that they were created almost exclusively by and for women. From the beginning, gendered reading practices have remained at the heart of both the success and the controversy associated with the existence of literature circles/book clubs in America.

The rapid expansion of "clubs" for women during the latter half of the nineteenth century is well-documented by Anne Ruggles Gere (1997) in a book entitled *Intimate Practices: Literacy and Cultural Work in U.S. Women's Clubs, 1880–1920*. Gere's is an important study for at least two reasons. First, it offers a detailed, complex portrait of women's clubs, making visible the scope and quality of their cultural work. Coexisting with more or less elite, highbrow clubs, were a wide spectrum of socially active clubs, some of them comprised of freed slaves, others formed by working-class mothers, and still others convened in immigrant communities. A common feature of these various collaborative ventures is a tendency to "describe their purposes in terms that modified, expanded, or redirected the meanings attached to *culture*" (p. 178). This emphasis on making a difference not only for themselves but for the benefit of a wider community points to the second reason why Gere's book makes an important contribution to our understanding of the history behind the current revival of interest in book clubs in America. She describes how a tension arose between competing views of what it might mean to live a life that includes literary reading when, at the turn of the last century, the study of modern languages and literature began to be defined as an academic discipline. This phenomenon, also researched by Gerald Graf (1987), required that "the study of literature" be clearly distinguished from the mere "appreciation of literature" (p. 101).

For the first time, a category of amateur or common reading was introduced as distinct from the scholarly, professional reading sponsored by universities. The latter according to Gere "drew on philology, emphasized mental discipline, and sought to make English studies intellectually rigorous enough to justify its place in the academy" (p. 212). Almost overnight, the emphasis on reading for self-development through social engagement that for some time had been the hallmark of women's clubs of all types was relegated to second-class status as the male-dominated literary establishment redefined what could count as "serious" reading. Gere (1997) and Graf (1987) have thoroughly documented this transformation for those who may desire more information about the immediate effects that followed from the construction of English as an academic subject. For our purposes we think it sufficient to point out that it makes perfect sense in light of this research that the brief history of the reading group in America offered by Laskin and Hughes (1995) would feature an abrupt shift from a focus on turn of the century "women's literary clubs" to "the next flowering of book clubs in America," namely, "the so-called Great Books movement, which swept the country after World War II" (p. 9).

Whatever one's opinion of the Great Books movement, which reached its zenith during the 1950s, it would be difficult to argue that it did not represent an effort to expand the reach of the academy through publishing lists of criti-cally approved (i.e., canonical) literature and advocating for prescriptive, teacher-led inquiry practices in places other than traditional classroom set-tings. A lingering effect of this effort is discernible in the current crop of mass-produced reading guides available online from major publishers (McGinley, Conley, and White, 2000). Against the backdrop of this broad sphere of influ-ence centered in university English departments, we think it is possible to frame the current resurgence of interest in book groups as a recovery of possi-bilities that had been more or less eclipsed by several decades in which literary culture in the United States was dominated by academic discourses.

Laskin and Hughes (1995) cite a claim made by sociologist Elizabeth Long whose research suggests that during the 1960s people "split off from the Great Books regimen to form more relaxed, wide-ranging book groups" and that these are the forerunners of the current resurgence of interest in book groups. This brings us back to the question about whether there is anything new in the concept of a student book club. We think the answer to this question is no and yes. No, because book clubs are an old idea connected with family and local literacies, which are being rediscovered and reinvented for a post-indus-trial age. Laskin and Hughes point to the "special kind of socializing" people find in book groups that provides a respite from fast-paced and stressful lifestyles. This hypothesis is supported by Jenny Hartley (2001) whose re-search led her to conclude that "running against the tides of all-encompassing mass media, long-distance link-ups and global horizons, reading groups partly owe their success to their commitment to the smaller scale and direct contact between people" (p. 14).

On the other hand, we also believe there is something new and unprec-edented in the way some people are constructing book clubs at the present time. People seeking a book club experience today can choose from a greater range of possibilities than has hitherto been available and at least some of those options represent a departure from anything seen in the past. A longstanding conflict between academic and popular discourse is being reconfigured in some groups to allow for discussion of a broader range of issues and experiences. We would call such groups "hybrids" because they appear to combine a sense of personal and social engagement with a respect for close reading based on practices of disciplined attention to language and textuality. One reason we wanted to write this book is to spread the word about our direct experiences with book clubs that transgress limiting assump-tions and allow for experimentation with new ideas and practices.

Elizabeth Long (2003) has found evidence for just this sort of experimenta-tion among book clubs she studied in the city of Houston, Texas, during the 1990s. Among many interesting findings, she notes the different ways groups use the adjective "serious" to describe what they do. Of particular interest to us are those who redefine "serious reading" in a way that "privileges the moral seriousness of discussion rather than the formal qualities of a given genre or individual book." (128) Long goes on to say that this move, in turn:

> relies on uncoupling the quality of discussion from the abstract notion of literary worth as something inherent in a given text that is, if 'worthy,' automatically morally or aesthetically elevating. . . . [T]his position privileges the distinction between reading and not reading rather than that between worthwhile reading and 'trash.' Both cultural moves challenge the autonomy of high or academic literary culture while maintaining allegiance to literary culture and moral seriousness in general. (128)

These groups as described by Long resonate with our experience as readers who are also teachers and help us identify what we hope to replicate in our classrooms through implementing student book clubs.

Long identifies readers who "automatically defer to cultural authority" but also "stand at some distance from it because they are amateurs who look to books for the pleasures of deep emotional involvement, meaningfulness, or the illumination of their experience rather than for the more rationalist pleasures that come with analytic distance." (130) Adult book clubs that produce this kind of hybridity in which academic influences are combined with deep personal investment in reading stand as the prototype of what we hope to achieve in our classes through the use of student book clubs. Our goal is to create contexts in which students can forge something positive in their lives out of the inevitable—and we would add perpetually unresolved—tension between the private and public pleasures of reading. One of the most significant effects of the work we did for part one of this book was the realization that each of us, though in different ways, has learned how to manage the tension between personal and academic influences on our reading. At the same time, we have learned to embrace our status as amateur readers along with the implications this entails for our role as teachers.

As we noted above, the birth of English as an academic subject was marked by a conflict between those who favored the professionalization of literary study and those who resisted the subsequent devaluation of "common" readers and reading. We probably wouldn't go so far as Helena Echlin (2000) who calls literary criticism a "hoax" (p. 534) or as Daniel Green (2001) who argues that "the very idea of literature as an academic subject seems a contrivance designed expressly to destroy all interest in the actual writing that brought the subject into being in the first place" (p. 273). At the same time, we share their frustration with the way academic reading and writing have become synonymous with literary history and criticism. We see in student book clubs an excellent tool for resituating literary study within a broader view of what it might mean to live a life that includes reading. We are excited by the possibility that student book clubs might be framed as a bridge linking academic and non-academic contexts so as to enhance the experience of reading literature in both settings.

What is a Student Book Club?

We want to use the foregoing brief history of book clubs in America as a point of departure in order to make a case for the special kind of book club we are envisioning. Historically, the term book club has been used to refer to a small group of up to a dozen or more adult readers—typically but not exclusively women—who gather periodically to talk about books. (Clearly, this definition excludes commercial uses of the term for the purpose of marketing books.) Further generalizations run the risk of defining the term too narrowly. Adult book clubs are usually, but not always, peer led and informal. The size of these groups as well as the requirements for membership are highly variable as are the types of books that are read and discussed. It would appear that the purposes for convening book clubs as well as the quality of the conversations they sponsor are as diverse as the individuals who desire to read in the company of other adults. (Hartley 2001)

We do not want to lose sight of seemingly limitless variations in the kinds of reading experiences that might be obtained through participation in a book club. At the same time, as we noted previously, books and other resources designed to encourage and support the formation of adult book clubs clearly fall into one of two categories, those that aim to mimic academic reading in non-academic contexts and those that more or less deliberately reject protocols for reading typically found in classroom contexts. It appears clear to us that these contrasting points of view are a product of the increasing professionalization of literary study that has taken place during the past 100 years or so. One important effect of this trend in both academic and non-academic contexts has been the marginalization of reading practices, which we associate with being an amateur reader.

The resurgence of interest in book clubs during the past decade has meant that many adults are now reevaluating the literature instruction they received in school and taking a stand either for or against the influence of scholarship (i.e., literary history and criticism) on what and how they read. Another effect of this trend has been that many teachers like Cheryl, Holly, and Jenny have felt pulled in two directions with respect to "independent" versus "required" reading within the school curriculum. In Part 3 we address this issue in light of developments in reader response theory since the 1970s as part of our argument for framing student book clubs as the basis for a more unified approach than is typical in schools at the present time. For instance, most teachers we know gravitate strongly toward one or the other of two extremes exemplified by Romano (2000) whose vision of "living literature" discounts the value of high theory and scholarship for most readers and by Appleman (2000) who makes nearly the opposite claim that recent scholarship ought to play a central role in the design of any credible literature curriculum.

We want to be clear about our choice not to ignore literary history and criticism in our work. It should be equally clear however that we do not want to force feed students a diet comprised solely of questions and concerns derived from the work of literary scholars and other professional readers. The stance we take calls into question the way critical reading is often defined in opposition to personal response. Thus, we believe our concept of student book clubs complements the work of Daniels (2002) and others (e.g., Beach & Myers, 2001; Burke, 2002; Nystrand & Heck, 1993; Sumara, 1996), all of whom seek to define a middle way in which multiple purposes for reading can co-exist so as to open up a range of possibilities for individual readers depending on their needs and desires. Daniels' work is particularly significant to us because of his prominent place among advocates for bringing "literature circles" into classroom contexts beyond the primary grades (e.g., Chandler, 1997; Dale, 1999; Flint, 1999; Hill, Johnson, & Shick-Noe, 1995; Noll, 1994).

We see Daniels' approach to classroom-based literature circles as similar to Atwell's (1987/98) workshop approach to teaching reading. Both situate themselves *in the middle,* helping to bridge the distance between students' more or less innate inclinations as readers and the kind of critical reading valued within the academy. Significantly, in the second editions of their widely read books, both Atwell and Daniels grapple with their role as teachers by seeking ways to intervene without negating the agency of their students as readers of literature. Both wish to maximize student choice regarding what, when, why, and how to read while simultaneously opening up new possibilities within that field of activity. Both seek to promote collaborative reading, Daniels through small, peer-led reading groups he calls "literature circles," and Atwell through a workshop approach that folds together experiences with reading and writing to get kids talking to each other about their ideas and goals.

Our concept of student book clubs stands beside the good work of Atwell and Daniels to offer another alternative for teachers of Grades 7–12 in particular, who care about helping their students become life-long readers but find themselves either by choice or by necessity working within a traditional literature curriculum that places great emphasis on literary analysis and other scholarly reading practices. The student book clubs Cheryl, Jenny, and Holly have developed to enhance their teaching in very different contexts and which they describe in Part 2 of this book do not offer students the same degree of choice about what, when, and why they read that is the hallmark of both a literature circle as envisioned by Daniels or a reading workshop as envisioned by Atwell. Student book clubs are convened for the express purpose of helping young readers engage with curricular materials but in such a way that they retain or develop a sense of personal agency that typically is absent from teacher-directed literature instruction.

There is yet another and related sense in which our work differs from Atwell and Daniels without necessarily being in conflict with the point of view they express. Philosophically, our take on being *in the middle* suggests that it is impossible to be anywhere else. In other words, we take seriously the world of critical, "professional" reading without seeing this as necessarily opposed to the wider world of non-academic, "personal" reading. From this perspective, we think it is possible to frame scholarly reading as a subset of amateur or life-long reading. As we said earlier, our goal is to model ways students might resolve the tensions between multiple purposes for reading because we want them to be aware of the options available to them as adult readers. The student book clubs we describe throughout this book constitute zones of possibility within which students can experience the process of building responses out of their initial reactions and through exercising choices about what and how to respond begin to realize that there is never just one way to read a text. In addition students learn that the tools of literary analysis may be useful even in situations where one's goal is not necessarily to produce a "scholarly" reading. In short, we believe it is possible to teach students how to read productively as amateur readers in connection with the goal of helping them choose a path of life-long reading without over- or under-emphasizing the value of exclusively literary terms and concepts.

In our role as teachers who are also readers, we have developed the concept of a student book club to create a space that demystifies the reading process in which young readers can begin to locate their reactions and responses within a range of possible lines of questioning that includes but is not limited to questions connected with literary history and criticism. Rather than impose on students a regime comprised of academic skills and knowledge in the abstract, we aim to guide them toward understanding why they may choose to respond in one way rather than another. In addition, we want them to compare their choices about how to respond with choices made by other readers that may be similar to but also may be very different from their own. Throughout this book, we will be making a case that what we are teaching is, after all, a form of critical thinking, moreover, one that actually has the potential to make a difference in the lives of our students.

Part 1

Teachers as Readers

"The real voyage of discovery consists not in seeking new landscapes but in seeing with new eyes."

—Marcel Proust

Chapter 1

Revaluing Amateur Readers and Reading

Ask ten people to explain the difference between reading for one's own purposes and reading as an assignment for school and you will hear a variety of reactions. No one, however, is likely to deny there is a difference. Is this a problem we should worry about? We would say no and yes. No, because we do not believe reading experiences should be homogenized to look and feel the same across all contexts. In fact we embrace the idea that academic and non-academic settings offer different sets of possibilities for reading alone and with others. The problem as we understand it lies in the adversarial relationship that many people, including many teachers, assume must exist between reading for academic purposes and reading that is focused on more personal needs and concerns.

We see evidence of what the poet/essayist Wendell Berry (2000) derides as the "religion of professionalism" (p. 130) in the way literature curricula present to children and adolescents an extremely narrow understanding of what it might mean to live a life that includes reading. Even well-known reader-oriented scholars like the literary theorist, Stanley Fish (1980) and the philosopher, Richard Rorty (1989) at times fall into the trap of assuming that the only worthwhile reading experiences are those that conform to the expectations of a professional elite, which is to say they privilege novelty in reading (produced in conformity to interpretive norms, of course) and devalue reading that fails to rise above merely ordinary experience. At the same time, we agree with Dennis Sumara (2002) that "reading literature in school still matters."

The approach we take in this book is aimed at confronting this disjuncture in order to re-imagine what might become possible through reading in and out of school contexts.

Research findings published by J.A. Appleyard (1990) indicate that adults who are not literary specialists and who choose to live lives that include reading are "pragmatic" in the sense that, over the course of a lifetime, reading is for them likely to serve a variety of purposes (e.g., "escape," "searching for truth'" and "discovering usable images"). During the past ten years, additional research including self-studies published by adult readers (Birkirts, 1994; Lesser, 1999, 2002; O'Brien, 2000; Pearce, 1997; Schwartz, 1996; Sumara, 2002) as well as more formal studies (Atwell-Vasey, 1998; Flecha, 2000; Long 2003; Rummel & Quintero, 1997; Sumara, 1996) has enhanced our understanding of the pragmatic, hybrid nature of adult reading practices. We believe this body of work makes possible a new appreciation for amateur readers and reading which in turn suggests alternative ways of understanding the relationship between school-sponsored and self-sponsored reading practices.

We are encouraged in this effort by what Mihaly Csikszentmihalyi (1990) has learned from years of studying the psychology of optimal experience. As he points out,

> [O]riginally, "amateur," from the Latin verb *amare*, "to love," referred to a person who loved what he was doing. Similarly, a "dilettante," from the Latin, *delectare*, "to find delight in," was someone who enjoyed a given activity. . . There was a time when it was admirable to be an amateur poet or a dilettante scientist, because it meant that the quality of life could be improved by engaging in such activities. But increasingly the emphasis has been to value behavior over subjective states; what is admired is success, achievement, the quality of performance rather than the quality of experience (140).

To read this as a dismissal of high expectations in school and in life would be a mistake in our opinion. Neither Csikszentmihalyi nor we are opposed to achievement! His point and ours is that one can respect both the quality of performance as a *product* and the quality of experience as a *process* while recognizing that for most of us these only rarely amount to the same thing. Furthermore, there are certain activities that can truly enhance one's quality of life even when—and sometimes because—they fail to count as "great performances." We would argue that literary reading offers a prime example of this type of activity.

In writing about her own gendered reading practices, literary critic, Lynne Pearce (1997) comes out, so to speak, by admitting that the reading performances she produces in order to gain status in her professional life are different from and in some respects less important to her than the relationships she develops with books in the context of her personal life. This "confession" is unusual only in that it was made by someone with a legitimate claim to being an elite, professional reader. The truth is that all four of us and a great many of our friends and colleagues readily acknowledge a very real tension between the experience of "reading as a teacher" and what many of us refer to as "just reading." We are grateful to Pearce and others who have helped us reclaim our (amateur) love for reading by giving us new language for naming what this is and why it is important. For example, Sven Birkirts (1994) writes,

> If anything has changed about my reading over the years, it is that I value the state a book puts me in more than I value the specific contents. . . . Reading a novel is not simply a matter of making a connection to another person's expression. Over and above the linguistic connection, the process makes a change in the whole complex of the self. We are for the duration of our reading, different, and the difference has more to do with the process than with the temporary object—the book being read. As with meditation, both the pulse rate and the breathing seem to alter; the interior rhythms are modified in untold ways (p. 81).

Birkirts' emphasis on "serious reading" as "above all an agency of self-making" (p. 87) resonates with Geoffrey O'Brien's (2000) claim that "there are styles of reading as there are styles of writing, as many as the reader can invent" (p. 71). Similarly, Dennis Sumara (2002) argues that literary reading can be framed as a "focal practice" aimed at "creating experiences of self-identity" (p. 8). These authors and others have helped us revalue our status as amateur readers who also happen to be educators concerned about teaching and learning in schools.

Running through this important body of work is the notion that literary reading can become a form of engagement with life. This notion recalls Kenneth Burke's (1937) famous description of literature as "equipment for living" but, even more so than Burke, the authors we are citing here have helped us to reinvent ourselves as readers and as teachers. Lynne Schwartz (1996) writes, "Reading is escape—why not admit it?—but not from job or troubles. It is escape from the boundaries of our own voices and idioms. . . . If we make books happen, they make us happen as well" (pp. 111, 118). The various experiences with book clubs we describe in the chapters to follow are connected with particular ways of thinking about reading. For instance, we talk about reading as an event that is folded into other aspects of our lives. We say a lot about the value of exploratory talk, about listening, about making and sustaining conversations, which sometimes requires one to make risky moves. We talk about gathering reactions during the course of reading as the basis for creating "works of reading." We talk about interpretation as a tool for generating personal insights rather than as the end point of reading. Much of what we say will seem at first glance to be at odds with what passes for business-as-usual in school contexts, but ultimately our goal is to underscore the power of shared experiences with reading and to show how these might become part and parcel with what passes for a literary education.

We are familiar with the argument that focusing on personal experiences with literature is soft and self-indulgent, that is, lacking in the necessary rigor that would make this practice of reading worthy of respect (e.g., Appleman, 2000; Lewis, 2000). In a sense, this entire book is a response to that argument as we redescribe the domain of the "personal" to include a view of amateur reading that embraces many of the conceptual tools and practices that have been developed in academic contexts but without limiting ourselves to the narrow band of questions and concerns dictated by literary history and criticism, especially as these typically come into play in secondary school literature curricula. As we have said several times thus far, our purpose is not to advance one position by demonizing others.

Our goal is a complex understanding of what it might mean to live a life that includes literary reading. This is not to deny that our argument is informed by a particular theoretical stance or to evade our obligation to explain what that stance entails. For those who are interested, we address these questions at length in part three of this book. Here, we want to stay close to our own and others' lived through experiences with reading.

A project described by Wendy Atwell-Vasey (1998) in *Nourishing Words: Bridging Private Reading and Public Teaching* is relevant to ours because she too worries about the fact that literature curricula in schools are constructed in a way that aligns rigor with scholarly reading practices that exclude much that she—and we—find valuable. In a sense, this situation harks back to the turn of the last century and the process described by Gere (1997) whereby book clubs organized by and for women became marginalized as a direct consequence of the campaign to legitimize the study of English language and literature within universities, in other words, "to make English as hard as Greek" (p. 213). As described by Gere,

> Clubwomen's need for interpretation looks different from the academy's. The insistence on an open mind, the attention to didactic features in literature, the receptivity to personal opinion, the prizing of affective and spiritual responses to texts, the organic approach to system, the emphasis on accessibility instead of difficulty, and the foregrounding of performance create an image quite different from academic interpretation. (242)

At the heart of this controversy lie gendered reading practices. We agree with Atwell-Vasey that these should be recognized as such and evaluated for their actual effects on reading experience rather than on abstract and we think sterile debates over the desirability or even the possibility of neutrality and objectivity in reading.

Proposing a metaphor of "nourishment" to describe what literary reading provides, Atwell-Vasey (1998) uses interviews with practicing secondary school English teachers to foreground the limitations of traditional classroom approaches to literary reading and teaching. Her interviews vividly portray a lack of continuity across the experiential domains we describe in this book using the phrases, *teachers as readers* and *readers as teachers*. Academic reading, whether framed in terms of traditional approaches to literary criticism or more contemporary approaches to critical literacy, is skewed toward a view of literary interpretation as an end product. Teachers are expected to guide their students toward proper interpretations of critically approved texts and help them summarize the results of this work in the form of "literary analysis papers."

Atwell-Vasey is critical of what she perceives as a dominant "masculine" point of view in the way literature instruction is conceived but she does not dismiss it out of hand as inherently wrong or misguided. Nonetheless, as the teachers she interviewed repeatedly point out, a profound conflict does exist between school-based conceptions of reading as a public performance and the purposes that motivate them—and most adults—to seek experiences with books in their private life. Atwell-Vasey's study is especially relevant to our own because she refuses to settle for merely documenting the divide between academic and non-academic purposes for reading. We share her emphasis on "bridging private reading and public teaching."

In conceiving of a literary text as a "potential space for enterprise," Atwell-Vasey's research aligns well with the self studies by accomplished adult readers mentioned above, in particular the one published by Dennis Sumara (2002), who also uses spatial metaphors to disrupt commonsense assumptions about literary reading and teaching. "Literary experience is a place," he writes. "By learning to attend to its details, readers can improve the quality of their lived experiences" (p. xiv). We also see a further connection here with Elizabeth Long's (2003) research. "Over and over," she writes, her

> participants speak of a process that couples reflection about literature with self-reflection in the company of others who bring similar reflexiveness, but different selves, into the process. And over and over, they speak as well of the surprising closeness that emerges from this kind of talk. (111)

All of these scholars emphasize bodily awareness in emphasizing what many teachers know to be true but which is rarely if ever acknowledged in academic contexts, namely, that it matters when, where, and with whom one reads.

Our work similarly places emphasis on the quality of our own lived-through experiences with literature and that of our students as we seek to expand the range of possibilities that are open to us as readers and as teachers. We are hopeful that the co-existence of gendered reading practices, for so long a source of conflict, may now begin to be viewed as a stepping stone to a more complex view of literary reading, one that allows for a multiplicity of stances including a recovery of respect for amateur readers and reading. We conclude this chapter with brief profiles of ourselves as teachers who have chosen the path of becoming life-long readers. Although we share a broad philosophical outlook on literary teaching and learning, our stories are different in significant ways that shape the different angles of vision reflected in the individual chapters that appear in Part 2 of this book.

Teachers as Readers: Individual Profiles of the Authors

Mark Faust

Mark lives with his wife and two daughters in Madison, Georgia. He teaches at the University of Georgia in Athens where he holds a position as an associate professor in the Department of Language Education. Mark previously taught English language arts in secondary schools for eleven years. He likes to talk about how the experience of reading literature in the company of teenagers changed forever and for the better his beliefs about what to read and why.

A few years ago, Mark became interested in the concept of literature circles, which led him to develop an innovative university class for practicing teachers who shared this interest. The idea was simple. Provide teachers with an opportunity to participate in a literature circle with other teachers for a semester. At the same time, encourage them to reflect on this experience to the end of building a desire as well as the confidence to integrate literature circles into their own classroom practice. Dubbed "the book club class," it continues to attract new students each year and has made a real difference in the lives of many.

As mentioned in the introduction, Cheryl, Jennifer, and Holly are all veterans of "the book club class" and the idea to write this book grew out of an ongoing conversation they were having with Mark concerning the pros and cons of designing literature instruction that includes opportunities for collaborative reading. They kept coming back to questions about how each had become a life-long reader and in particular to questions about the role of schooling in that process. The concept of a student book club as distinct from a literature circle evolved from a shared realization that their choice to live lives that include reading represented a transformation not a rejection of what they had learned in school.

For his part, Mark sees his current passion for collaborative reading as a delightfully unexpected development in his life.

> It's odd that someone like me should have become a strong advocate for the idea of collaborative reading in schools. Growing up, I never thought of reading as something people might do together. Despite the fact that like many people I have fond memories of being read to as a child, reading on my own always felt like a solitary activity. Picking up a book put me in a place far from the madding crowd, a place where I could indulge myself a little, play with ideas, and give my imagination some room to move. Throughout my school-age years, I more or less dutifully completed reading assignments for English classes, which is to say I never questioned the validity of literary history and criticism or doubted that my teachers were helping me to become a better reader. Nonetheless, I did not perceive any connection between the reading that was assigned for school and the reading that captivated me during my solitary hours.

Becoming an English major in college only served to reinforce this divide between academic and personal purposes for reading, but in a way that brought about a reversal in Mark's sense of himself as a reader. In a manner that parallels what Cheryl, Jennifer, and Holly also say about their education, Mark discovered the thrill of literary interpretation and the accompanying—he would now say, illusory—feeling of mastery over complex literature. Fortunately, this phase was comparatively short lived.

Further study, especially of reader-response theory and criticism, combined with the sheer impact of being around young people every day produced another profound turn in Mark's outlook on literary reading and teaching. He writes,

> What I wanted from students was their questions. What I offered them was guidance towards recognizing questions they didn't even know they had or didn't know it would even be possible to ask. My goal became one of helping them learn, in Rilke's words, to "live the questions themselves" while resisting

easy answers. The irony is that once I started to do this, I was constantly amazed by the questions my students raised and the power of their ideas when engaged in making connections between what we were reading together and their properly teenage interests and concerns. Why can't we teach kids to read with a balance of humility and resourcefulness appropriate to their time of life? As an adult, I am happy to acknowledge my "incompetence" as a reader (Somer, 1994). This stance keeps me honest and open to new ways of thinking and doing. Like the character in Italo Calvino's (1979) novel about reading novels (*If on a Winter's Night a Traveler*), who suggests that "Reading is going toward something that is about to be, and no one yet knows what it will be . . .," the most satisfying reading experiences for me are those in which I am able to use an author's words to make something that is both engaging and unexpected. Each time I open a book, I must learn how to read that particular book at that particular moment in my life to the end of realizing possibilities that neither myself nor the author could have fully anticipated in advance.

Mark's relatively recent discovery of collaborative reading has added a whole new chapter to his personal history as a reader. He is grateful to the many teachers who have participated in his book club class and shared their enthusiasm for reading in ways that blend academic and personal styles of reading to produce experiences that are magical and profound.

Cheryl Hancock

Cheryl lives and teaches middle school language arts in Bogart, Georgia, still a relatively rural area but close enough to Atlanta to have become a more diverse and complex place in recent years. As she explains in more detail later on in Chapter 4 of this book, her students come from a variety of backgrounds and bring a variety of needs to her classroom. Her stance as a teacher is informed by her own past difficulties as a student, which makes her well suited to empathize with young people seemingly not destined to choose lives that include reading. She writes:

When I asked my eighth grade students what a life-long reader might be, I received quizzical looks, blank stares, and disinterest. When a verbal response was offered, it consisted of questions about what I meant by "life-long reader." *But that's what I asked you*, I thought quietly. I thought back to my own analysis of what a life-long reader might be, after being asked the first time in graduate school. I didn't have a clearer idea, and

> here I was expecting eighth graders to have a clue! In front of
> my students, I confidently smiled in secret anticipation of what
> they would soon learn about reading from my class!

For Cheryl, student book clubs represent a way to make reading inviting to reluctant readers and at the same time introduce the basic skills they will need to be successful in school. She has learned that basic skills by themselves cannot motivate many students particularly those who are ill equipped to meet the demands placed on them by the school curriculum. Through a combination of patience and encouragement, Cheryl makes reading engaging for students and only gradually introduces more complex tasks and levels of thinking.

Cheryl learned to read at home at a very young age thanks to her mother's enthusiasm for books. She has many fond memories of a childhood that included reading. But something happened during her teenage years that changed everything. Cheryl was drawn into a lifestyle that turned her off not only to reading but to anything having to do with school and at age sixteen she became a high school dropout. Four years later, divorced and the mother of a child, she began to put her life back together. She found herself reading self-help books and feeling a desire to resume her education. After completing a program leading to a GED, Cheryl enrolled in a community college, where, for the first time in her life, she experienced a sense of empowerment through reading and understanding literature.

> I began to crave the debate, the analysis, and the pure enjoy-
> ment of making meaning, comparing situations with my life,
> and seeing how the same issues impact others. I was getting
> personal with the characters, becoming friends or enemies,
> frustrated that I couldn't talk back, and sad when they died.
> Finally I owned an outlet where I could be heard, where I could
> agree and disagree with others' opinions. Another member may
> contribute enlightening comments, serious thoughts, an unex-
> pected point of view, and at the same time give me the insight
> I needed to make further connections. For me that is the pin-
> nacle of the pleasure of reading.

The confidence and positive self-image Cheryl derived from succeeding in school propelled her to continue her education and eventually to become a teacher herself.

She continues to this day to be an avid reader, especially of poetry, and wants to do everything she can to help as many of her students as possible discover that reading for school does not necessarily require them to ignore their personal investment in what books have to offer. Cheryl loves to read books about women who, like her, have overcome obstacles in their lives and she tries to help her students connect with books that relate to their interests and concerns. Student book clubs provide her with a perfect vehicle for building engagement while setting the stage for more complex literate practices in her classroom. In Chapter 4, she describes her approach to creating student book clubs gradually in order to minimize the fear of failure, especially among students who have known little else in school. She has found to her delight that, once such students begin to feel some confidence, many begin to see themselves as readers and even bring her books they have chosen to read on their own.

Jennifer Cockrill

Jenny lives with her husband in Atlanta, Georgia, and teaches at the Atlanta Girls' School. This is a new position for her and it presents a somewhat different set of challenges than those she describes in the chapter she wrote for this book. Nonetheless, she remains committed to the idea of using student book clubs in her classes and is looking forward to the opportunity afforded by her present position to investigate the role of gendered reading practices in classroom contexts.

Jenny describes herself as having always been a model student who only recently has begun to question the values and practices associated with reading for school. Although her personal history differs markedly from what we have just read about Cheryl, there are some underlying similarities between them especially with respect to their current reading practices. Jenny was also raised in a home where reading was valued and has fond memories of reading aloud with her mom books like *The Boxcar Children* well into her pre-teen years. Although her transition to reading for school was effortless, and more or less seamless, in sharp contrast with experiences described elsewhere in this chapter, Jenny does recall feeling at times as though school represented a parallel universe in comparison with the rest of her life. Nevertheless, it is only in retrospect that she sees her early literary education as limiting and culturally biased. She believes this accounts at least in part for her continued allegiance to a traditional curricular format even as she looks for ways to broaden the scope of her goals as a teacher.

In describing herself as an adult reader, Jenny emphasizes the role of visualization and the sound of a narrator's voice, a practice she associates with the way her mom would pause and savor an engaging scene as they read together. She also sees herself as needing to feel as though a reading experience is going somewhere, that at some level she is "getting it." When pressed to define what she means by "getting it," she uses language similar to that deployed by Hunt and Vipond (1992) when they talk about "point-driven" reading. Jenny attributes this aspect of her style of reading to her dad, whom she interviewed for this project.

> My father feels that novelist Lee Smith has got "it" and expresses it beautifully. When I push him to explain "it," his response cannot quite capture a clear definition. He speaks about how Smith understands and writes with great accuracy and sensitivity about the South in the 1930s–40s and the soul of Appalachian folk. My father feels a personal connection with her work, which in turn helps him feel connected with his own family history. When I ask how he knows she has got it, he can only tell me it is an instant connection and recognition that he understands through a character's stories.

Understanding her parents as amateur readers who had a profound influence on her development as a reader has led Jenny to reconsider her goals as a teacher of literature. It is clearer to her now how her mastery of literary history and criticism is folded together in productive ways with a rich legacy of reading for amateur purposes.

In Chapter 5 of this book, Jenny describes how she uses student book clubs to create conditions in her classroom conducive to helping her students make similar connections with their own histories as readers and to helping them develop their own individual reading styles. At the same time, she believes very strongly that the tools of literary analysis and essay writing are essential to academic success. She portrays herself as on a mission to reduce the tension most students see between reading for their own purposes and reading for school. While still very much in an experimental mode, her work so far with student book clubs is exciting and will be of interest to secondary school teachers who, like Jenny, hope to achieve a better alignment between literature instruction and the goal of helping students grow into life-long readers.

Holly Isserstedt

Holly teaches twelfth grade English at a large, comprehensive public high school located near her home in Atlanta, Georgia. Unlike Cheryl and Jennifer, she had already experimented with collaborative reading in her classes before enrolling in Mark's book club class. Her move in this direction was prompted by a profound sense of disillusionment with her teaching that began with a moment she describes as follows:

> A turning point occurred for me several years ago in one of my classes. A student who was habitually late to class began the following familiar and worn-out inquiry as a means of avoiding

an assignment she was already ten minutes late beginning. It went something like this: "Why do we have to read this?", "What is the point of reading this?", "Why do you make us read when we hate it so much?" Normally, my response would be to reestablish my authority with a comment that silenced the student and kept the class on task. But for some reason, my student's questions that day hit home. This time, I could not dismiss them as easily as I had so many times before. What stuck me as unusual, was that instead of the droning questions of a reluctant student I had heard countless times before, I heard a non-reader asking a reader why this was an activity of value. It occurred to me that in all my time in front of a classroom teaching literature and in effect, requiring my students to read for hours each week, I had never stopped to consider what it was exactly that I wanted them to do and why. The only place to begin was to first pose the questions of myself: Why do *I* read? Why is it important to *me*? I knew that until I could answer these questions, I had very little hope of convincing my students that their reading was worthwhile endeavor.

Holly's quest to reinvent her teaching in response to these questions led her to experiment with collaborative reading, an experience she describes in Chapter 6 of this book. For her, Mark's book club class provided support and encouragement for something she was already trying to do with her own students.

Holly's journey as a reader and teacher is similar to the others mentioned in these profiles. She grew up in a home where reading was considered as natural as breathing, early in life developed a love of reading as a solitary pleasure, became captivated in college by the allure of literary theory and criticism, and now inhabits a complex space where academic and personal purposes for reading combine to produce experiences not common either in or out of the classroom.

Until a few years ago, I did not recognize what I now know to be true about reading. My reading life had always seemed to exist in another universe parallel but not connected with my "real life." In other words, I perceived my reading as something independent of my other activities. It was not until recently that I began to see how my life as a reader influences and informs all other aspects of my life, particularly my teaching. In the same way, I have come to understand and value all the ways my lived experiences affect how I read.

Holly's enthusiasm for student book clubs stems from an understanding of her unique position as a teacher who not only is a life-long reader, but who sees herself as a role model for her students. Having embraced the image of herself as an amateur reader, Holly acknowledges that reading for scholarly purposes is not the same thing as reading to engage with one's life concerns. At the same time, she acknowledges that what she knows about literary history combined with the habit of "close" reading she learned in school enhances the potential of reading to make a difference in her life.

Holly's success in redefining what it might mean to "read critically" in school contexts so that students can begin to see the connection between this and their personal lives makes her chapter an appropriate culmination for the second part of this book. She would be the first to say, however, that her approach is meant to be suggestive not prescriptive and this goes for the book as a whole. The four chapters focused on classroom practice that comprise Part 2 are meant to suggest practical strategies for bridging the revaluing of amateur reading undertaken in this and the chapter to follow with the (re)definition of critical reading offered in Part 3.

Chapter 2

Schooling (and) the Amateur Reader

Upon completing the personal profiles we wrote for Chapter 1, we spent a long afternoon talking about our work. That conversation opened with each of us commenting on what we had written about the role of schooling in our development as readers. Although it is clear that as young adults we all experienced some degree of tension between our independent reading and the reading we did to complete assignments for school, it is equally clear that as adult readers we have managed to resolve that tension in productive ways. How each of us reads today can be traced back to both strands in our past experience leading us to ask the question, how might we do a better job as teachers of helping adolescents realize and resolve that tension in their own lives? We ask you to approach the following discussion in light of that question and also as a necessary bridge to the descriptions of our classroom practice that comprise the second part of this book.

Above all, we describe ourselves as amateur readers. We read literature for the sheer enjoyment of the experience and the related insights concerning life we are able to derive from it. Literary history and criticism, while interesting to us, are not the driving forces behind our personal choices about what to read and how to read. This is not to imply, however, that we choose to disregard the obvious fact that we are all English teachers by profession. Far from it. We simply want to assert that our being teachers of reading and literature should not necessarily compel us—or our students—to deny our status as amateur readers. Another way of putting this would be to say that the critical tools employed by university professors and other professional readers are going to be useful for us only to the extent that they are somehow connected with our choice to live lives that include reading. This chapter explores some of the consequences we think these assertions entail for us as adult readers who also happen to be teachers of reading.

The first and perhaps most significant point this project requires us to address is the distinction we make between the pragmatic focus of amateur reading and the scholarly focus of professional or academic reading. This does not mean we think being an amateur reader necessarily precludes the use of practices usually associated with academic reading. We do claim, however, that those practices serve somewhat different purposes for us as amateur readers than they do for those who seek to join the ranks of literary scholars. We would describe our own reading practices as a "hybrid construction," which is a fancy way of saying we have found ways to interlace what we have learned in school with what we have learned through the experience of being life-long readers. As we try in this chapter to look past our individual differences in an attempt to name what we share in common as adult readers you will notice that we place a great deal of emphasis on this notion of "hybridity."

For the most part, academic reading at the high school and college level centers on using the tools of literary criticism to situate texts in light of literary history. How do various aspects of a complex text work together to produce a unified whole? What makes it a good example of a poem, novel, play, or other writing? Why is it important, that is, what is its place in the context of literary history? Clearly, these are significant questions for literary scholars and our conception of appropriate classroom instruction does not ignore them. The fact remains that most teenage and adult readers do not find those concerns particularly engaging. Generally, readers are interested in using books to connect with themselves and others through focusing on more personal concerns and insights generated by their reading of literature. Typically, literature instruction in schools leads students to conclude that the words academic and personal describe incompatible ways of reading. Our aim is to show that there is no reason why this has to be the case by constructing a portrait of amateur reading as a productive combination of various influences not excluding school-based literature instruction.

Based on what we wrote for Chapter 1, it should be clear that none of us sees the relationship between academic and non-academic purposes for reading as necessarily an adversarial one. Mark appears to come closest to this position when he says, "reading for school and reading on my own amounted to completely different experiences." On the other hand, both Holly and Cheryl celebrate their exposure to techniques of close reading in academic contexts even as they explore its limitations in relation to their present concerns as adult readers. Jenny admits to moving easily between the worlds of academia and her personal life while growing up. She is perhaps the most "well schooled" of the four of us and the one for whom the book club experience has brought about the most radical transformation of her perspective on reading. We find that our status and concerns as amateur readers locates us on a continuum somewhere between the academic elite—those who actually produce literary history and criticism—and that (unfortunately) large population of aliterate people—those who know how to read but choose not to.

Through participating in adult book clubs and conversing with many adult readers over the past few years, we have come to the conclusion that who we are and what we do as readers is not at all uncommon. In fact, we would hypothesize that a large proportion of adult readers fall into the category we are calling amateur reading and that, allowing for individual differences in styles of reading, most use books as we do to obtain experiences that are pleasurable and rewarding. It now appears to us that the contrasting and stereotypical images of rigorous "literary analysis" versus frivolous "beach reading" accurately describe no more than a tiny fraction of the millions of reading events taking place every day among those who would describe themselves as life-long readers. In Part 3 of this book, we draw upon literary theory in order to contest the claim made by many in the academic community that teaching young people about literary history and criticism is synonymous with teaching them how to be thoughtful, critical readers. At this point, our goal is merely to raise questions about the relationship between schooling and life-long reading by offering a synoptic look at our own practices as adult readers.

The Pragmatic Focus of (Teachers') Amateur Reading

Looking back over what we wrote for Chapter 1, we find ourselves in the middle, so to speak, with respect to a "discrepancy" aptly described by English professor and critic, J.A. Appleyard (1990) at the outset of his investigation into "the experience of fiction from childhood to adulthood." His observation matches well with what we say above about academic versus personal purposes for reading. Appleyard writes:

> This topic became interesting to me a few years ago, when I discovered that most of the college students I was teaching used literature for purposes that my classroom canons of interpretation . . . had obliged me to disavow. I wanted them to think about how books and poems were structured and how

they worked, what values they implied, how they reflected or criticized the culture in which they were produced. The students seemed to want to discover messages about the meaning of their lives, to find interesting characters they could identify with in their fantasies, or to use the ideas of an author to bolster their own beliefs and prejudices. (p. 1)

Appleyard goes on to situate his own reading practices within this "discrepancy" wondering aloud about the possibility of formulating a "comprehensive theory" that would allow his own and his students' approach to reading in their personal lives "some standing as legitimate responses to literature" (p. 2).

Appleyard ultimately answers his own question by delineating two distinct roles that mature readers might choose to inhabit: "the pragmatic reader" and the "reader as interpreter." We are grateful to Appleyard for helping us think about our dual role as readers and as teachers but, for reasons we hope to make clear, our "solution" to the problem does not mesh completely with his. Where he envisions two distinct roles, we see a single more complex or hybrid space encompassing all of the various influences on what we experience as readers of literature. When reading for our own purposes we are unable simply to "forget" that we are teachers but by the same token we are never able to completely shut down our personal investment in a reading event in order to fully mimic the stance supposedly required for the purpose of "analyzing" literature. The point is that we never cease being teachers and readers, a fact that distinguishes us from who we used to be as much as it separates us from the students in our classes whether they are readers or non-readers. We find ourselves less concerned about the issue of legitimizing multiple ways of reading than we are about asking what do we really have to offer our students. Why should they want to read like us?

It is fashionable these days to describe serious reading as a practice of selecting one or another from an array of available critical "lenses" (see, for example, *Critical Encounters* by Deborah Appleman, 2000). Our contrasting view—we account for the theory behind this view in Part 3 of this book— posits a single complex field of reading practices within which questions derived from literary history and criticism co-exist in more or less productive ways with interests and concerns stemming more directly from one's real life experiences. We agree with Sven Birkirts (1996) that "serious reading is above all an agency of self-making" (p. 87). Moreover, we subscribe to his claim that the difference between "serious" and less serious reading is not well served by language that reproduces a stark contrast between academic and personal orientations. In his view and ours, serious reading has the potential to modify "our natural angle of regard upon all things; we reposition the self in order to see differently" (p. 80).

Through our experiences of reading collaboratively with other adults in a variety of contexts, we have come to realize that there are differences as well as similarities between what we do and what many other adults (who are not teachers) typically do, namely those who (for whatever reasons) have chosen to live lives that include reading without being persuaded that literary history and criticism has anything to offer them. What distinguishes us from other adults who are amateur readers? We would point to our predisposition as English teachers to pay attention to language, our own and others', so that for us reading is not framed as a mastery project, an act of appropriation, but as a gesture toward the possibility of engaging with other points of view. Our purpose in this chapter is to expand on this insight through naming what we do as amateur readers always with an eye to positioning ourselves as role models even for people who may never care about the finer points distinguishing literary movements or the evolution of writing as a craft.

We hold that a person does not need to possess a comprehensive knowledge of literary history and criticism in order to read for enjoyment and to gain insights from their lived-through experiences with literature. At the same time, each of us can point to ways our own experience has taught us to make good use of techniques for close reading developed by literary critics notably during the past century. Embedded in the profiles we wrote for Chapter 1 are many passages suggesting that the four of us have managed to resolve this tension by allowing our reading to become a hybrid construction wherein academic and personal purposes for reading co-exist within a single reading event. The following sections develop this idea in more detail beginning with a closer look at what characterizes the personal and academic strands that combine to produce the hybridity that in turn produces reading events we would argue have the power to make a difference in a person's life.

Amateur Reading and the "Flow" Experience

We turn now to Mihaly Csikszentmihaly's (1990) book, *Flow: The Psychology of Optimal Experience*, for help in clarifying what we mean when we say that literary reading cannot and should not be divorced from our personal lives and concerns. Csikszentmihaly spent years gathering data from people worldwide concerning what they believe are the most enjoyable experiences in their life. This research led him to the conclusion that for most of us pleasure is not synonymous with enjoyment. In contrast with merely pleasurable experiences, "enjoyable events occur when a person has not only met some prior expectations or satisfied a need or a desire but also gone beyond what he or she has been programmed to do and to achieve something unexpected, perhaps even unimagined before" (p, 46). This conclusion did not surprise us as much as Csikszentmihaly's findings that "optimal experience and the psychological conditions that make it possible seem to be the same the world over" and that the "phenomenology of enjoyment has [just] eight major components" (p. 46) Together these eight components produce enjoyable experiences Csikszentmihaly describes using the word, "flow."

In general, flow experiences are connected with states of mind existing somewhere between what people experience at one extreme as anxiety and at the other as boredom. Such states of mind are marked by "deep concentration, high and balanced challenges and skills, and a sense of control and satisfaction" (83). Flow experiences rarely if ever arise spontaneously and even then only among people who have already cultivated the requisite physical and mental aptitudes. Csikszentmihaly's project is significant for us because we concur with the many people he interviewed worldwide who linked reading with the experience of "flow," that is, as an activity producing enjoyment as opposed to being merely pleasurable.

We will briefly describe the eight components of the "flow experience" and point to ways we think they directly pertain to literary reading. As we go along, we will raise questions concerning the potential role the study of literary history and criticism might play so as to produce a positive rather than a negative effect. These questions will constitute a background for the concluding sections of this chapter in which we position ourselves as readers who have learned how to successfully navigate the tension between personal and academic purposes for reading.

1. *Literary reading is "a challenging activity that requires skill."* We believe that the project of learning how to read takes a lifetime. Both the challenges involved and the skills required in order to be successful change during the course of a lifetime of reading. A potential problem with literature instruction in schools arises when the challenges that are identified and/or the skills that are taught conflict with what young readers need in order to experience literary reading as desirable. For example, understanding figurative language such as an author's use of metaphor and literary devices such as foreshadowing can enhance the experience of reading but only if this understanding is presented in such a way as to enhance not inhibit flow.

2. *Literary reading involves "the merging of action and awareness."* Csikszentmihaly writes, "One of the most universal and distinctive features of optimal experience takes place when people become so

involved in what they are doing that the activity becomes spontaneous, almost automatic; they stop being aware of themselves as separate from the actions they are performing." (p. 53) Here again, we would argue that the content and the quality of this "merging of action and awareness" changes over time for individual readers. We believe learning to read is a life-long process, one in which schooling can and should play an important but ultimately limited role. What "goes without saying" for a mature reader late in life will differ from the same phenomenon as experienced by a teenager. By the same token, what an individual chooses to focus on at a conscious level is likely to reflect both the age of that reader and the subject matter of what he or she happens to be reading.

3. *Literary reading is connected with "clear goals."* In what sense is literary reading a goal-oriented activity? What's the point of reading? Obviously, multiple purposes for reading exist even if one narrows the range to exclude all but explicitly literary reading. Why not openly acknowledge this in schools? Why not give young readers opportunities to articulate their own goals—such as identifying with favorite characters, reliving scenes they find engaging, and formulating questions about character motivation—at the same time as we attempt to introduce them to more sophisticated possibilities associated with critical thinking? And even then, activities focused on prompting critical reading should reflect the interests and concerns of actual readers.

4. *Literary reading produces "feedback."* It is well known that competent readers constantly look ahead and look back as they make sense of the sentences immediately before them. Thus, to some extent, good readers use the process of reading itself to produce useful feedback. The question that arises here concerns the potential role of teachers as providers of "feedback"? Another question concerns the potential role of other readers in a person's individual reading process? The approach to collaborative reading, which is the major focus of this book, points to potential benefits that arise from classroom practices that encourage students to provide feedback for each other.

5. *Literary reading requires "concentration on the task at hand."* Here we would repeat what we said above for #2 and add this question: Is it possible that school assignments and activities can actually interfere with the "task at hand" if by that we mean using literature to obtain a "flow experience." Reading is itself an activity that should not be eclipsed by other activities only tangentially related to the "task at hand." In our view, most literature textbooks designed for school-age

children do just that by overwhelming each selection with ancillary ideas and information.

6. *Literary reading involves "the paradox of control."* Csikszentmihaly writes, "What people enjoy is not the sense of being in control, but the sense of exercising control in difficult situations. . . Only when a doubtful outcome is at stake, and one is able to influence that outcome, can a person really know whether she is in control." (p. 61) We strongly believe that enjoyable experiences with reading are connected with a sense of agency on the part of readers and will say a great deal more about this in the discussion to follow.

7. *Literary reading involves a "loss of self-consciousness."* Csikszentmihaly writes, "Loss of self-consciousness does not involve a loss of self, and certainly not a loss of consciousness, but rather only a loss of consciousness *of* the self. What slips below the threshold of awareness is the *concept* of self, the information we use to represent to ourselves who we are. And being able to forget temporarily who we are seems to be very enjoyable. When not preoccupied with ourselves, we actually have a chance to expand the concept of who we are. Loss of self-consciousness can lead to self-transcendence, to a feeling that the boundaries of our being have been pushed forward." (p. 64) As we will point out shortly, a "loss of self-consciousness" through literary reading is far from a unitary phenomenon and becomes manifest in various ways depending on how the "task at hand" is defined by particular readers.

8. *Literary reading involves "the transformation of time."* Csikszentmihaly writes, "The objective, external duration we measure with reference to outside events like night and day, or the orderly progression of clocks, is rendered irrelevant by the rhythms dictated by the activity." (p. 66) A key word for us here is the word rhythm. In what sense can literary reading be characterized as rhythmic and what bearing could (or should) this understanding have on curriculum development in school contexts?

We want to underscore the fact that Csikszentmihaly himself makes no explicit connection between the "flow" experience and literary reading nor does he explicitly address concerns about the relationship between "flow" experiences and learning in academic contexts. Moreover, among his many adult research subjects who described reading in their private lives using language consistent with that Csikszentmihaly attaches to his concept of "flow," none explicitly mentioned the relevance of literary history and criticism. However, in a previously published study, Csikszentmihaly and Larson (1984) did address this issue when they observed that literature instruction in schools tends to treat reading from a cognitive viewpoint that ignores the quality of actual reading experiences. That study clearly supports the leap we are making here based on the fact that we ourselves see such a strong connection between our personal reading practices as adults and what Csikszentmihaly calls the "flow" experience. Just as significant to us is the obvious fact that we see nothing about the "flow" experience that necessarily precludes academic purposes for reading if by academic we mean drawing upon resources provided by the history of scholarship connected with literary history and criticism.

In contrast with scholars like Appleyard who set up an opposition between personal and academic purposes for reading literature, we see Csikszentmihaly's delineation of "flow" as a perfect vehicle for bringing both sets of purposes together into a productive space. Let's be clear about this. We follow Appleyard to the extent that experience has taught us that direct instruction aimed at teaching students to "think about how books and poems are structured and how they work, what values they imply, how they reflect or criticize the culture in which they were produced" is not likely ever to generate anything like a "flow" experience. On the other hand, and here's where we depart from Appleyard's contention, we are convinced that such teaching can enhance "flow" experiences once they are underway, that so-called interpretive questions about how books "work" can co-exist in productive ways with pragmatic concerns about how, for example to "use the ideas of an author to bolster one's own beliefs and prejudices."

This brings us to the critical issue of defining what can be classified as critical reading. Most English teachers we know like to claim that their curriculum helps young people develop skills as critical readers and critical thinkers. We agree that this should be a priority as far as the relationship between schooling and life-long reading is concerned. But in our own teaching we want to stop short of subverting our ultimate goal—namely, that our students may choose to live lives that include reading—by focusing exclusively on academic knowledge and skills that all-too-easily suppress rather than enhance the "flow" experience in conjunction with literary reading.

Once again, Csikszentmihaly provides language that relates to our dual role as teachers and as adult role models for young readers. "Most things we do," he writes, "are neither purely autotelic nor purely exotelic." (p. 67)

> The term 'autotelic' derives from two Greek words: auto meaning self, and telos meaning goal. It refers to a self-contained activity, one that is done not with the expectation of some future benefit, but simply because the doing itself is the reward. (p. 67)

Obviously, then, exotelic means focusing on the outcomes rather than the experience itself. "Flow" experiences are predominantly autotelic but may include an exotelic dimension as well. We would say that "flow" experiences are hybrid constructions in that they combine one thing and another to produce a third space marked by both influences but constituting something different from either one of them treated in isolation from the other. In Part 3 we will discuss the remarkable sychronicity between this way of thinking and Louise Rosenblatt's transactional theory of literature as exploration. Here we want to stay close to our own experience as readers and as teachers in order to begin building our case for "student book clubs" as a valuable tool for respecting the potential of literary reading to become a "flow" experience.

Before moving on, we want to insert one more quote from Csikszentmihaly's book because it explicitly addresses a concern many of our readers are likely to raise in response to what we have said so far.

> Often children—and adults—need external incentives to take the first steps in an activity that requires difficult restructuring of attention. Most enjoyable activities are not natural; they demand an effort that initially one is reluctant to make. But once the interaction starts to provide feedback to the person's skills, it usually begins to be intrinsically rewarding. (p. 68)

One objection that has been raised concerning the influence of "reader-response theory" at the secondary level—the same objection is raised concerning the influence of "whole language theory" in the primary grades—is that these theories enable and even encourage teachers to abrogate their responsibility to be teachers. These objections stem in part from the idea—an all-too-prevalent idea in our view—that the ideal educational setting would be one in which teachers became irrelevant and students simply taught themselves. Nothing could be further from our understanding of the ideal relationship between schooling and the development of life-long or what we would call amateur readers.

In the sections to follow, we hope to make it quite clear that we see nothing "natural" about what we do as readers of literature. The practices we will be describing have been learned through years of experience that include experiences in school. We would call what we do "authentic" only to the extent that it is connected with our desire to obtain a particular and in our view unique experience of "flow" through the reading of literature. The teaching practices we will be recommending in part two of this book derive from our understanding that one needs to do more, much more, than simply hand kids books in order to promote reading that is likely to result in "flow" experiences. For those students who come to us never having known an experience of "flow" in conjunction with reading, our goal should be to help them make that connection. For those who show up at our door already able to produce "flow" experiences with books on their own, our task is to help them enhance that experience as much as possible without inadvertently suppressing it. We think our concept of student book clubs which we discuss at length from our different vantage points in the "Readers as Teachers" section of this book can play a significant role in both endeavors and thus become a key factor in helping all adolescents—not just those enrolled in Advanced Placement classes—understand why they might want to choose lives that include literary reading.

The remainder of this chapter is devoted to a more detailed account of specific literate practices we associate with being an amateur reader. We elected to organize this part of our discussion with reference to key words that will be familiar to readers of Nancie Atwell's (1987/98) celebrated book *In The Middle*. Atwell's workshop approach to teaching reading is compatible with our concept of student book clubs and we share her vision of the classroom as a place where academic and personal concerns are folded together. We agree with her that readers thrive when they have *choice, response, time*, and *community* and we use these key words to open up different spaces in which to talk about how we use books and why we think reading literature makes a difference in our lives.

Amateur Readers Choose What, When, Where, and How to Read

There is never a time when any of us is not reading something. Even before we finish one book, we are already thinking about the next one in line. Many factors play a role in our choices about what to read next. Suffice it to say, none of us reads in order to shore up our knowledge of Restoration Drama, for example, because we somehow missed that period in college. Neither do we read, for example, to fine tune our understanding of the narrative technique Tolstoy used in writing *War and Peace*. And don't expect to see any of us rushing to the library to bone up on enjambment so we can better appreciate T.S. Eliot's poetry. Perhaps this weakens our credibility as English teachers but, then again, we are not claiming to be anything more—or less—than rank amateurs when it comes to reading literature.

How exactly do we find books to read? Like other adults, we respond to the marketing efforts of publishers. We look at catalogs, scan the shelves in bookstores and browse the Internet. Mark admits that his love affair with Paul Bowles' novels began with the highly publicized film adaptation of *The Sheltering*

Sky. We heed recommendations from other readers whose opinions we trust. Sometimes we just get in the mood to read a particular genre or about a particular topic. Jenny has a special regard for books written by southern authors. Cheryl often looks for books that will help her think about an issue that matters to her, such as relationships between mothers and daughters. Of the four of us, Holly is perhaps the most voracious and eclectic reader. Our point is that there are many factors influencing what we choose to read, most of them quite ordinary, but somehow absent in school contexts where even "outside reading" choices (that is outside the prescribed curriculum) are often dictated by authority figures.

Choosing when and where to read is also an important aspect of our individual reading styles. Jenny and Mark prefer to do professional reading in the morning. Neither Cheryl nor Holly prefers to read in the early morning at all. We all like to read in the evening before bed and reserve this time for books and magazines that bring us pure pleasure. Each of us can identify special places we associate with reading a book: a comfy couch, hammock, and the bathtub. These places are not neutral sites. Each holds its own qualitative feel that becomes part of what we experience as readers. Cheryl caused us all to nod when she brought up the fact that she brings a book with her wherever she goes and often reads while waiting in line and in restaurants. We find it interesting and significant that we connect many of our most memorable reading experiences with particular times and places in our lives.

As teachers, we know we cannot replicate these conditions in our classrooms but we can and do encourage our students to become readers by showing that we value their independent reading and by seizing opportunities to model what we do as adult readers. We all have experimented with various approaches to "sustained silent reading" (SSR) in our classes. Cheryl takes her eighth graders to the library on a regular basis so they can choose books to read. Holly has a large bulletin board in her classroom where she invites students to "rant and rave" about their independent reading. Jenny encourages independent reading and gives students opportunities to share their favorite books using alternatives to the standard essay form or book report.

Perhaps the most important arena of choice we value as adult readers, however, and the one that is most neglected in school contexts is the choice about how to read. In their zeal to emphasize the acquisition of new knowledge and skills, teachers often ride roughshod over the importance of helping students develop an individual reading style through choosing how, as well as what, to read.

We are grateful for the teachers we had—although we wish there had been more of them—who helped us engage with reading as creative participants in a process of imagining people and places, making them spring to life in our minds. Those same teachers helped us develop an ear for language, a writer's and our own as we learned how to connect the magic of story telling with the allure of ideas. We learned that literary reading involves many subtle choices about what is worth one's attention and what questions it makes sense to ask. In the next section, we take a closer look at our choices about how to read.

Amateur Readers are Responsive Readers

When our conversation turned to the topic of how we read in comparison with other adults we know, Jenny recalled a comment made by her dad who claimed he could always tell very quickly whether or not a book had "it." This prompted us to ask what his comment might imply about what we, as adult amateur readers, require of books and also to consider what books require of us. Books that have "it" we decided are books with which we are able to have an intense, engaging experience, which is to say, we are able to use the author's words to generate a "flow" experience. Here again we find the concept of hybridity helps us come to terms with the paradoxical nature of reading experiences that are uniquely our own and at the same time utterly dependent upon someone else's words. What we respond to when we read is in part but not completely our own creation.

For a while our conversation revolved around a passage Holly wrote in her essay for Chapter 1: "The value of reading comes not necessarily from what I keep, what I am able to carry with me after the last page is turned, but from what happens in the moment when I am reading. It is the immediate transformation that occurs while I am engaged with a particular book where I am able to cultivate something new—an idea, an insight, a revelation, an attitude—that might not have otherwise been were it not for the text." We all agreed that having a "flow" experience with reading is not synonymous with being mindlessly "lost in a book." For us, the sensation of being in the moment, of being completely wrapped up in a lived-through experience with reading is one of acute activity and attention to what we are doing.

"Reading," asserts one of the characters in Italo Calvino's (1979) novel about reading, *If on a Winter's Night a Traveler*, "is going toward something that is about to be and no one yet knows what it will be . . ." We never know exactly what to expect as we turn the pages of a book, what will transpire as we look ahead and also back within the space of a reading event. There is a rhythm to our reading process that bears some resemblance to what Judith Langer (1995) describes as stepping in and out of an "envisionment." However, we would qualify her description somewhat to emphasize the continuity between what we prefer to call moments of *reaction* and moments of *response*. For us, it's not a matter of stopping the "flow" in order to reflect on what we are reading. We prefer to think of it as expanding the scope of engagement through exercising our authority to question the experience we are having in a manner that actually enhances the intensity of the flow experience for us.

It is a truism that a question presupposes some prior understanding of the topic being investigated. Understanding what we are reading enables us to react—with our senses, emotions, and intellect—to what we imagine is happening before us. Mark recalls an experience reading the novel *To Kill a Mockingbird* with ninth grade students who wanted to talk about the incident in which Atticus Finch amazes his children by destroying a rabid dog with one shot from a distance of 100 yards. Initially students wanted to focus on the incident through sharing stories about their own experiences with rabid or otherwise diseased animals. Rereading this passage however prompted one student to question why Atticus wants to conceal his marksmanship ability from his children. Others chimed in and the whole conversation moved to another level without breaking the flow that had been established earlier. We think this is a minor but telling example of how questioning and ultimately critical thinking can follow from more or less humble reactions and observations.

Conceiving of reading as a flow experience does not rule out critical thinking, if by critical thinking one means a process of raising questions about one's initial beliefs and assumptions going in to an experience. One of the problems with textbook questions about literature is that they tend to exist in isolation from any actual reading event and thus have the effect of impeding "flow" rather than enhancing it. Questions that arise during the course of reading are our primary means for generating a response, that is, a more or less complete thought aimed at accounting for whatever it is we are sensing, feeling, or thinking as we read. And it works the other way as well. We would go so far as to say that any conceivable response to a literary work is connected with one or more specific questions.

One never knows at the outset of a reading experience what questions are going to arise and become relevant within the space of that unique event. Nonetheless, we found it interesting to learn that each of us is more likely to raise some types of questions than others, which we think says something about our individual reading styles. Jenny, for instance, tends to focus on characterization when she reads. The questions she usually finds engaging are those that invite reflection on voice and character development. Cheryl, on the other hand, reads to "test my beliefs," thus leading to questions aimed at clarifying and validating ideas that are important to her. Mark also spoke about "reading for ideas" though with less concern for validating his own beliefs than to broadening and even complicating his understanding of how to think about matters that concern him. Holly mentioned her practice of using reading to put her own thought processes into relief so as to develop critical self-awareness. None of this should suggest that a person is going to be interested in only one kind of question but we think it does point to an important way that reading events are situated with respect to individual needs and desires.

We will have a lot more to say about this matter of reading events being situated when we develop our theoretical stance toward reading as a process in Chapter 7. Here we want to observe that our tendency to formulate responses through questioning and attention to language probably marks us as teachers and distinguishes us to some extent from some adult amateur readers we know who seem to do little to build on their reactions when they read so that their responses tend to be less studied and more spontaneous than ours. Our hypothesis would be that this phenomenon could be explained in part as an effect of schooling. There appear to be many adults who, having rejected the practice of literary analysis as too difficult and/or simply uninteresting, are not aware that there are other ways of becoming thoughtful, critical readers. Our concept of student book clubs, which we unveil at the conclusion of this chapter, addresses this and other concerns about the relationship between schooling and life-long reading. We see student book clubs as an important tool for positioning ourselves as role models for young readers.

The four of us routinely (re)read all or parts of the texts we find engaging. For us, (re)reading, along with questioning, supports our reflexive stance whereby we aim to transcend our immediate reactions in order to explore possible responses. Thus, we have learned to approach books with an attitude of patience and a tolerance for uncertainty. The purpose of reading for us is not to achieve mastery over a given author or text but to make use of an author's words to create insights that are relevant to our concerns as individuals. This is not to say however that we view reading as a form of talking to ourselves (although it is that too!) More than anything else we use reading to encounter voices other than our own, to take a second look at what we may have thought was familiar and in the process invent new possibilities for thinking about our world.

Amateur Readers Expect Reading Events to Evolve In and Over Time

In retrospect, we notice that the issue of reading speed never came up during our conversation.Unlike many adults we have met over the years, we just don't think of ourselves generically as either "slow readers" or as "fast readers." By the same token, we hesitate to label a book as either a "quick read" or as one requiring more time and effort. We would prefer to say that it depends on the person. How quickly each of us gets through a book or parts of a book is always relative to what we happen to be reading as well as the circumstances surrounding that reading. In this section, we want to step over the issue of reading speed to embrace a slightly more complex view of the role played by time and temporal awareness with respect to reading, one that takes into consideration both the duration of particular reading events and the various ways those events are embedded within an individual's life history as a reader.

No one would disagree with the claim that reading, especially literary reading requires an expenditure of time and effort. Trying to spell out exactly what is entailed by this claim, however, is an altogether different matter. Commonsense notions summed up in the phrase, reading comprehension, for example, imply that the ultimate goal of reading is constant and complete clarity, a flawless transmission of content from writer to reader via a text. These notions persist despite overwhelming evidence—anecdotal and research based—that this is simply not how people read. In fact, one of the things we know for sure about struggling readers is that they tend to approach reading as a mastery project beginning with the mastery of individual words, then sentences, then paragraphs, and so on. School has taught them to believe that meaning is there on the page if only they look hard enough. Frank Smith (1997, 2002) and others have done extensive research documenting the debilitating effect of well-intentioned but seriously flawed teaching practices that are responsible for disengaging kids from other more productive ways of approaching the experience of reading as an event that evolves in and over time.

Again allowing for individual differences, the four of us, as noted in the previous sections, assume a strong sense of personal agency as amateur readers when it comes to choosing what, when, and how to read. Another aspect of this sense of agency is the expectation that reading events will take time to evolve. We open a book hoping to enjoy a lived-through experience in an imaginative place where we will have an opportunity to make something out of our—sensory, emotional, and intellectual—reactions to the voices of an author, narrator, characters, and sometimes other readers. We approach a literary text not as an object to be deciphered and interpreted but as a place to be explored. For the duration of a reading event we constantly revise our sense of where we think we have been and where we think we are headed, folding the two together to sustain the experience of "flow." Even before we arrive at the final page we already have done a lot of re-reading both in the sense of actually revisiting particular passages and in the sense of reworking our memory of all that has carried us along to a provisional moment of completion. We say provisional because even if we choose not actually to re-read a book (though we often do so choose) the reading experience we have just been through will continue to evolve as a memory in relation to additional life and/or reading experiences that may come our way.

There is another important way that lived-through experiences with reading evolve in time. Reading may indeed transport us to imaginary places but those places are still influenced by their proximity to our real-life situations. In other words, the circumstances surrounding a reading event can and do make a difference. Jenny vividly recalls what it was like to read *On the Occasion of My Last Afternoon* by Kaye Gibbons during the weeks following her marriage. The narrator's search for a better understanding of her past as a married woman spoke to Jenny in ways it probably would not have at any other time in her life. Holly nearly brought tears to our eyes as she recounted the experience of reading *The Things They Carried* by Tim O'Brien with her dad who had just returned from a journey back to Vietnam. It was the one and only time in her life that he opened up to her about his experiences as a soldier there in the 1960s.

We think it is crucial for teachers to respect this fact that our present lived-through experiences with reading are always connected more or less explicitly with our past history and our future prospects as readers. Each of us can cite many instances when finding the right book made an important difference in our lives. Cheryl read a book called *Edwin and the Iron Shoes* by Marcia Muller during the breakup of her first marriage and it changed her life to read about a woman who breaks free from a stifling relationship. Reading Emerson's "The American Scholar" touched Jenny's heart and mind at a time in her life when she was ready to embrace the idea of reading literature as a serious pursuit in her life. Holly spoke about reading *Charlotte's Web* as a young girl trying to understand and cope with her parent's divorce. The story helped her come to terms with change and the heartache of letting go at that time in her life.

We believe each reader has a story and that it is important to acknowledge this fact in school contexts. At the same time, we believe schooling, specifically the opportunity to experience guided collaborative reading, has the potential to enrich each reader's story. Just as the notion of reading as a hybrid construction helps us to account for our experience of making something unique to ourselves using someone else's words, we think it also addresses the way two pathways represented by schooling and life-long reading can combine to produce something new and unprecedented in a person's life. In the next section, we develop a perspective on community that supports an understanding of hybridity as two-dimensional, that is, operating across reading events in and over time.

Amateur Readers Recognize the Value in Reading with Others

Most people who become life-long readers can point to early experiences of being read to by parents or older siblings. Even those who do not develop the habit of reading until late in their lives usually can point to a mentor figure that provided them with crucial encouragement and support. It would appear that life-long reading exists as a social experience before it can exist as the more familiar private experience it becomes for most adults. For many, the social dimension of reading goes underground, so to speak, even to the point of seeming to disappear as it did for us only to be rekindled later in life sometimes as it was for Cheryl and Mark through becoming a parent oneself, or through participating in a reading group, even if a group of just two, as in reading with one's husband or wife—all four of us can testify to this. Our point is that the social dimension of reading with others appears to remain a dormant or barely realized possibility in the lives of many people who, like us, would identify themselves as life-long readers.

Putting one's reactions into words with others during a shared reading event inevitably underscores the fact that people—even people with very similar backgrounds—see and hear different things when they read. For some, this is the most eye-opening aspect of participating in a book club in which members feel free to be honest in describing what they are thinking and feeling. Of course, once a conversation is initiated on this basis, similarities as well as differences emerge and each person leaves the group with a richer mix of impressions to work with if they choose—or are required—to formulate a personal response to the reading. In this context, consensus doesn't have to mean everyone agrees; it may simply refer to a situation in which two readers begin to appreciate their very different reactions to an author's words. And of course there is always the possibility—in fact the likelihood—that the process of sharing reactions will have an impact on how each ultimately responds. We would point to this as yet another angle on our notion of reading experience as a hybrid construction.

Another factor that arises when people undertake to read books together, one frequently mentioned by participants in Mark's "book club class," concerns the quality of the relationships that develop between readers. The process of sharing reactions often leads to conversations that connect people with each other as well as with the book under discussion. Holly tells a wonderful anecdote about her participation in a book club with other teachers at her school. About midway through the year she was struck by the realization that she had become engaged in the lives of other people who otherwise would have remained mere faces in the crowd, people she might have chatted with in the teacher's lounge, but not the complex personalities she was encountering each month.

Reading in company with others, especially with those who represent different experiential backgrounds opens up the possibility that some readers will be prompted to take a second look at their own beliefs and assumptions, a move that we would argue constitutes an important form of critical thinking. Finding those with whom to share such experiences often means looking no further than one's own family, a point beautifully expressed in a recent essay by Mary Catherine Bateson (2000). Jenny remembers reading *West With the Night* by Beryl Markham with her dad and realizing how much their gendered perspectives influenced their reading. Holly shared a similar experience reading books with her mom in which each struggled to come to terms with generational differences in their ways of reading.

A good deal of research has been devoted to understanding how the act of writing itself generates new ideas. In other words, we know that writing involves more, much more, than merely transcribing thoughts completely worked out in advance. When it comes to reading, however, many shy away from the notion that comprehension involves a process that can affect the outcome. The fact is, we would claim, that a large part of our own process of learning how to read has been connected with learning how to talk about our reading. Beginning with early childhood when the only reading experiences available to us were social experiences on through adulthood, our ability as readers has grown step by step with our ability to verbalize complex responses as part of what we do as readers.

As paradoxical as it sounds, reading, which most regard as an intensely private experience, is utterly dependent on its social foundations beginning with the language that makes it all possible on through the various ways that reading either requires or invites encounters with voices other than one's own. What we have said so far about the dimensions of our own reading experiences with respect to choice, response, time, and community points to various ways that an act of reading does and indeed must transcend the limited actuality of an encounter between one reader and an author's words. Knowing this about ourselves as readers helps us situate ourselves as teachers of reading in ways we make explicit throughout the second part of this book.

In Chapter 3, Mark discusses the effect of his "book club class" on a group of teachers who, having never experienced anything like it before, wrote eloquently about how it opened their eyes to new possibilities for thinking about reading, teaching, and learning. Then, in Chapters 4, 5, and 6, Cheryl, Jenny, and Holly respectively explain in detail how they used their experiences in Mark's class to develop the concept of a student book club, which in their hands became an effective tool for teaching students how to be amateur readers and thus overcome the disconnect many assume must exist between reading for school and reading for their own purposes.

Part 2

Readers as Teachers

*"I expect readers to read in my books something
I didn't know, but I can expect it only from those
who wish to read something they didn't know."*

—Italo Calvino

"Half-Cultivated Fields": Teachers as Readers in University-Sponsored Book Clubs

"Mine was, as it were, the connecting link between wild and cultivated fields; as some states are civilized, and others half-civilized, and others savage or barbarous, so my field was, though not in a bad sense, a half-cultivated field."

(*Henry David Thoreau,* Walden)

Mark Faust

What exactly do parents and teachers mean when they express hope that children will mature as life-long readers? Who is a life-long reader? How do life-long readers use reading to enhance the quality of their lives? In the first part of our book we offered some personal reflections on these questions in light of our evolving practices as adult readers who happen also to be teachers of reading. In this next part we turn our attention to the different ways each of us is attempting to connect what we believe about life-long reading with our classroom practice as teachers of reading and literature.

Throughout my career as a teacher and teacher educator, I have always taken seriously questions concerning the relationship between schooling and life-long reading, but five years ago, this issue took on new meaning for me. At the time, I was participating in several book clubs with other adults and I found myself brooding over the wide gulf separating the lively, engaging conversations I was experiencing on a regular basis and the stilted, teacher-directed "discussion" I was observing in schools also on a regular basis. This experience prompted me to reevaluate my own past experiences as a student in high school and college in light of my current practices as an adult reader.

It became a matter of urgency for me to prompt similar reflection among the teachers enrolled in my classes. I was willing to grant that teachers need to accept responsibility for introducing young readers to quality literature and teaching them how to read critically. Nonetheless, there appeared to be a huge gap when it came to helping students see why these practices might make a difference in their lives other than in relation to passing tests. Experiencing the power of collaborative reading for myself combined with being intro-duced to new books such as *Literature circles: Voice and choice in book clubs and reading groups* by Daniels (1996, rev. 2002) and *Curriculum as conversation: Transforming traditions of teaching and learning* by Applebee (1996) inspired me to take the next step, which was to propose an innovative new course at my university designed by and for teachers interested in having a direct experience with a book club as a first step toward experimenting with this concept in their own classroom practice.

The "Book Club Class"

Since spring 2000, the course known colloquially and referred to henceforth as the "book club class" has been offered five times producing a total enroll-ment of 74 mostly middle and secondary school language arts teachers. Sixty-six or about 90% have been female. As we discuss in our introduction this predominance of female voices is significant given what we know about the complex history of gendered discourse in literary study. Although women still comprise the largest population of adults participating in book clubs, and my book club class is obviously no exception, there are signs that this landscape is becoming more diverse (Hartley 2001). Moreover, as teachers nationwide learn more about the value of collaborative reading and, like Cheryl, Jenny, and Holly, experiment with book clubs in their classes, one can at least hope that the book club experience may become less exclusively a girl thing.

Despite or perhaps because of its billing as an "experimental" course, the book club class tends to attract people who are not only interested in book clubs but who also value a non-traditional instructional format, that is, teach-ers who are willing to question "business as usual" (Sheridan 1985) in the language arts classroom. Nonetheless, as the chapters following this one make abundantly clear, opting to introduce book clubs in middle and high school classrooms does not require a wholesale revamping of the curriculum. Cheryl, Jenny, and Holly explain how to fold the book club experience along with its power to motivate young readers into one's class without abrogating the responsibility to address matters of concern to most secondary school teachers. For several years now each has been experimenting with ways to construct book clubs in middle and high school that replicate the open-ended, peer-led structure envisioned by proponents like Harvey Daniels while acknowledging realities such as required reading and the need to teach critical reading and writing. They have successfully transposed the more or less free-wheeling experience they got from my book club class into contexts involving a much greater array of constraints.

Allowing for differences in the size and makeup of the groups, the basic ground rules for the book club class have remained consistent since its inception. First and foremost, the teachers themselves decide what they want to read. Typically groups choose contemporary fiction such as *The Poisonwood Bible* by Barbara Kingsolver and *The Hours* by Michael Cunningham but notable exceptions include *All Over But the Shoutin* by Rick Bragg and *The Orchid Thief* by Susan Orlean as well as poetry by Billy Collins and Mary Oliver (a more complete reading list is available in my file in the Appendix along with a syllabus and samples of handouts). Each teacher participant is invited to recommend a book to the group and to make a "sales pitch" prior to the casting of votes to determine the level of interest among group members for each selection on offer. The number of books read during a semester varies depending on the size of the group and the nature of the reading selections.

Participants also are free to determine how they want to share and discuss their reading over a period of twelve to fourteen weeks. A simple survey enables me when necessary to divide each class into two or three groups (the survey inviting participants to indicate their preferences, e.g., what types of books they would enjoy or at least be willing to read? Would they prefer open-ended or more structured conversations? What others should know about them as potential conversation partners is also available in the Appendix). In addition, I make it clear from the beginning that my role as instructor does not include any responsibility to facilitate discussion. The task of initiating and sustaining conversation in the book clubs is solely the responsibility of those enrolled in the course.

So far, the "book club class" has supported the creation of eleven autonomous groups with the largest comprised of ten members and the smallest four members. Once book clubs are formed during the second week of class, they function as independent units within the overall structure of the course, which includes some required writing and discussion aimed at theorizing and contextualizing the book club experience as a resource for classroom teachers. In addition to reflecting on their own preferences and practices, students conduct an inquiry project that revolves around interviewing other adults who would describe themselves as life-long readers. Although these additional requirements are framed as supplemental and thus separate from the primary experience students obtain in their book clubs, most participants find the various aspects of the course work together to complicate their dual identity as readers and as teachers of reading/literature.

Personal versus Academic Reading

What distinguishes an "academic" from a "personal" response to literature? A substantial majority of the teachers who enroll in my book club class subscribe, at least initially, to a fairly rigid definition of "academic" responses, which they associate with literary history and criticism. Academic responses are supposed to be text-based and rigorously objective. Critical thinking in the context of classroom discussion of literature typically is understood to involve building defensible interpretations of literary texts. In contrast, they describe personal responses as reader-based, subjective, and marked by the absence of critical thinking.

Given these presuppositions, most participants approach the book club class enthusiastically as an opportunity to share personal responses without being burdened by any pressure to produce the kind of academic responses typically expected by their professors in the English department. A small but significant minority express hope that the book club experience will provide a context in which to advance from "merely" personal toward more academic responses. Almost all embrace the notion that the labels academic and personal describe different purposes for reading. In this vein, almost all participants begin the book club class believing that students in school should be allowed to experience both kinds of reading, that is, they believe that some form of "independent reading" as well as instruction in "critical reading" needs to be included in a comprehensive high school literature curriculum.

By the end of the semester-long class and reading a half dozen or so books collaboratively with their peers in a book club environment, reflective writing and exit interviews clearly suggest that, for most, the sharp boundary separating academic and personal responses has become much less distinct. While allowing for the inevitable nuances of individual opinion, I think it is fair to say that all arrive at a more complex view on the matter as compared to their stance at the beginning of the semester. For these teachers, the book club experience had opened up a third area or hybrid space that could not adequately be described as either academic or personal. Noting the value in exploratory talk and questioning that is simultaneously text-based and reader-based, they claim to have realized that critical thinking does not necessarily require one to relinquish one's personal investment in a reading event.

Likewise, participants report that their book club created opportunities, unique in their experience, to pursue a line of thought or develop an idea that illuminates *both* an aspect of text *and* a personal connection. I will return to this idea of a third area or hybrid space at the end of this chapter as a way of anticipating the chapters to follow because I think this is exactly what Cheryl, Jenny, and Holly are proactively trying to create for their students. Prior to doing that, I want to underscore just how pervasive this tendency to isolate personal and academic responses actually is and then, using teachers' own words as much as possible, highlight ways that the book club class disrupts this assumption.

The disconnect expressed by many teachers who have participated in the book club class over the years, including the four of us, between the purposes that motivate us to read in our personal lives and what is required of us as teachers of academic reading in schools is reflected in disagreements among professionals regarding the best approach to teaching young people how to read and enjoy good literature. We have already touched on this controversy in our praise of amateur reading that appears in the introduction to this book as well as in our reflections on life-long reading in Part 1. For readers who are interested, Part 3 of this book situates the distinction between personal and academic responses in relation to reader response theory. There we clarify the theoretical basis for a longstanding conflict among educators between various "text-based" and "reader-based" pedagogies in order to illuminate the commonplace assumption that a choice needs to be made between reading for personal and academic purposes. In this chapter, I touch on ways the book club experience is being framed by advocates outside the academy in order to underscore just how pervasive the distinction between academic and personal reading has become in our culture.

The kind of either/or thinking about academic versus personal reading so prevalent in school contexts is clearly evident in recently published guides designed for adult readers seeking advice about how to form book clubs in their communities or workplaces. *The New York Public Library Guide to Reading Groups* by Saal (1995) provides a good example of a text-based set of suggestions about "how to have a good discussion." (31) Of paramount importance, according to Saal, is the avoidance of "literary anarchy" (32) by "focusing intently upon the book itself." (35) "The book and the book alone is the thing. No biographical material is allowed to contribute to the discussion." (34) Citing protocols derived from the famous Great Books Program developed by Mortimer Adler, Saal assumes that good literary conversation should transcend the personal concerns of individual readers. A similar stance is taken up by Jacobsohn (1994) who argues that the primary purpose of a good discussion is "to analyze a text "its form and function" and, only secondarily to "discuss it's personal applications." (68) "Remember," she writes, "your questions and responses should emerge from the text, and discussion should be redirected back to the text." (68) Searching the websites of six major publishers, I found a similar emphasis in their recommendations for book discussion groups. Without exception, these revolve around lists of questions for discussion that clearly position readers as more or less passive recipients of meanings presumed to be intended by authors and conveyed by texts.

At the opposite end of the spectrum, *The Reading Group Book* by Laskin and Hughes (1995) typifies a thoroughly reader-based approach to defining what book clubs are about. They write, "We want to talk about subjects that make our brains feel alive. . . Book groups at their best are a bit like school without teachers, tests, or term papers—a kind of dream classroom where you can sip wine and nibble snacks, where it's perfectly acceptable to say that you adored a character in a novel because she reminded you of your sister" (xvii). Truly "unforgettable meetings" are those "in which the book was a springboard for a wider-range discussion. . . . The point is, anything goes—and often, the more contentious the better." (xviii)

A large-scale, international survey conducted by Hartley (2001) suggests that adult reading groups mirror the spectrum of practices found in classrooms but that a majority lean toward those described by Laskin and Hughes rather than the strictly text-based recommendations mentioned by Saal and Jacobsohn. According to Hartley, many respondents stress that, in their book club discussions, they use books as "a jumping off point, a springboard which can take the group in unforeseen directions. The point is that the group chooses the direction, and the book isn't isolated for study as it may be in a university seminar" (90).

Despite a clear leaning toward reader-based practices, Hartley's (2001) findings overall point to a complex mix of reading practices among adults, a phenomenon that deserves to be studied more closely, especially in light of the growing popularity of "book discussion guides" distributed by mainline publishers. In an extensive analysis of 120 such guides, McGinley, Conley, and White (2000) found that almost without exception, these documents legitimize "a highly formal English-class version of reading in everyday social life" based on "formalist ways of reading and understanding the text in itself." (208) Hartley's findings are interesting because they suggest that adult readers do not necessarily subscribe to the either/or thinking described above. Adult readers, like us and those interviewed by Appleyard (1991), are just as likely to adopt a "pragmatic" focus on reading for purposes not well described by approaches dominated by either a text-based or a reader-based orientation. Similarly, my own findings suggest that when adults, even adults who are language arts teachers, read together in a book club, they may well engage in practices that undermine their own beliefs about reading insofar as these are tied to a long history of thinking about literary reading in terms of binary oppositions between "text" and "reader," "social" and "personal," and ultimately between "academic" and "non-academic." This is exactly what happens for most of the teachers enrolled in the book club class over the years, many of whom began to see implications for their own classroom practice based on what they experienced in their book clubs. In this context, the teachers found themselves discovering new ways of thinking about what it might mean to be "on task" in an academic setting as well as new ways of understanding their personal reading and what it might mean to be a "life-long reader."

As far as I can tell, every one of the teachers who enrolled in the "book club class" over the past three years found it a worthwhile experience. Nevertheless, my data do not support an idealized view of book clubs in school. While some groups were more successful than others in fostering conversation and fellowship among participants, all presented challenges for the teachers most of whom possessed little or no experience of anything other than formal teacher-led discussion and "independent reading." Participating in university-sponsored book clubs disrupted their familiar ways of talking about books and many of the teachers expressed some discomfort, particularly at the outset, as they found themselves entering a conversational space that included limitations and possibilities calling for negotiation.

In my view, the conversations engendered by the book club class resemble what post-colonial theorist, Homi Bhabha (1985), refers to as the "third space," a "place of agency and intervention" within which new identities are fashioned out of concepts that were once understood to exist in binary opposition to each other. Related to this concept of the "third space" is the notion of "hybridity" advanced by the Russian linguist and philosopher Mikhail Bakhtin. As it is currently being used in the field of education, "hybridity" generally refers to spoken or written language that draws from two or more distinct sources to produce new and different ways of thinking about teaching and learning. Since the 1980s the term has been taken up in a variety of educational contexts. For example, Kris Gutierrez and colleagues (1999) use the word hybridity to theorize the tension that results when children representing different ethnic backgrounds challenge the "official language" of their primary school classroom by bringing in ways of speaking and acting derived from their local communities. Similarly, the book club class typically produces conversations that transgress conceptual boundaries separating "text" and "reader," "social" and "personal," and "academic" and "non-academic." In the sections to follow, I quote from participants in the book club class—their comments appear in italics—to illustrate the tension that arises when teachers engage in literary conversations that are neither personal nor academic, as those terms are usually understood.

The sections to follow are organized into three broad categories: (1) risk-taking and exploratory talk, (2) sustaining literary conversations, and (3) making connections. Within each category I allude to the possibility that teacher book clubs might constitute a kind of "third space." Readers looking for a more detailed discussion of hybridity and book clubs as a third space will want to consult Part 3 of this book where, as I mentioned before, we construct a theoretical rationale for making the book club experience a standard feature within programs of literature instruction in schools.

Risk-taking and Exploratory Talk

Advocates for classroom-based book clubs as a form of "independent reading" embedded within or alongside other curricular mandates tend to de-emphasize risk as a factor in making book clubs work (e.g., Chandler, 1997; Dale, 1999; Daniels 2002; Flint, 1999; Hill, Johnson, & Shick-Noe, 1995; Noll, 1994). They suggest book clubs in school should be as non-threatening as possible so as to encourage readers to open up and share what they think and feel about a particular book. Implicit in this recommendation is a desire to minimize students' fear of misreading or failing to "do justice" to a text. Proponents of the book club experience as a form of independent reading usually aim for a risk-free environment in opposition to what many perceive as the more risky environment produced by a teacher-led discussion conducted for the purpose of providing literature instruction.

In contrast with the mainstream view that books clubs are or should be risk-free, teachers enrolled in the "book club class" quickly discover a need to think differently about risk. Many find themselves seeking alternatives to what Meyer (1993) aptly refers to as "the illusion of mastery." The task of having to make conversation led many to address concerns Meyer frames as follows: "Can we establish an 'authority' that is not based on the illusion of mastery? Can we locate an academic discourse that is not aggressively combative and competitive but that promotes a community that engages in dialogue, not debate?" (p. 52) Redefining risk and developing patience for exploratory talk are key elements whereby teachers enrolled in my book club class forged a practice of reading as "ongoing revision." (p. 56) In the chapters following this one, Cheryl, Jenny, and Holly each describe how they addressed this issue of creating a safe space not as an end but a means for teaching critical thinking.

All of the eleven teacher book clubs my class has thus far sponsored confronted several types of risk the teachers described as quite different from the risk of being "wrong" or of displeasing an authority figure. One type was related to sharing personal thoughts and preferences with others in a social setting: *I looked forward with a little anxiety about sharing my poem. Most amazingly, I felt pride and joy when the others appreciated my chosen poem. (Molly)* Another type of risk emerged in conjunction with feelings of responsibility to the group: *I found myself reading the novels differently. I must admit that I am a better reader when I know other people are reading the same text I am and that we are going to discuss it. (Ellen)* A third type of risk was connected with the possibility that disagreements might result in the conversation becoming adversarial. The fact that all eleven book clubs negotiated this risk early on was a crucial factor in their success.

> I love being challenged to see things in a different light. That's what was happening in our group. (Sykora)

> We are all students of literature as much as we are teachers, so we've agreed not to be afraid to get too intellectual or scholarly, but also not to engage in a mr/mrs smarty pants competition. (Melissa)

> I caught myself sharing more than I thought I would. (Aleigh)

The ability to engage in risk-management produced an ethic of care that many of the participants recognized as essential to the success of their book clubs.

> [Being in a reading group] challenges us to think about what we say before we say it and to think whether or not what we say will affect someone else negatively or positively. (Sharon)

> We dove into our differences and the differences in our kids in our upcoming classrooms and how great it is to be different but how careful with each other we should be. (Paula)

Confronting and managing potential sources of risk appears to be a prerequisite for the emergence of tentative, exploratory talk, which in turn becomes a valuable source of subject matter that can be used to build conversations and keep them going.

The kind of exploratory talk I observed at the outset of book club class discussions aligns well with what Barnes and Todd (1995) identify as "conversational moves" associated with learning through talk. For example, participants would initiate discussion of a new topic by making a comment, claim, or by posing a question. This often elicited further comments aimed at validating and/or elaborating on what had been said. The person initiating the topic frequently would reformulate their thoughts indicating that they had accepted the qualifications coming from the group. Often, examples or illustrations were solicited in order to extend the previous contribution. Out of this back and forth, new comments, claims, and/or questions would emerge. For the most part, the teachers were comfortable with skirting a variety of matters before making a commitment to follow up on any of them.

Many participants wrote about their joys and concerns regarding exploratory talk. Curiosity about others' experiences with the reading was sometimes offset by feelings of impatience over reactions that to some seemed irrelevant to the emerging conversation. On balance, however, exploratory talk was valued as an important precursor to more focused conversation.

> Our exploratory talk helped us segue in and out of sustained conversation, and it felt as though we comfortably floated along a stream of reactions and responses. (Angie)

> I like the discovery phase of reading. . . . The discussions took twists and turns that were sometimes unexpected. (Sara)

Being productive, the teachers discovered, could mean something other than merely sharing personal reactions and/or sticking to the text. Over time, their ability to negotiate sources of risk and their willingness to engage in exploratory talk ultimately produced a more complex conversational space (Barnes & Todd, 1995) than is generally authorized either by reader-based or by text-based concepts of good discussion.

Sustaining Literary Conversation

Book clubs require patience and time for participants to make and sustain conversation. My observations have led me to the conclusion that this process often occurs in the form of lateral connections that typically are overlooked in the context of more vertical, goal-oriented classroom discussion. At the same time, successful groups learn how to define and manage conversational drift, the tendency to digress in more or less interesting ways. They also recognize the need to negotiate boundaries with respect to roles and possible topics of discussion: *We shifted roles from quiet observer to animated story-teller to advice giver to policewoman keeping us on track and within the bounds of our established rules, for we all sensed 'ownership' of the group. (Ellen)* Open-ended conversation requires participants to monitor the tone they take toward each other: *I learned how to be patient when others are sharing pieces of their lives, especially when they might be so different from mine. (Annie)* Many reflection papers addressed the issue of paying attention to the flow of one's own reactions in conjunction with listening to others talk about theirs: *I learned something about my negotiation skills. There were times when I wanted to share a perspective about a particular topic and found that the conversation had either moved on before I could contribute or that the topic had changed. I simply wrote down my thoughts, and usually found an opportunity to relate it to the conversation at a later time. (Meghann)*

The challenge of sustaining a conversation for up to two hours meant that the groups had to learn how to restart when the talk subsided. With varying degrees of success, the teachers learned to use interruptions in the flow of conversation as an opportunity rather than a threat. *Today we talked about silence and the role it has played in our group. I think that silence and the attitude with which we regard it is important to a book club. . . . The silences that we allow give us the pause we need. (Kristin)* It never ceases to surprise me when the majority of teachers enrolled in the class say that they have never experienced anything quite like the ebb and flow conversation in a book club.

Conversations across all the groups were energized and sustained when one person validated another's comment by adding to it or connecting it with something else. This strategy, much more than expressions of doubt or disagreement, defined what it meant for a group to consider itself "on-task." Some individuals worried about this as they felt a desire for more probing and questioning of each other's ideas. On the whole, however, and despite the reservations expressed by a few participants, the book clubs represented in this study were marked by a spirit of cooperation as the teachers worked hard to make something useful and interesting out of whatever was offered up during the course of the conversations.

> *It was amazing how in our discussions we found ways to link our common reading experiences. (Emily)*
>
> *Even though each person comes from a different background, we found common ways to connect. (Tara)*
>
> *We sometimes joked that it felt like we were in therapy, but essentially, we were gathering strength from each other in terms of validation. Just knowing that you and someone else agree or disagree, but your voice is heard and accepted as intelligent is in itself a great feeling we all need at some point. (Lisa)*

Consistently, the teachers wrote in their reflection papers about the excitement they felt over the opportunity to develop their personal reactions to a book in light of what others had to say. *Meeting with the group opened some very provocative questions and clues that I never would have imagined about this short story. We fed off each other's ideas. (Sharon)* At the same time, most were not interested in hearing about experiences that seemed disconnected from the flow of conversation about a book: *Some days we were right 'on task' with our discussion and reactions to the book. We connected the work to our personal experiences and political/religious views, and then we would connect back to the work. Other days we would really get off track in a conversation that stemmed from one thing to another and then wonder how we got there. (Amy)*

Good literary conversation across all the groups came to be defined as both text-based and reader-based. Academic discourse, while not actively discouraged, rarely defined the focal point of discussion. Nonetheless, most participants grew impatient if the conversation drifted too far from the collaborative project of making sense of the reading. A desire to address gaps in understanding expressed in the form of questions and comments, mostly about character and situation, clearly displaced art appreciation as the dominant concern across the groups. Most of the time, this pragmatic focus on meaning making allowed for a variety of conversational modes: *Our conversations ran the gamut, ranging from very serious and incorporating some traditional elements of literary analysis to whimsical lighthearted conversation peppered by laughter and even punctuated by teary emotional moments. (Kris)* Paying attention to the text became intertwined with paying attention to each other as the teachers used literary conversation to build connections among themselves as well as between themselves and the books they read together. *The books we read in the class will always be connected with the three other faces I have been seeing every Wednesday evening. We've shared our lives, our histories, our perspectives. It is a connection that I am thankful for during this hectic time in my life. It has rekindled my joy in female friendship and the thrill of a great book. (Linda)*

Making Connections

Among the most intriguing outcomes of the class for me is evidence that book clubs can facilitate connections between people as much as they connect readers with books and that the best conversations do both. *There has been nothing in my life that quite compares to this process of building a community of readers that began as strangers and somehow serendipitously became bonded through the pages of a book. (Tara)* And, *We were growing into a band of intertwining stories and life-experiences, each of which was valuable and intriguing, each of which we will take with us when the class is over. (Ellen)* The connections with other readers came as a surprise for a number of the participants. *One of the most important learning outcomes for this course, which I would say is an unexpected one, is the relationship and trust that is established. (Aleigh)*

On occasion individuals used the book clubs to connect with their own ideas and to critically evaluate their initial reactions to a book. *The discussions that I began in my group reached into my personal life and opened up issues in an interesting way. (Heather)* One of the few men to enroll in the class wrote, *I never realized how stereotypically 'male' many of my responses were! (Keith)* Although the rigorous pursuit of critical thinking one finds in many classrooms was not the dominant mode of conversation, many of the teachers nonetheless wrote about reevaluating their ideas and opinions in light of what others had said in their book club. Many alluded to blurring the boundaries between personal and social in this context. *I really enjoyed the conversation when we discussed political topics like feminism, classism, racism, etc. because hearing other people's reactions and experiences really personalizes these topics for me. (Alecia)* Ultimately, many of the participants found themselves thinking differently about the role of reading in both their personal and their professional lives. *Overall, I think the past ten weeks have expanded my notion of what it means to be a reader. (Amy)*

Over time, even the boundary separating individual points of view became fuzzy as the teachers realized they were co-creating something important that in the end belonged to no one of them in particular.

> *Words are shared. No one owns the words.* (Molly)
>
> *A book can be a social event, a shared experience.* (Sara)
>
> *We sometimes created a whole more powerful than any one of us.* (Kirsten)

Likewise, for many, the lived-through experience of reading became folded into that of reading with others producing a kind of "third space" in which familiar binary distinctions were redescribed in terms of both/and.

> *As I read in the days leading up to our weekly meetings, I found myself wondering what the other group members would think about a particular line or section of the book.* (Beth)
>
> *I'll probably always think of Ellen when I read Welty.* (Angie)
>
> *It is a rare privilege to glimpse the private lives of these co-readers and read both inside and outside my own experience for a given time.* (Rose)

My choice to highlight connections rather than differences across the eleven book clubs is motivated by a desire to underscore what becomes possible when unquestioned assumptions separating reader and text, personal and social, and, indeed, non-academic and academic reading are not allowed to determine in advance the course of a literary conversation. For the past three years,

I have been amazed by the energy with which so many teachers seized the invitation to transgress these boundaries; in many cases surprising even themselves with never-before imagined possibilities. *I have a thirst for this kind of conversation that is rare in life—conversation that transcends the bibble-babble chatter and cuts right into the unspoken thoughts we all have. The oddest thing is that since I was never around people who talked about these kinds of things, I've never learned to articulate myself very well. . . I've realized that my educational experience simply didn't give me any opportunity to form this kind of reflection and thinking. (Melissa)*

Reflection: What is a Proper Reading

How does one discuss the material without including the individual? I tend to be in the middle of this tug of war—I want to do both. I have a great curiosity to know how other people read things. I learn so much about the other person AND the book/author through another person's eyes. Is this a 'proper' reading? Who defines what is 'proper'? (Aleigh)

Exit interviews with participants revealed that most did not view their positive experience with book clubs as necessarily negating the value either of personal independent reading or teacher-led discussion to enhance critical thinking. Instead, they referred to the potential role book clubs might play as an additional way of reading, one that stands between text-based and reader-based orientations in such a way as to enhance the value of both for a broad spectrum of readers. For example, the one teacher who was most adamant about the limitations of her book club conversations expressed herself this way: *Call me an English major, but I think there is a place for that deeper literary conversation. It should come after the personal reactions.* Significantly, however, she situated academic discourse as a tool for enhancing reading experiences already in play rather than as a set of predetermined conclusions. This concern is precisely what Cheryl, Jenny, and Holly address in the chapters following this one. How can teachers model reading practices that fold together personal and academic concerns in ways that enhance their students' experiences with literary texts?

Another teacher, who also expressed some concern over what she saw as the failure of her group to fully realize the potential in the conversations they started, still left with a very positive view of her experience: *Not only are reading and interpretation skills enhanced, but also important life skills such as cooperation, acceptance of differing opinions, and communication. I hope that my students will attain an appreciation for reading and discussing a work of literature, not just read to answer the questions on a test. I hope they will come to understand that the very same words can evoke multiple emotions and thoughts in various individuals. I hope they can conceive of becoming a life-long reader, or at least understand why many of us are! (Tara)*

Overall, many participants claimed that the course helped them to develop a more complex understanding of reading as an event that can evolve in unexpected ways over time. Many of their comments resonate with Sumara's (2000) call for a more complex view of reading that overcomes rigid binary thinking rooted in outdated Cartesian epistemological assumptions. Repeatedly, I noted comments to the effect that the participating teachers were leaving the class feeling less constrained by competing definitions of what might count as a "proper" reading. Aleigh, the teacher quoted above who referred to feeling caught in a "tug of war" ultimately joined many of the others in arriving at a more complex view of proper, one allowing for a multiplicity of legitimate purposes, including both informal dialogue and critical thinking.

Like the adults Appleyard (1991) interviewed for his research, the teachers I have met over the years through participating in the book club class are well-described as "pragmatic" readers, many of whom reveled in the opportunity to choose what and how to read and then to use books to address questions and concerns that arose in the context of their shared reading experiences. In this context, the teachers redescribed the boundary between academic and non-academic in ways Schultz (2002) argues should be the norm if we want to help young people make necessary connections between schooling and life. Also relevant are Fiske's (1989) investigations into the way people actively resist the efforts of authorities to prescribe and limit their responses to all manner of cultural phenomena. Writing about her group's discussion of *All Over But the Shoutin'* by Rick Bragg, Ellen wrote, *we continue to probe, to ask questions of the author's intentions. It would be wonderful to meet him and then give him a piece of my mind!*

I make no claims about laying to rest knotty questions about the relative value of academic discourse versus more "authentic" ways of reading. Nor do I want to suggest that the divide between academic and non-academic contexts for reading either can or should be completely erased. I would, however, point to ways in which the current popularity of collaborative reading in the form of book clubs may signify a new opportunity for teachers and teacher educators. Experiencing book clubs for themselves in the book club class has helped many teachers begin to think differently about reading and their role as teachers of literature. *My book club has grown into an integral part of my life for the past sixteen weeks and enriched my worldview, influenced my teaching philosophy, and fanned the flames of my love for reading; it has been a joyful, empowering experience that has created connections with others. (Sara)*

Summary and Recommendations

Like most language arts teachers, every one enrolled in the book club class claimed that helping young people grow into life-long readers is an important goal of their teaching. A primary motive for taking the class is expressed in the desire mentioned by many to learn how to use book clubs in their own teaching as a means for achieving that goal. What most did not expect is that participation in a book club would expose them to new possibilities for thinking about reading and themselves as readers. This finding suggests that book clubs have the potential to be as valuable for teacher educators as they appear to be for classroom teachers. The experience of reading with other teachers in a book club led many to raise questions about the necessity of thinking about academic as opposed to non-academic purposes for reading. Many, like Cheryl, Jenny, and Holly, found themselves becoming less bound by conventional ways of thinking dictated by binary logic and more open to ways of seeing literature and life as connected in the context of reading with others in book clubs. The long-term effects of this experience as well as its potential links with other aspects of a teacher's self concept and classroom practice are both an avenue for further research and an exciting prospect for those who would like to see a better fit between literature instruction in schools and the choice all people must make about whether or not to live a life that includes reading.

Over the past several years I have experimented with various ways of constructing this experimental class. The biggest challenge has been finding ways to provide opportunities for pedagogically oriented reflection that do not threaten the integrity of the primary focus of the course which is the book club experience. Initially I tried locating this discussion at the end of the course. That didn't work because after twelve weeks of reading together, the teachers resisted having to disband in order to complete the requirements of the course. Following that experience, I tried setting aside special days designated for the necessary conversations centering on "naming" what we were doing and planning exigencies related to introducing book clubs into mainstream schools. That approach turned out to be somewhat less problematic from the teachers' perspective but still not what I was looking for. Finally, I hit upon an approach that seemed to work pretty well (see the syllabus in the appendix to this chapter for more details).

Beginning at the mid-point of the semester, we set aside the last 40 minutes of class for discussion focused on a sequence of specific topics related to the challenge of "transposing" the format for conversation developed in book club class so that it could be useful for teachers and students in schools. This approach worked because it allowed for plenty of time early on for teachers to develop an identity as a group and address the important issues I talk about in this chapter. By the mid-point of the semester, groups were humming and 90 minutes turned out to be plenty of time to have a meaningful conversation. We took care of the needed shop talk and still were able to keep the groups intact for as long as possible, that is, right through the last day of class!

A key element I would not touch is the autonomy I gave to teachers to choose what to read and how to conduct conversations. Nonetheless, and partly due to the experience of working on this book, I am considering the possibility of creating an optional strand that would provide teachers an opportunity to experiment with extending their conversation over a particular book in order to follow through on their initial reactions and questions thus moving toward a more critical stance than has been engendered in the book club class thus far. This option would provide a first-hand experience with what many veterans of the class say was a must if they were going to be able to make book clubs part of their teaching repertoire especially at the secondary level, namely, they had to be able to connect the book club experience directly with the curriculum. Devoting class time to "independent reading" even of a collaborative nature was simply not an option for many.

Defining the book club in school not as a place existing outside or running parallel to the literature curriculum requires the kind of thinking exemplified by Cheryl, Jenny, and Holly in the three chapters that follow. In different ways each has found that it is not only possible to connect book clubs with curricular goals but that book clubs help students meet those goals without having to sacrifice their personal connection with the experience of reading with others. They have discovered ways to construct book clubs as third areas that exist in productive tension with other aspects of the literature curriculum. Following a brief introduction to the concept of the book club as a third space, I will conclude this chapter by anticipating the discussions to follow. Just as the experience of participating in the book club class became a springboard for my colleagues to experiment with the concept in their own teaching, I hope this chapter prepares the way for our readers to learn from what these experienced teachers have to say about the challenges and rewards of modifying the school literature curriculum in light of what the book club experience has to offer.

Modifying the Curriculum: The Book Club as a Third Space

Henry David Thoreau's (1854/1981) famous account of his experiment at Walden Pond is a book that bridges academic and non-academic contexts in a very personal way for me. In discussions leading up to our decision to undertake this project, I found myself returning to Thoreau's metaphor of the "half-cultivated field." I allude to it here as a means for distinguishing book clubs as "half cultivated fields" from the fully "cultivated fields" of literary history and criticism as well as the (more or less) "wild fields" marked by unbridled individual responses to literature. Just as Thoreau used his experience at Walden Pond to put the rest of his life into perspective, I believe collaborative reading experiences in book clubs can become a means for putting other, and equally important aspects of a literary education into perspective. This metaphor strikes me as an ideal way to situate book clubs within a comprehensive vision of literary reading and teaching. I find that opening up this third space puts the other two in perspective for teachers seeking to negotiate the challenge of helping students connect with literature on a personal level while encouraging them to broaden their perspectives on literature and life. Seen in this way as a third space, a book club becomes fertile ground for producing hybrid language practices that transform what it means to read and discuss a book.

Envisioning a broad-based, comprehensive approach to literature instruction, as variously cultivated fields of activity would help bring schooling into line with adult reading practices, which, as is well known, tend to be eclectic and pragmatic in character. We are not opposed to the idea of introducing young readers to literary history and criticism. Neither would we want to eliminate the experience of what is usually referred to as independent reading. Our goal is to expand the menu of possibilities we offer to young readers including the use of book clubs to open up a third area or hybrid space where they can connect with literature on a personal level in a context that exposes them to experiences that have the potential to enlarge their perspectives on literature and life.

In the chapter following this one, Cheryl talks about her experiments with student book clubs in a middle school classroom. Adolescent readers, she discovered, require a lot of instruction and modeling up front before they are able to participate in student book clubs that do more than provide a venue for sharing reactions to books. She describes how this effort is paying dividends for her as well as the students in her classes. Her success with student book clubs has opened Cheryl's eyes to the possibility of connecting reading and writing through a workshop approach to instruction.

In Chapter 5, Jenny describes her experiment with implementing student book clubs at a suburban Atlanta private school. Her challenge, quite different than that Cheryl faces every day, was to motivate her above-average students to think beyond the confines of a curriculum within which they had learned how to be successful. Where Cheryl now sees student book clubs as a tool for helping many of her students overcome a history of failure, Jenny sees student book clubs as a tool for helping her students redefine what might count as success in an academic context.

Part 2 concludes with Holly's chapter in which she contextualizes both perspectives through describing her work with two very different twelfth grade classes in a racially diverse suburban public school. Framing the concept of a student book club differently for her "basic" level classes as compared with what she did with her Advanced Placement class, Holly was able to promote critical reading and discussion in both contexts. Perhaps because she has had a longer history with thinking about book clubs, Holly's work exemplifies possibilities toward which Cheryl and Jenny are aspiring as they begin to restructure their own classroom practice. As a whole, we hope that Chapters 4 through 6 suggest a variety of options and points of entry for readers of this book depending on their level of experience and the climate within which they work.

Appendix to Chapter 3

ELAN 7700: Creating Literate Communities

Spring Session 2003

Time & Location: 5:00-7:30; meets initially in Rm 116 Aderhold Hall
Professor: Dr. Mark Faust
Mail & Messages: 125 Aderhold Hall
Office Phone: 542-4515
Office Fax: 542-4509
Email: mfaust@coe.uga.edu
Office Hours: By appointment

"Ordinary people don't know how much time and effort it takes to learn how to read. I've spent eighty years at it, and I still can't say that I've reached my goal." (Goethe)

"Criticism is the province of age, not of youth. They'll get to that soon enough. Let them build up a friendship with the writing world first. One can't criticize until one knows." (Robert Frost)

"The real journey of discovery lies not in seeking new landscapes, but in seeing with new eyes." (Marcel Proust)

"I expect readers to read in my books something I didn't know, but I can expect it only from those who wish to read something they didn't know." (Italo Calvino)

"The purpose of art is to lay bare the questions that have been hidden by the answers." (James Baldwin)

Course Description

This course number (Creating Literate Communities) was developed to provide professors and students with opportunities to explore different ways of construing what a "literate community" is and how such communities are "created" in different contexts. For example, the existence of schools, classrooms, workplaces, families, and other social contexts is connected with a wide array of "literacies," i.e., shifting definitions of what will count as "literate behavior." The particular version of ELAN 7700 being offered this spring foregrounds adult reading groups as one type of literate community. Thus, the centerpiece of the course will be the creation of one or more functioning teacher reading groups. In addition to participating in the reading group, students will contribute to an ongoing collaborative investigation into their own and others' reading practices in this setting as well as the larger context that goes with living a life that includes reading. The overarching purpose of the course will be to address two questions: What can we learn about the kinds of reading experiences that become available through participation in a reading group? and What exactly are we talking about when we express hope that our children will become "life-long readers"?

The course will be divided into three overlapping phases to facilitate (1) preliminary conversation and formation of the reading groups, (2) development of the reading groups and individual inquiry projects, (3) reflection and conversation focused on practical considerations connected with implementing "literature circles" in academic contexts.

What follows are a few additional key questions that students can expect will be addressed either directly or indirectly during this course: What makes a reading experience pleasurable for you? How would you describe your ability to have pleasurable experiences with reading to someone who doesn't already know what you're referring to? How do your present experiences with books compare with those you had when you were younger? How would you account for your experience of some books as "better" than other books? Do you recognize a distinction between 'just reading' and 'literary analysis'? How (for you) does the experience of reading a book for the first time differ from reading the same book more than once? How would you characterize the relationship between reading and writing in your life?

Required Reading

Reading group(s) will decide what to read based on a process of negotiation among group members.

Course Requirements

Participation: Everyone is expected to attend each meeting on time and to be an active, respectful participant in class discussion and in the reading group. This doesn't just mean being prepared to talk, but also to listen and to engage productively with others over matters of concern to the group as a whole. In addition, everyone is expected to use the following protocols as part of their individual engagement with the readings: (1) select passages to foreground by highlighting, underlining or by some other means, (2) make notes "reacting" to the readings in the margins or in a notebook of some kind, (3) generate and write down questions for private reflection and/or public discussion.

Position Paper: (due 1/16). What does the phrase "becoming a life-long reader" mean in the context of your life? What for you is pleasurable about reading? How does reading help you to live your life? Compose a paper (up to 500 words, typed with double spaces please) in which you share some of what comes to mind when you think about these questions.

(10 points possible)

Inquiry Project: (due 1/23). Everyone is expected to conduct an interview project to investigate what it means to live a life that includes reading, and if possible reading with others in a book club or other social setting. To get started, find and interview at least two adults who could be described as "life-long readers." Ask your subjects to identify what and when they read. Ask them to explain why they have chosen to live a life that includes reading. What factors do they think contributed most to their becoming life-long readers? Find out if they have had any experiences reading with others in book clubs or other social settings, and, if so, ask them to describe these experiences? I advise you if at all possible to tape-record interviews but it is not necessary to transcribe them. After studying data generated by your interviews, write a brief report of findings (up to 500 words) and make copies for others in your reading group. A range of options for organizing these reports will be discussed in class.

(20 points possible)

6 Mini-Reaction Papers: (papers are due at the end of class on days featuring literature circle discussions). Each reading group is instructed to conclude their conversation no later than 7:15 to allow time for individuals to write down some reactions (describe/comment/question) to what was said and how they think the group functioned.

(30 points possible)

5 1-Page Handouts: (1) Pretend you are addressing a person other than one of us and write up to a page describing your experience with literature circles this semester. Please do not assume that negative reactions are unwelcome. It is perfectly okay to mention problems and/or limitations you have encountered so far (due 3/13); (2) List at least three reasons why you think an experience with literature circles might be beneficial for high school students. Give us a brief explanation for each of your ideas (due 3/27); (3) List any ideas you have about introducing the concept of literature circles to high school students with respect to forming groups, selecting books, and negotiating risk. (due 4/3); (4) List any ideas you have about introducing the concept of literature circles to high school students with respect to managing class time and providing structure/scaffolding. (due 4/10); (5) List any ideas you have about introducing the concept of literature circles to high school students with respect to assessment and evaluation. (due 4/17).

(25 points possible)

Reflection Paper: (due 4/24). How would you describe the overall quality of the conversation that took place in your reading group? What was it like for you to be a participant in your group? Are there particular aspects of the conversation that you found exciting and useful? Did you ever find yourself feeling frustrated or disturbed? How was this experience different from other experiences you've had reading with others in school or elsewhere? Compose a paper (up to 500 words, typed with double spaces please) in which you make a case for or against the value of reading with others in the kind of informal settings created for this course.

(15 points possible)

Grading

Everyone is expected to keep up with all the course requirements and to maintain a high level of commitment to making the course a success. Students who meet this expectation can in turn expect to receive a grade of A on their transcript.

93-100   A
85-92   B
77-84   C
70-76   D
Below 70   F

Course Outline

1/9   Course intro.

1/16   *Position Papers due.* Preliminary discussion and decision making.

1/23   *Inquiry Project due.*

1/30   Literature Circles

2/6   Literature Circles

2/13   Literature Circles

2/20   Literature Circles

2/27   Literature Circles

3/6   Literature Circles

3/13   Literature Circles (5-6:30)
       Discuss *Handout #1* (6:45-7:30)

3/20   (spring break)

3/27   Literature Circles (5-6:30)
       Discuss *Handout #2* (6:45-7:30)

4/3   Literature Circles (5-6:30)
       Discuss *Handout #3* (6:45-7:30)

4/10   Literature Circles (5-6:30)
       Discuss *Handout #4* (6:45-7:30)

4/17   Literature Circles (5-6:30)
       Discuss *Handout #5* (6:45-7:30)

4/24 (AERA) *Reflection Paper due.*

5/1   Discuss Reflection Papers
       Course Evaluation

ELAN 7700: Creating Literate Communities

A sampling of 25 books selected by participating teachers since 2001:

All Over But the Shoutin by Rick Bragg
The House on Mango Street by Sandra Cisneros
The Hours by Michael Cunningham
The Red Tent by Anita Diamant
The Count of Monte Cristo by Alexander Dumas
The Cider House Rules by John Irving
The World According to Garp by John Irving
The Poisonwood Bible by Barbara Kingsolver
Paradise by Toni Morrison
The Bluest Eye by Toni Morrison
Proud Shoes by Pauli Murray
Going After Cacciato by Tim O'Brien
The Orchid Thief by Susan Odean
The Body of Christopher Creed by Carol Plum-Ucci
Close Range by Annie Proulx
The Feast of All Saints by Anne Rice
The Widow's Mite and Other Stories by Perrol Sams
Me Talk Pretty One Day by David Sedaris
The Killer Angels by Michael Shaara
A Thousand Acres by Jane Smiley
Gulliver's Travels by Jonathan Swift
Slaughterhouse Five by Kurt Vonnegut
Divine Secrets of the Ya-Ya Sisterhood by Rebecca Wells
Quite a Year for Plums by Bailey White
Mrs. Dalloway by Virginia Woolf

ELAN 7700: Creating Literate Communities
Spring Semester 2000

<u>READING SURVEY</u>

1. How many hours of free time do you spend reading each week?

     0-7_____   8-14_____   more than 15_____

2. How often do you choose each of the following "genres" of reading?
     0=never   1=rarely   2=often   3=regularly

     Put one number in each space below:

     _____magazines/periodicals   _____short stories
     _____action/adventure   _____horror
     _____literary classics   _____science fiction
     _____reference books   _____historical fiction
     _____biography   _____mystery
     _____non-fiction (science, history,   _____romance
          philosophy, etc.)
     _____newspapers   _____young adult
     _____western   _____poetry
     _____comics   _____letters
     _____fantasy   _____essays

3. Circle YES/NO

     Yes or No   Do you ever put down a book and not finish reading it?
     Yes or No   Do you tend to finish one book before beginning another?
     Yes or No   Do you like to read books more than once?
     Yes or No   Have you ever participated in a reading group?
     Yes or No   Do you normally talk to others about your reading?
     Yes or No   Do many of your friends share your attitudes toward reading?
     Yes or No   Do you like to "stop and think" while reading?
     Yes or No   Do you tend to "visualize" what you read?
     Yes or No   Do you like to "analyze" what you read?
     Yes or No   Do you like to write about what you read?
     Yes or No   Do you frequently use some form of writing to enhance your
                     experiences with books?
     Yes or No   Do you come from a family of readers?
     Yes or No   Were you read to as a child?
     Yes or No   Can reading be valuable for you without also being pleasurable?
     Yes or No   Do you believe that some books are "better" than others?

ELAN 7700: Creating Literate Communities
Spring Semester 2002

<u>Survey for the purpose of forming reading groups</u>

1. Preferred genres (you may check more than one)

_____ novels

_____ short stories

_____ poetry

_____ drama

_____ essays

_____ non-fiction (science, history, biography, etc.)

_____ "popular fiction" (e.g., books that can be purchased at
            Walmart)

_____ young adult literature

_____ "multicultural" literature: please specify the cultural
            tradition you are most interested in :

_____

2. Do you teach in a primary, middle, or secondary school? (circle
    one), or describe your present occupation if not teaching:

3. Quality of conversation (you may check more than one)

_____ I can enjoy a meandering, unfocused conversation.

_____ I am interested in hearing about the personal
            connections others make with a book.

_____ I get impatient unless a conversation is clearly "going
            somewhere."

_____ I am anxious to "interpret" what I read using the
            "tools" of literary criticism.

_____ I really want to experiment with potentially unfamiliar
            ways of reading and talking about books with others.

4. Is there a particular "thematic focus" you would like to explore
with your group? If so, please specify below:

5. Do you have a preference when it comes to deciding whether
everyone in your group reads the same titles?

_____ Everyone reads the same material prior to discussing it.

_____ Group members select reading on their own to share
with others during reading group meetings.

_____ I'd like to experience a little of both.

6. Summarize your expectations for this class by describing what would
have to happen for you to feel the class was successful, valuable, enjoyable,
etc.

ELAN 7700: Creating Literate Communities

Spring Semester 2000

Tentative Protocols for In-class Book Discussion Groups

We agree to the following:

1. to keep up with the reading and to keep our "reader's notebooks" up-to-date so we will have "reactions" to share with the group.

2. to be active listeners who frequently ask for clarification and/or elaboration directly or indirectly as in "Let me see if I understand what you're saying."

3. to practice an ethic of care. This means that, in addition to being considerate of each other in what we say and how we say it, we all will make an effort to monitor the discussion so that no one feels left out.

4. to refrain from rushing into summative proclamations about literary merit or meaning and to focus instead on exploring what it is like to be a reader of the particular book under discussion.

5. to do our best to make room for silence.

6. to do our best not only to tolerate difference but to make good use of our differences as they become apparent during the course of the semester.

Protocols for Our Whole-Group Inquiry Project

We agree to the following:

1. to engage in an ongoing endeavor to "name" (generate meta-awareness) what we talk about and what we do as individuals and as a group.

2. to take turns serving in the role of "recorder/reactor" who will make notes about the flow of discussion on a given day. The "recorder/reactor" will use her/his notes as well as the suggestions of others to create a handout that partially documents what happened during the discussion.

3. To set aside the last 5–10 minutes of each book discussion as time to take note of what was said and what happened. These jot-notes will be passed on to the "recorder/reactor" to assist her/him in creating a handout.

4. To set aside a portion of our "reader's notebooks" for the purpose of reacting to the book discussion experience as distinct from our reactions to the books themselves.

ELAN 7700: Creating Literate Communities
Spring Semester 2001

<u>Mid- Term Survey</u>

Use a separate sheet of paper to respond to the following items:

A)   Briefly describe the status of your "inquiry project" (e.g., Have you identified and contacted people to interview? Have you settled on certain questions you will address in the interviews? Do you have a clear timeline in mind for completing the project by April 18?).

B)   Briefly describe how you are using the "reader's notebook" (e.g., Have you found that you do pretty much the same thing for each entry or not? Does it seem like you will end up doing different things in connection with different books? Have our conversations on Wednesday evenings in any way influenced what you write?).

C)   Briefly describe your impressions of the reading group conversations so far (e.g., how would you "name" what is going on each week? In what ways have you found the conversations exciting, useful, interesting, annoying, frustrating, confusing, etc.?).

X-Sender: mfaust@sage.coe.uga.edu
Date: Thu, 3 May 2001 12:10:18 +0100
Reply-To: 7700 Reading Groups <ELAN7700-L@LISTSERV.UGA.EDU>
Sender: 7700 Reading Groups <ELAN7700-L@LISTSERV.UGA.EDU>
From: Mark Faust <mfaust@coe.uga.edu>
Subject: last handout
To: ELAN7700-L@LISTSERV.UGA.EDU

Here's the promised final handout based on ideas presented in class
regarding options for teachers seeking to implement reading groups in their
classes. Thanks again to you all for making the "book club" class a success
this semester. I'd love to hear about anything you try in your own classes
along these lines during the coming years. How about if we keep this list
active so we can share ideas with the whole group?

FORMING GROUPS

let the "books" choose the groups
kids self-select into groups
micro-managing, i.e. teacher's choice
student "roles" (a la Daniels) drive the formation of groups
kids name others they want to work with and teachers use this info to
construct groups
random sorts via lottery or counting off
check "online" resources for forming groups across town or across the
nation (I've even heard about links with reading groups abroad)

BOOK SELECTION

free choice
teacher constructed lists
what's available in the book room
lists organized around a theme
books by popular authors
students identify books they would like to re-read

Note: Keep in mind the NCTE publications called Books For You and High
Interest Easy Reading. These are excellent, annotated bibliographies of
books that would appeal to young readers.

DISCUSSION

use role sheets (cf Daniels)
let kids figure out how to make the groups work (but give them elbow room and
opportunities to discuss what works and what doesn't)

use prompts (quotes, opinionaires, surveys, checklists, key lines, etc.) (but be sure to keep the prompts open ended so that they do not supersede student "reactions")
use personal reflections, logs, response journals to stimulate discussion
technology (lists, chatrooms, etc.)

EVALUATION

see Daniels, chapter eight!!!

As you experiment with some of these options, keep in mind that you can broaden and complicate the issue of "validity" for your students (I used to do this with students as young as ninth grade) without communicating to them that "validity" is a non-issue, i.e., that "anything goes."

Good Luck!!!!!!
And have a great summer!

ELAN 7700: Creating Literate Communities
Spring Semester 2002

Highlights from the last set of "reaction papers" but first a reminder about the five crucial factors teachers need to think about as they plan to introduce the concept of literature circles in their classes:

TRUST BUILDING FACTOR

GROUP FORMATION FACTOR

BOOK SELECTION FACTOR

TIMING FACTOR

EVALUATION/GRADING FACTOR

Listen for comments that speak to our ongoing conversation about how best to transpose the "book club experience" into our secondary school classrooms.

"I don't think students would benefit from an interaction after the completion of the novel only. They need much more time to read a novel and would lose much information before a discussion could take place. It would be important for them to discuss, share, and predict as part of their learning experience. I also believe the *practice* of being in the groups many times would create ease of discussion and comfortable situations."

"I found that we approached this last book in a somewhat different way than we had our earlier readings. I believe this was a function of the nature of the book, our personal life experiences, and where our group has evolved over the course of the semester. . . . . I doubt we would have *experienced* this novel in quite the same way as a group had it been our first read, or even if we had each read it alone. Reading a book about the bonds among four women was perfectly timed by our group of four women."

"I read ahead and finished the novel. . . I felt my total knowledge of the book and its outcome totally inhibited me from saying much of anything. . . .I wonder if this issue could arise for high school students."

"I am sure that I gained insights about the characters in this novel that I would not have reaped had I not been part of this reading circle."

"We spent quite a bit of time examining the language of the book. Although we did not discuss in terms of specific literary terms like metaphors and similes, we all shared favorite passages that exemplified the beauty and flow of the words. Is it important for high school students to be able to name what they like about the novel? Or do you let that conversation flow naturally and somehow identify it when you debrief with the group or as part of a larger group discussion?"

"When groups have total control over what they will read, is it ever appropriate to think about a central theme for book choices? Do reading groups ever make those kinds of choices?. . . I would be interested in doing pairings of contemporary novels with classic novels in the high school classroom."

"Now the big question, how does this translate into the classroom? . . . Since I don't really even know the level, age, or grade of my future students, it's hard to create specifics. I know I won't be reading whole books and then discussing them. I think a large part has to do with the personalities of the students and then the personalities of the groups they create. Very rarely will there be a group of high school students that connect like the four of us women have. . . . . All the books we've read will be forever connected with the *social event* that is Buffy, Linda, Tara, and Holly."

"I find myself most fulfilled when we make connections and relate experiences instead of exploring the symbolism and inherent philosophies in [a book]. . . . . Many times when we go the direction of the college English discussion, the discovery is observed and time spent on that subject is brief as we fumble through the pages trying to come up with a clever response."

"The more I think about it, the more valuable I feel like our time together is. Never would I have been able to contemplate the social structures of the people in Pride and Prejudice and the strength of their *world views* compared to our own, and never would I have been able to have had explained to me Chinese marriage traditions If I hadn't been involved with these people for our common purpose—to experience literature in a new way."

"The short stories allowed for more substantial conversation. As far as literature circles go, it seems that *less is really more*. This would be an important point for me to remember when I implement this activity in the classroom.

"I would really like to read this book again someday, considering the things we have discussed."

Chapter 4

One Day A Week:
Nurturing Student Book Clubs
In A Middle School Classroom

Cheryl Hancock

I am in my fifth year teaching and my third year teaching eighth grade language arts. The school where I work is small, about 60 teachers and around 700 students. It is located in a lower- to middle-class, rural, industrial town in North Georgia. Many of my students come from families who have lived here for generations. Once a factory town, there are now many farms, horse ranches, and small businesses. The effect of suburban sprawl from neighboring Atlanta has changed the demographic picture to some extent, as has the influx of immigrants including Hispanic and Humong. The new challenges presented by this increasing level of diversity have made the leadership in my district more open to innovative practices like the ones I will be describing in this chapter. Nevertheless, from the standpoint of their attitudes toward teaching and learning, not much has changed since I started teaching.

A majority of students still come to my classroom from traditional, conservative backgrounds where quiet is valued and literature study means answering textbook questions on required reading. Reading is highly regarded though not well understood as a process of meaning making. In most classes at my school, students are simply read to or asked to read aloud in whole group settings, and much of what students are allowed to read is restricted to what is available in our outdated textbooks. As a former student of teacher-centered classrooms where the dominant mode of instruction was the lecture, I know what it's like to be bored to tears. In fact, I myself lost interest in reading altogether as a teenager and only discovered its true potential later in life. My personal history that I described in Chapter 1 combined with the positive experience I had with collaborative reading in Mark's book club class two years ago led me to become interested in student book clubs as a classroom strategy. I became very excited about the potential of this approach to allow students room for creativity and independent thought while at the same time meeting curricular expectations.

In my classroom, students are introduced to ideas such as writing in a journal and forming their own questions. Being asked to express their own, individual ideas separate from what parents and teachers tell them to think is a new experience for most. Even before I began experimenting with student book clubs, I discovered that my students become excited when what they say is valued. The idea of implementing student book clubs is the latest in a series of attempts on my part to direct students away from stifling teacher-directed study, question, and recitation. As a life-long reader myself, I want my classroom to become a stepping-stone for students to become life-long readers as well. One thing I have learned and will talk about in this chapter is that change is difficult. Finding ways to share my newfound enthusiasm for collaborative reading with my students has not been easy. Over the past couple of years, they have taught me to respect the fact that human beings tend to be attached to what is familiar, even if it is unpleasant, and to resist reaching out to new experiences.

After being appointed department head at the end of last year, I now have an excellent opportunity to share my ideas about student book clubs with other language arts teachers, as well as teachers of other subjects who have expressed interest in the concept. As a consequence of my efforts, a number of other teachers in my school are experimenting with collaborative reading in their classes. This work has taken on a variety of aspects that would be an interesting study in itself. For the purpose of my contribution to this book, however, I will focus on my individual effort to help students make the transition from reading group/literature circles to fully integrated student book clubs. While I do not place much stock in labels, I share with my co-authors a belief that there is an important distinction to be made between open-ended, peer-led book discussion groups like those described by Daniels (2002) and the kind of collaborative reading envisioned by our concept of student book clubs where there is more focus on meeting specific curricular goals. My goal is to enhance my students' experience with the required reading, while also creating opportunities for them to listen to each other and have choices about how to read and discuss a text. I believe that respecting the process of reading in this way can make assigned reading more enjoyable at the same time as it helps students develop important social skills and discover their own voices as readers. My approach to introducing the concept of student book clubs aims to move students gradually toward the higher-level thinking that is required for academic success and I strive to do this without stifling their personal investment in reading.

For many students at this age, brain development hampers their range of thinking, prohibiting for many the ability to think in abstract terms. In this light, I begin by teaching my eighth grade students how to move away from strict and limited concrete thought toward more abstract thought. Variables connected with their relative maturity means that some of my students are not ready for abstract thinking but even those in that category benefit from being exposed to new possibilities in a non-judgmental context. It is in this beginning place where most are quiet, unsure that what they speak will make sense, need reassurance as they experiment with new ideas. With lots of praise and positive reinforcement, the process becomes more familiar and less threatening. In my classroom, scaffolding plays a big role in making this transition possible.

When students are learning how to use student book clubs, I use various types of scaffolding to help students pay attention to themselves as learners and readers. We spend time on vocabulary, language skills, and literary concepts but in a way that connects this work with critical thinking about books in relation to our depending certainly on age and growth individual worlds as well as the world around us. I am continually asking students to help me understand their thinking process by asking simple but profound questions. "What was it like for you to be a reader of a particular selection?" "What were you really thinking and feeling as you read?" "What about this reading is puzzling you?" I insist that my students never disregard another's reasoning and instead focus on listening to each other and themselves. While this is not always easy, there are moments when I can see in a student's eyes that they suddenly realize their thoughts can count for something. I know that when it comes to reading, school will never mirror life, nor can we expect life to mirror the constructs of school. However, the type of activity I am referring to can bring the two spheres together and create a more realistically useful learning experience.

Student book clubs create an excellent place for students to interact with reading as well as the other students in the class, but also to question others and their own ways of thinking. Where else do students have the opportunity to interpret the world if not for schools and open-minded classroom teachers? If students are to form their own opinions, create ideas, or develop an individual belief system distinct from what has been influenced by parents, culture, community, or friends, an outlet must be provided somewhere. As a student myself, I am constantly troubling my assumptions and seeking another direction in thinking about concepts, life, and the world. As a teacher, my aim is to model reading practices that encourage and support students in becoming freethinkers who use books in a way that makes sense, where reading is productive. I will have more to say about this idea of reading as productive from various angles in the sections to follow.

Expectations

Through participating in Mark's graduate school book club class, I began to see the potential value of student book clubs, not only in my own reading life but also in my teaching. The sparks of energy created during informal, open-ended reading discussion amazed me. I noticed a place for small role assignments (especially the time-keeper!) in our adult circles since the flow of conversation can lead both to useful new connections as well as to tangential discussions that distract even the most dedicated adults from keeping focused on the book. Mostly, I learned to listen to and hear, my own voice, and ultimately found that I had something relevant to share, which is what student book clubs force my students to discover. I could put my insecurities on the back burner and contribute to the meaning being created within the group. I learned to interact with a book instead of passively taking in words without making meaning.

Needless to say, my involvement with the idea of book clubs became fairly intense and I discovered a real urge to share this experience with my students. I also encouraged book clubs among colleagues at my school and joined one with friends. Witnessing for myself just how the flow of discussion and the exchange of ideas could enhance my experiences with reading (and how I relate to the world) became the spark that ignited my passion for a new approach to teaching and learning with my students. I wanted my students to read this way, to interact, to dive in, to engage with each other, and to test their beliefs through such discussions. These book clubs were missing from my past adolescent experience. What might I have accomplished if I had been introduced to them earlier in my life? How might I have questioned my world and my experiences with reading?

When I introduced this concept to my students for the first time, however, their becoming an equal and active part of a group was not as natural as it had been for myself and other adults in the college class. My young students, some who resist reading completely, did not immediately become as excited over this wonderful idea. In reality, I could not expect students who had never heard of these concepts to automatically understand the purpose (or for my excitement to rub off on them). I had shy and fearful students who were not comfortable with speaking out. There were also those students who for years had been expected to quietly listen while a teacher told them what to think. At first, the dynamics of the groups I tried to form were tentative and sometimes artificial. I could not expect students to adjust immediately to the idea of thinking for themselves. At the same time, I knew my excitement had carried over to them previously with other new ideas, so I remained hopeful that I might succeed with this one too.

My students felt awkward, unsure of themselves and the assignment, when I asked them to sit together in small groups and "discuss" the book our class was assigned to read. The students who resisted speaking out in a whole group situation also regressed in smaller, more intimate groups. Complicating this more, I wanted to incorporate writing into the objectives. Many of my students questioned every aspect of the task seeking a specific, tangible assignment with specific right, wrong, or multiple-choice answers! Such was their comfort zone. Realizing my students needed a guide, something they could look at and hold in their hands, I would have to provide some tangible scaffolding if this idea was going to work.

This scaffolding process would require focus and dedication, and my role as facilitator would be large. Until my eighth grade students saw for themselves how great student book groups would work, they would initially need to be co-dependent; I'd have to lead them on for a while. They required the usual worksheet, something to touch, work on, that was tangible in that it actually looked like a traditional assignment. I had to begin with the students' traditional comfort zone and work toward independence. The new ideas needed to be introduced gradually to avoid complete rejection.

In the first place, I keep reminding my students, and myself reading is a *process*. I learned that a gradual approach to introducing student book clubs, one which began with informal reading groups that met once a week with very few expectations other than participation, could lead to the formation of powerful groups in which previously resistant students become active readers. I want to help my students realize that their interactions with reading empower them to reflect on their own thinking, in short, to make a difference in their lives. Story structure, vocabulary, inference, and comprehension all come into play but in a way that transcends merely preparing to pass standardized tests. What can occur in student book club discussions extends into real-world, authentic learning at the same time that curricular goals are met. What students take from the reading and incorporate into her or his own thinking creates a transformation that is immediate within the student. Through extending in this way, they begin to see that reading is a journey that doesn't necessarily end on test day.

My goal was to redefine the relationship between academic and pleasure reading (allowing for the reality that some students see reading for pleasure as no less foreign than academic reading). To begin, I introduced the student book club idea to my students as a simple reading group (an activity with which most were familiar from primary school) once a week, mainly on Fridays. I framed it as a kind of reward for taking care of business during the week. I carefully selected an intriguing story to draw them in and pique their interest, then created a tangible and relevant structured assignment incorporating strategies that gave them discussion starters and a purpose. Students seeking a worksheet grade were satisfied that what we were doing "counted" yet the assignment also required individual opinion through response. As students began to see the activity as fun, I hoped I would be able to add some new expectations, such as rereading, making new connections, and formulating their own questions.

Small Group Dynamics

Many times I have found myself in the middle of a debate with other teachers about the amount of success students are able to have in a small group. Small groups do not *always* work since there exist many variables that cause groups to become dysfunctional. Finders (1997) describes groups of girls in a co-ed school who consider themselves popular and call other girls "woof-woofs" who do not fit into their perception of what is popular. The mere fact that name-calling occurs creates a negative feeling for the girl with the negative label. Then, how will this group "work"? Finders describes a setting in which students are asked to write about their summer vacation. "Students shared their trips to the mall to buy new school clothes and their last summer excursions. Dottie did not share what she had written about her father putting their dogs to sleep because he had recently lot his job, and they could no longer afford to feed them." (106)

Finders has helped me to keep in mind that all students come to school with whatever it is that defines them at home, that is, they are not blank slates eager to scribble on their empty templates. They come from families who may or may not have money, who may or may not be a different culture than the majority of others, who may or may not have significant differences that cause others to label them, to judge them, to identify them as "woof-woofs." The classroom can be a dangerous place for many teens of all statuses,' from the popular segregating the one chosen to be ousted, to the jocks picking on the geeks, to mom or dad losing a job, to any and all different kinds of circumstances. We have heard about students who take over and do all the work supposedly accomplished by a group, those who are shy and uncomfortable in groups, those who would rather work alone, and those who rely on others to decide what answers to write.

On the other hand, there is much to be *gained* in small groups. There are many positive aspects of small groups, especially when there is continuity and students have the opportunity to build trust. For instance, the smaller groups allow for more individual speaking and less drowning of voices that might rather be silent. Giving each student a role means each has equal responsibility. There is less of a stigma with testing the discussion waters in a small group. Some students cannot bare the slightest hint of ridicule in front of the whole class. Labels are lessened in small groups especially when alliances are separated and no tension exists to live up to another's expectations. Students are more likely in smaller groups to be open-minded, offer suggestions or aid in someone's understanding, question each other, or allow themselves to be questioned.

My experiment began with examining every kind of group make-up to see what worked best for which class. As most teachers know, every class is different depending on the chemistry of the students. I have divided the class into groups of four or five based on my own sense of who might (and who might not) work well together while explaining that the composition of the groups could change depending on how situations developed. Eventually I hoped to allow students to form their own groups according to interest. Again, my intentions were always to try to create the safest space possible within our restricting surroundings in order that students should feel comfortable with experimenting with these new concepts and ideas.

To facilitate group formation and management I developed an interest survey (see my file in the Appendix). Students filled out the surveys individually and I persuaded them to be "honest." Creating this silent survey helped me to form groups based on similar interests and reading preferences. Taking them out of their social "comfort zone" did not hurt them. In fact, reflecting on these uncomfortable situations helped some students gain new self-awareness or a new friendship. Negative chemistry *can* produce good chemistry. Experimentation is the key. Realistically, students of opposite social groups may resist this type of arrangement, but the teacher can do much to help these groups engage by valuing cooperation over competition.

Teacher as Facilitator

As facilitator first of reading groups and then of fledgling student book clubs, I adopted various stances. Typically, I walked around the room observing students and making available input at many different intervals. I became the portable group member, floating from group to group adding when needed and contributing only "warm-bodied" observation and the occasional nod when the group sustains itself. However, the teacher does play an important part, more than just being the facilitator, for if the facilitator just does nothing or gives out text he or she has not read, the student book club assignment can become meaningless and fall apart. I have found that it is crucial to begin with assessments that recognize and value participation and cooperation. Over time as students became comfortable with the reading group format I modified my stance as facilitator. I gently pointed out instances where their ideas could be extended or clarified or led to potential sources of disagreement. I also began to model a process of asking probing questions associated with what our textbooks call higher-level thinking. Gradually, our Friday sessions began to look more like literature discussions than the informal "bull" sessions they were at the outset of my experiment.

In the first place, I positioned myself as a classroom monitor, watching out for interactions that interfered with discussion and productive conversation. I also was always ready to support positive gestures made by students. Inevitably, one student turns to another for help with the role sheet, and that's where the discussion sparks. But, if the conversation gets off the topic, for instance when students begin talking about the weekend and there's obviously no connection, the teacher can steer it back to focus by making a simple positive comment about a student's paper noticing a well-written question or unique definition for a chosen vocabulary word. I can also maintain the order that may be needed when members begin to fight over being heard, become too loud, or need a change of topic. I own the knowledge to manipulate this type of strategy because of planning and prior knowledge. A teacher's previous experience in book clubs or college classroom discussion will help as well by containing immediate responses and rebuttals for extending discussions.

The second type of role I played was to make myself available to provide additional background information or knowledge on a subject. I sometimes added a perspective based on my life experience to the group discussion or made subtle, questioning suggestions. I also provided alternate ways of thinking about a same issue or challenged a student's comment if I felt the student was ready for this experience. Asking basic questions such as, "Why do you think you think that way?" "What do you mean by that?" or "How does that pertain to the character here, or to yourself," can create a student's expanded thinking and help create more meaningful associations and discussions.

A third role that came into play with increasing frequency called for me to intervene to help students realize the potential in a conversation they had initiated. When a group seemed to need a push, I would walk over and suggest an idea for a discussion question, such as "How could this situation create questions?" "What do you think the society demands of the characters?" "How does the setting influence the characters to think in certain terms?" I also ask them to think about ways a teacher asks *quality* questions to the students, as well as what makes a quality question. I was asking students to interact with their reading, to question quality is, what makes a good story *good*, and what it is that makes us think twice about an idea. At this level, students have begun to read like adults becoming in a sense co-authors as they engage with a text and make meaning through their own questioning, not a teacher's direct guidance.

Ultimately, as students learned to become more independent in the reading groups, my role as facilitator became less important. I was able to relinquish leadership though not completely. I became the observer and provider of supportive comments and positive feedback, observing with more intensity the occurrences as the discussions became more detailed and interesting. At this point I introduced them to the term, "student book clubs," and we discussed the differences between what they were doing now and what they had been doing in "reading groups" earlier in the year. I commended them for reaching farther and accomplishing more than what they had been taught to expect from themselves.

Assessment can occur at different levels depending on the classroom and environment. In my eighth grade classes, the completion of the role sheet, which I will discuss next, was the key. When the work was completed, I could be sure that the student did interact with the group in some way. Completed role sheets also provided data I could use to gauge progress. I also took notes on students' behavior as I circled the room. If a student refused to work (though a student can rarely avoid putting opinions into this type of discussion), this fact was reflected in a note on his or her paper describing the lower grade. Opposite this, a teacher may take note of exceptional interaction and grant a completion grade of a role sheet that may be in whatever way incomplete or inarticulate, so frustration does not hamper progression. This allows for students who are not "writers" to display work verbally. Also, this approach allowed me to validate a student's questioning or being "stumped" as a sign of quality thought in addition to demonstrations of understanding through more tangible productions such as oral or written essays.

Role Sheets: An Evolving Strategy

Since my students are young, they are still learning *how* to read, and role sheets give them a place to begin reading and discussing productively. Also, young students can rarely be allowed the same level of independence as might be appropriate for older students. My young students require more structure in the beginning, or they will easily stray off task discussing an array of irrelevant issues. As I mentioned previously, role sheets stand alongside other forms of scaffolding that communicate to students exactly what I expected of them. From that starting point, I was able to revise the role sheets or the way we used existing role sheets so as to guide and also mark our progress toward student book clubs.

Through the college book club class, I learned about similar types of group member roles. We used them in our groups to a small degree, but as adults, we didn't need a sheet of paper and specific written instructions to complete our assignment. Neither were the roles as in-depth nor as specific as those I developed for my young students. The roles were only suggested and minimally structured because we could manage ourselves, and we became so engrossed in what was occurring among us, that we tended to lose sight of what we were engaged in as academic work. We designated someone to bring us back on task when we began to go off on multiple tangents. Our timekeeper kept track of our allotted class time, since it seemed everyone had a page to turn to or quote to analyze.

We rotated the few roles so members shared responsibility. Required reflections after each session allowed for depth of reflection on happenings within the group. Some of my reflections, for example, produced statements such as, "I felt a responsibility to be a contributing member and always bring something to share." Also, "I was able to have interesting conversations about a piece of literature I really enjoyed without feeling pressured to use the most academic speech or to have the best interpretation of its meaning." Defining minimal roles for our adult groups worked because we were accountable for ourselves, being adequately motivated by responsibility, and our similar interests aided in overcoming vulnerability. We were liberated and lost control of ourselves discovering an unlimited flow of ideas and a new definition to the words "pleasure reading."

Young students, however, who have never been allowed freedom with their thoughts or who feel uncomfortable and insecure sharing, require more guidance. To initiate the reading groups, I borrowed from the role sheets recommended by Daniels (2002) in his book on literature circles. These formed the basic template I used and modified in my effort to move students from the more or less independent climate of reading groups where expectations were minimal to student book clubs where my expectations for engagement with assigned material would be more substantial.

I developed each role sheet with a specific assignment in mind based on the purposes and needs of my individual classes. The role sheets provide structure while allowing each student a different outlet of expression. Specific examples of the role sheets I used, including those I revised over time, can be found in the appendix to this chapter. Here I want to offer an overall summary look at the various roles I envisioned for my students.

1. *Passage Finder: Locate passages meaningful to you and the group members from the story.* For example, was there a line that jumped out at you? Did a character say something that grabbed your attention? The sentence or passage does not have to be a quote a character says. The narrator may make a statement that strikes you as important. Locate these passages, and then describe what they mean to you or another group member. Ask your group members for passages they found important or to identify the speaker of the found passage.

   > This role is great for students to be able to point out "quotable quotes," clichés, idioms, or just great statements made by characters they admire and explain them. Again, in this way students identify passages they consider important and can discuss how and why the passage is meaningful. The students will have to search within themselves rather than have a teacher tell them what is important.

2. *Literacy Scout: Discover words (language) unique to the story you are reading.* The words can be those that are unfamiliar or unique to the story, such as slang or terms used generationally. For example, in *The Outsiders,* the word "greaser" is used to describe a gang of teenagers. What does it mean in the context of the story? You are to define the word using the dictionary, and then define the word in the context of how it is used in the story. Ask your group members for help finding extra words. Describe why you picked each word.

   > Instead of the usual assignment: defining the vocabulary word using the dictionary, writing the part of speech, and writing a sentence, students are discovering words in the context of a story and defining them using this context. In this way, unfamiliar words become more meaningful and specific to circumstances, culture, language, and relationships inside the reading, and students can see that words can have multiple meanings. They identify how language affects how we think and feel about our interactions, as well as how we view the world.

3. *Summarizer: Summarize the story you are reading.* If you are not finished with the book or story, summarize up to the point at which you have read. Include details such as major characters' names, the setting, the plot, point of view, the climax, and so on, but summarize from your point of view. Ask your group members how they would summarize the story. In what ways do you see things differently?

Through summary, students explain what they read in the story in their own words. In this way, teachers can discover how the students are conceptualizing important points in the story rather than regurgitation of what they are told they read. The students have the choice on what ideas they see as important.

4. *Visual Illustrator: Fill in the lined page by writing down any and all images that come to your mind while reading the story or book.* What do you imagine the characters look like? (Think in colors.) What does the setting look like? Does the story give you any clues? How do the characters dress? In what time period does the story occur? What do the other members of your group see? How do others envision the characters' dress? Then, draw and color your ideas.

For those students who are visually oriented, allowing them this kind of visual expression is crucial. To an artist, art is equally or more expressive as writing is to a writer. Students, for example, may create a comic strip series of explanation of events, or they may create a collage of images depicting important story events.

5. *Questioning the Reading: On your paper, create good discussion questions that you might ask to start a quality discussion among the members of the group.* Questions should begin "How did . . ." "What do you think . . ." "Why did . . .", and "Predict what . . ." All questions must be open-ended. (No yes-no questions.) To test your question, ask a group member to answer it. If the answer is yes or no, you must revise your question. Questions can include descriptions of characters, qualities they hold, situations they are in, conversations they have with other characters, and so on. Ask your group members for more ideas. The more difficult time creating a response, the better the question!

Through devising these questions, students are performing critical thinking skills. They are creating their own questions instead of answering teachers' questions. Amazingly, students have heard and read teachers' questions so often, that this is an unusually easy and fun task. Also, students can identify with and enjoy what they might consider a leadership role. My expectations for this assignment evolved from merely supporting students' initial efforts to frame their own questions to looking for evidence of thoughtful engagement with the reading and with each other.

I found that the role sheets can be manipulated, or redesigned, to meet a particular teacher and/or students' needs. I combined the sheets after the students became "expert" at each one, so that each job is on each role sheet. The sheets can be constructed in great detail in the beginning, then less detailed after time, leaving more space for answers to become more in-depth. (Once students become proficient at student book clubs, the role sheets can be excluded.) Students saved the role sheets in a portfolio they used to aid in the development of essays or other authentic ways of expressing what is occurring to them. Collecting the sheets in such a portfolio provided a very graphic means whereby I was able to show students (and their parents) how much they had changed and grown as readers during the course of the year.

Initially, I required each reading group to staple all their papers together while reminding them that I would be checking to see that no answers were the same, not even close in wording. By the time we got to the stage being referred to as student book clubs, this wasn't even an issue. The amazing thing is how flexible and adaptable the practice of using role sheets can be. Exactly how the role sheets are used is less significant than the fact that they provide young students a beginning point, accountability, and focus the learning.

Once I established what began as reading groups as a normal feature of my class, I was able to adapt this strategy to the job of meeting a variety of curricular mandates including content knowledge such as story structure and the significant features of different literary genres as well as process knowledge including such topics as questioning, reviewing, predicting, envisioning, and evaluating. As long as students felt accountability for completing the activity and I roamed through the room facilitating, interacting, and observing, the activity supported independent reading and prepared for discussion of required texts. Once each student held an objective, a role, the "assignment" could be carried out and expanded depending upon the amount of effort the student applied. As the year progressed and students got used to reading collaboratively in groups I observed a qualitative shift in the tone of the groups. In place of the more or less random sharing and completing of tasks dictated by the role sheets I began to notice students listening to each other building real literary conversations over the assigned reading. I would say that what I was seeing marks the difference between a reading group or literature circle and a student book club.

Students and Theory:
They are Not Too Young

What do I mean when I say my students began to engage in real literary conversations? Once they are able to set aside their fear of failing to measure up, I find that today's adolescents crave any chance to talk about serious issues. I have had students come to me in private with stories about their encounters with prejudice based on race, class, and gender as well as conflicts within their families but it was a new experience for them and me to air these concerns in the classroom. They want to understand the world around them better and ask the "why" questions. Students of different cultures are examining the class-room power structures that define relationships between teachers and students, some feeling inadequate and fearful, most feeling uncomfortable and expecting authoritarian teachers who silence them and others. In the face of these problems, many young people who walk through my door continue to hope that school might be a place where they can sort out their issues and find real answers to their questions.

Heath (1983) tells us that students come to the classroom with their own cultural language that is "dependent on the ways in which each community structured their families, defined the concepts of childhood that community members could assume, and played out their concepts of childhood that guided child socialization" (11). Also, religious affiliations and activities, access to "goods and services," what type of neighborhood a child leaves, and other features of the community also affect the perceptions of student. The teacher should protect these students' ideas, value these issues, and take into account differences when considering the discussion the insight she or he may give to others in the group.

Furthermore, students discuss theory every day, though they may never realize it. Kutz and Roskelly (1991) tell us, "Teachers will see many silenced learners—mainly because . . . these learners fear making mistakes . . . [and] if left to their own devices, they'll pass quietly through classes, and their teachers will learn little about them." (53) Teachers have the perfect opportunity through student book clubs to create the interest students desire through this quality discussion. Talking about feminist issues can be as small as focusing on a fe-male character's dilemma in a reading or as large as discussing the women's movement and civil rights. For male students, the word "feminist" need mean nothing more than standing up for women's equal rights, not becoming a "woman" as some seem to think. Students told not to think will never wonder about class struggle, acceptance of cultural differences, those persons once poor who won Nobel prizes, or how to escape abusive or racially restrictive relationships to become successful, open-minded thinkers.

Ultimately, the purpose of student book clubs in my class transcends the curriculum. My aim is to stimulate thought and create opportunities for students to consider how the world works and to identify their place in it. Again I quote Kutz and Roskelly who write:

> We need to know things in particular contexts as well as through abstractions, through personal experience as well as through formal structures, through manipulating objects as well as through reading about them. When we allow multiple ways of knowing, and the language in which they're represented, into our classrooms, we'll support the developing thought and language of all of our students. (55)

Lisa Delpit (1998) makes a similarly important statement when she says, "Teachers are in an ideal position to play this role, to attempt to get all of the issues on the table in order to initiate true dialogue. This can only be done, however, by seeking out those whose perspectives may differ most." (292) All students have a story, each different and unique, and each extremely and personally important. She also comments that students are "experts on their own lives . . . we must not be too quick to deny their interpretations."

The traditional curriculum in force at my school positions students as passive receivers of meaning supposedly contained in great books. My class works within and against this system. Yes, I want my students to experience success but I also want them to think about what success means. In short, I want them to join me as meaning-makers, as co-authors of the books we read together. I have found that students understand the concept that their reading experiences are created through interaction with an author's words and that their voice can count for something in the process. Whatever an author might have meant during the writing of a text is not readily available to the reader, nor is it necessarily our job to focus on trying to figure that out. What is important is the discussion of ideas, the connections made, the expansion of knowledge that arises with students' interacting together around a book. Student book clubs facilitate this kind of discussion. In the next section, I will talk in more detail about what student book clubs *look* and *sound* like in my class. Discussions like these should not be held with whispers but with enthusiasm and quizzical stares from outsiders looking in through the doorway.

Self-Reflection through Journal Writing

The final assignment for the class period, saved for the last ten minutes of our 80-minute class period, was student reflection. I used journal writing to create a safe space and an avenue for self-reflection. When I talk about a safe space, I do not mean to imply an absence of standards and expectations. I have learned that students need to feel protected from abusive behaviors and comments as a prerequisite for taking the kind of risks I wanted them to make. My requirement for journaling in the beginning of the year was at least half a page. Many times students got "stuck" and could not adequately articulate emotions in one or two sentences. Toward the middle of the year, we changed to writing up to a full page. By this time many students were surprised by their increased fluency. I was able to learn a lot about their ideas and their reading process through reading their journals. This not only helped them to grow as writers but it contributed to my being able to make appropriate adjustments in the way I interacted with individuals and with the groups.

Sometimes I prompted journal writing using specific questions to elicit responses around particular happenings. At other times I provided an option of a question or allowed students to choose what to reflect on. Each reflection may be different, focusing on specific group events or individual beliefs or ideas. In the beginning they may be blunt, resisting the journal writing as extra writing they seem tired of completing. Then the groups and the students do seem to "blossom," and those students who were once pessimistic soon become optimistic and eager to be in the group setting again. Journal prompts often dealt with issues that came up during book club discussions. At other times I asked students to reflect on the process itself. Either way, they are writing to interpret their lives and ideas, not solely the text.

The types of questions I ask are varied consisting of open-ended essay questions or specific requests about the detailed interaction within the group. Here are some examples.

1. Identify one specific time where you helped someone in your group and what you helped them do.

2. Identify one specific time when you needed help and how someone helped you.

3. Identify one specific time when you contributed verbally to the conversation about the book or short story.

4. Identify one specific time when you made a connection with the story or stories that you had not thought of before.

5. Identify when your group went off on a tangent. What was the topic, and where did you go with it?

6. What is one thing you definitely enjoyed about your book club?

7. If you could suggest something for others to read, what would it be?

All the questions require critical thought about the occurrences within the group. I ask that responses be written in complete sentences, and I always tell them to answer the question, "why?" to every statement when thinking of a response.

Interspersed throughout the next pages are comments some of my students have made. They describe the inter-workings and happenings between members of the groups and how they gradually became self-sufficient, confident, and energetic but not right away.

> *Finding the vocabulary words is the toughest part and what I need the most help with. Sometimes I can't decide what a good vocabulary word is.*

> *Finding the right definition is hard sometimes because not every definition will fit the situation of the word.*

> *I couldn't decide on ideas for the summary, and the others helped me decide what to write. Sometimes they thought the same as me, and sometimes they didn't.*

> *The only part I liked was the drawing. That's what I do all the time and get in trouble for. Teachers don't like it when I draw instead of listen.*

Again, each time the class began the reading groups, members were required to choose a different role than they had the previous time, and they could help those who had never performed their new role, assisting with the instructions and examples. The students quickly became efficient at completion, focusing less on the role sheet and more on discussing the reading, giving opinions, making comparisons, and participating in techniques such as cooperative learning, reciprocal teaching, and abstracting. The students had something to teach others and an outlet to sounding and feeling smarter, to hearing their own voices. Also obvious were the personal connections being discussed and the creation of meaning with the text.

> *It was fun arguing with the others at the table when I mentioned all men being the same. That conversation went on for twenty minutes.*

> *I liked working with others because when I make comments, it's not in front of the whole class. Plus, I can argue with them without feeling wrong.*

> *Our group chose two stories that related the most to each other. The four stories were all similar, but we all agreed [these two stories] were closer.*

> *I like that we can talk together and ask questions. It's like we each get more time to talk things out in the smaller groups.*

Once the students knew what they were supposed to do, the conversations became livelier, and the activity became something they soon desired, which was reflected in the journals. Each time the role sheets were filled out more and more until the majority of students were completing in full the role assignment and even extending. The journals proved that the students became more relaxed and comfortable with sharing the responsibility, and they felt free to say anything. That was when I knew my students were doing what student book clubs intended for them. They were discussing the reading, asking questions, coming to conclusions, making connections, identifying contexts, and all of this was happening as a group. I saw proof of the students *enjoying* themselves.

> *The days we have book club groups, I always put my views in! And I don't worry about being wrong anymore.*

> *She didn't understand the directions, so I explained them to her. I felt good knowing that I could help someone else for a change.*

> *I like knowing others are there to help me with my work if I need it. Someone else remembered the page number when I forgot where I read something. I could help others too by explaining how to do something.*

> *I really enjoy reading now and being able to hear what other people think about the story. I tell what I think too. Book clubs help me to better understand the story too. [Discussing in the group] also made me feel smart.*

> *I started reading the same books as [my friend] so we could talk about them. I like knowing she's reading the same thing.*

Once the students become comfortable with their book club groups, I enjoy discussing with them what occurs during their interactions. I help clarify for them how to recognize the isolated skills we learn that work together to help them enjoy reading. But also, I want them to know what they see themselves doing among the discussions versus what I could tell them about the things I see. The reactions I receive tell me that they cannot always see their own learning. The ease at which I allow them to "just talk" leads them to believe they are not completing "school work."

Authentic Assessment Strategies

Probably the most sensitive issue connected with student book clubs is how to assess student learning. It has always been my opinion that grades do not accurately or fairly reflect a student's performance in school. In his article *Creating Tests Worth Taking*, Grant Wiggins (1992) makes a grand statement when he says, "Typical tests, even demanding ones, tend to overassess student 'knowledge' and underassess student 'know-how with knowledge'" (27). The idea of student book clubs is to get students reading and discussing books as adults would. In this way, no multiple choice or true/ false tests could adequately assess what is being learned.

Alfie Kohn (1999) offers a complementary perspective when he describes the results of praise, rewards, and punishment as creating "praise junkies" out of our students, and that "ability grouping is equally detrimental to adequate evaluation of assessing learning." Authentic assessment strategies force students to "show" what they know, to incorporate more than one task at a time. Students writing essays, completing portfolios, or completing oral performances are not isolating but combining skills in a "production" of owned knowledge.

Reading groups en route to becoming student book clubs allow for a multitude of "performance" assessment activities. First, in my description of the activity in my classroom, I describe individual role sheets and the students' completion of the individual assignments. Here, the students receive a completion grade for length and effort put into the role sheet. If any part of the sheet is left blank, the student could get half or partial credit. The assignment is considered as class work and is assigned a completion grade rather than a number or letter. In this way, students are less confined by the grade and more open to participate in the conversations.

Through the role sheets, I assess engagement and effort, which is apparent in the quality of questioning, the types of vocabulary words found and definitions following them, and the extent to which a student detailed a drawing. Effort as well as participation is subject to the teacher's opinion and knowledge of a student's personality, but it is also an *easy* grade to see. My note taking about participation becomes the basis for conferences in which students develop an honest appraisal of their contribution to the success of their group.

Another type of formative assessment I use in my classes is the reflection, or self-assessment statement. I worry less about the type of writing there, as long as it is developed, and I grade according to length and depth of thought. Students understand that I am not grading their ideas but their ability to make their ideas known to others through talk and writing. The idea behind the reflection assignment is to provide a place for students' thoughts and allow them the opportunity to discuss what they decided was happening within their student book club. While student book clubs indeed require interaction among students, a teacher can walk around the classroom and witness personally those students who are not contributing and help them become involved. With a teacher's gentle persuasion, no student can remain uninvolved for long!

My favorite type of assessment is the summative self-reflection essay writing that focuses on what was discussed, learned, even awakened, or changed inside their minds. Essays incorporate grammar and organization, but also content, thought, and interaction with peers and ideas. Presentations to the class may combine member's efforts, show individual transcending; include art, music, or any other cross-academic variable. Authentic assessment ideas such as these create the sense of ownership and responsibility students should take in evaluating their own ideas and ways of seeing the world.

Finally, twice each year I require students to construct a portfolio representing their development as readers. In December, their portfolios include evidence of increased fluency and ability to function in their group. By the end of the year, most portfolios include evidence not only of increasing fluency but also of a new level of literacy. Almost every student can cite instances where they helped someone else or were themselves assisted by another who may have suggested and idea or question to them. When students can show their parents the difference between the role sheet assignments they completed at the beginning of the year and those exhibited in their end of year portfolio, it is a proud moment for the student.

Having the class agree on expectations through rubrics can create consensus on the quality of work expected at any point during the school year. Inviting students to participate in the creation of rubrics gives them a chance to know the expectations of the assignment because they chose the rules, and they really appreciate the task, which can become quite fun. Rubrics work for all types of assignments, and I have found that when students are involved in the creation of guidelines, they are more likely to follow them. Rubrics should not be general but "task-specific" as Popham (1997) suggests in his article *What's Wrong—and What's Right—with Rubrics*. As with the essay, a rubric can be devised to specifically target content over grammar, or look at multiple parts with great specificity. Look for examples of rubrics and further reading in my file.

Teacher Reflection

As important as the students' learning, discussions that promote learning, debate that causes insight, and student reflection, is the final puzzle piece, teacher reflection. Keeping record of aspects of the group dynamics and discussion will tell if something is not working or working well, and the analysis can be saved to be reviewed at a later time. Many times I will read a book and decide not to mark a favorite passage. Later when I want to recall that passage, I have forgotten where it is, even the particular book in which I could find it. The same thing happens when teachers do not reflect in some recorded way on teaching practices. Many times we forget what didn't work (hopefully because we stopped doing it), and we never look at why. The "why" can reveal the most important learning for a teacher. The most wonderful aspect of teaching anything, whether student book clubs or math or science is the fact that lessons and plans can be changed, adapted, and manipulated to fit the needs of the different students in their different stages of learning as well as differences in culture, gender, and ability.

The type of reflection I use is journaling. I keep a sectioned classroom journal for discipline reasons, brainstormed ideas that occur at a moment's notice, for reflecting on activities and strategies that work as well as those that do not. Often plans work with flaws that a teacher wants to "tweak" or refine and may not be able to identify immediately. Often thoughts return and disturb my thinking later in the day (or in dreams at night). Reflection brings clarity to positively change an activity.

This type of recording can also allow detailed examples of reasons behind a teacher's thinking and reasoning. Delpit (1998) reminds us to remain open-minded to different students' learning styles and not associate everyone with one way of instruction. "To put our beliefs on hold [by questioning ourselves and how we've come to certain beliefs] is to cease to exist as ourselves for a moment—and that is not easy . . . because it means turning yourself inside out, giving up your own sense of who you are, and being willing to see yourself in the unflattering light of another's angry gaze." (297) A teacher should remember that she or he is not perfect, share power in the class with students, admit when she or he is wrong honestly and openly, and not put herself above flaw or fault. Modeling with this behavior promotes similar behavior in students.

Reflection can come in other ways as well. I regularly invite other language arts teachers to come in and interact with or just observe my classes. Afterward, they give me insight as to what they noticed in the room. Comments surround discussing interactions among students, discussion topics, whether they noticed the activity functioning well, and often advice on how I could change or add to the book clubs. I always value comments from others because they help me to understand where I am in my own learning as a teacher and whether I am remembering to be pragmatic with my students and their learning.

Of all the reasons for reflection, it is most useful for allowing progress through change. Student book clubs evolve, as does the teacher's method of instruction. I have begun each of the past several years with a different and completely new mindset. I begin ready to try new ideas with students. This upcoming year is no exception. Student book clubs have become for me another way of trying to make the learning produced in school *matter*. Along with the ideas of co-authoring, reciprocal teaching, and collaborative reading, students find reasons behind their learning, a way of articulating what was learned, and a feeling of school actually mattering in their lives.

Making School Matter

I am constantly questioning my ideas, my plans, and the ways in which I interact with my students. I believe teachers need to trouble the stereotypes, question our own ways of thinking, defend our ideas through language, and truthfully ask ourselves if what we're doing is working. I am constantly reminding my students to question their own reasoning while searching for supporting details by asking the question "why?" whenever writing. They find more detailed support for their defense, but most of all every possible reason for their ideas, making room for stronger arguments. Teachers should push students further than they might go alone to question what they know, comfortable labels, and limited home influences to become freethinkers—because they can!

To borrow from Kutz and Roskelly (1991) again, I would describe mine as an *Unquiet Pedagogy*. Since I began my career my teaching philosophy has revolved around raising the issues, arguing the truths, and questioning the answers. I teach all my students as if they were all gifted. I have high expectations and create challenging and "un-comfort zone" activities for open thought and debate beyond the obvious. With each experience I become someone new and my students have the opportunity for this type of transformation. I essentially want students to question their place in the world, who they are, how they got where they are, and where are they going. This is the general premise behind my teaching and how I use student book clubs. It is another try at *making school matter*.

I love that there is no one cookie-cutter approach to student book clubs. Through discussion, I have noticed even the titles (literature circles, reading groups, reading circles, book clubs, Sumara (2002) calls them Commonplace Book practices) change depending on the person or group defining it. But the great aspect is, I am more experienced than in previous years and in my fifth year teaching and my third year teaching student book clubs. As with most teachers, I can develop ideas at the spur of the moment, switch gears suddenly, and head off danger at the pass if something's not going right. Certainly, this takes practice, trial and error, which makes us all better teachers. Also, being more informed about the reasons *why* we do book clubs aids in defending any rationale.

One day early in the school year just past, I turned the attention of the class to a follow-up activity after the reading groups had met. Silence. I told my students "you should be talking to each other!" At that point, one student chimed in saying, "I'm not used to the teacher telling me to talk. They usually tell me to be quiet." My students associate talking with free time without realizing that in their daily lives, whether socializing or completing a puzzle on the dining room table, they are learning through communication and interaction, not being quietly observant. As my students became more comfortable with collaborating with each other in student book clubs, they began to recognize the power of talk in relation to their reading.

It is a fact that some of my students still struggle with book discussions and are still not yet "readers" even at the end of the year. Not every group progresses at the same rate toward the quality of conversation I associate with a successful student book club. Nonetheless, as the year progresses, I watch other students, many of whom began the year as non-readers, catch fire as they discover what reading can mean in their lives. Students, who would never speak out in a whole group, speak out and even in some cases assume a leadership role in their student book club. I watch students who were resistant readers write better reflections, become more eloquent in speaking about literary terms, and maybe just come in and ask, "Are we going to do student book clubs again this Friday?" But remember, I teach eighth grade, and many of my students are only now being introduced to this concept and their own abstract thought. I think of it as preparing my students for the book clubs of their future, their adult book clubs.

Across the hall from my classroom, the teacher there speaks softly to the students who in turn must be quiet enough to hear him. On most days, the classroom remains quiet from the time the students enter until the time they leave. I hear continually that the teacher is "nice" but "boring." In contrast, students in my book club classes are actively talking, interacting, sharing, moving around the room, and discussing their ideas from the time they walk in until the time they leave. I hear descriptions such as "getting away with free time," and "Mrs. Hancock's class is fun." The exchange allows the students the learning. And there is so much going on within the group exchange. I would be offended if anyone ever described my classroom as quiet, traditional, conservative, or as a "worksheet" class. Please describe it as unconventional and busy, just like the teacher inside.

Appendix to Chapter 4

Name _____   Survey for Student Book Clubs

1. Identify one specific time where you helped someone in your groups and what you helped them accomplish.

2. Identify one specific time when you needed help and how someone helped you.

3. Identify one specific time when you contributed verbally to the conversation about the book or story.

4. Identify one specific time when you made a connection with the story or stories that you had not thought of before.

5. Identify when your group went off on a tangent. What was the topic, and where did you end up going with it?

6. What is one thing you definitely enjoyed about your book club?

7. If you could suggest something for others to read, what would it be?

Name _____

Reading Interest Survey

Answer the questions as honestly as you can and in complete sentences.

1. What do you like best about Language Arts class?

2. How do you feel about reading? Why?

3. How do you feel about writing? Why?

4. What are some activities you have done in other classes that you would like to do again?

5. Describe the kind of class in which you feel the most comfortable.

6. Circle your reading interests.

Science fiction	Sports	History	Ocean voyages
Teen issues	Emotional issues	Non-fiction (true stories)	
Fantasy	Romance	Short stories	Poetry
Self-help books	Comics	Magazines	Newspaper
Novels	Relationships	Family matters	

Other: _____

7. When do you read?

At home?   At school?   On the weekends?   Before bed?

Name _____   Student Book Clubs

Important Passages.

On this paper, translate passages you found within the reading that were in some way meaningful to you or another group member. This could include a line a character said or a line from the narrator. The title may prove meaning to the story, or a character's insight may lead to other ways of thinking. Write down the line and describe how it is meaningful to you or another group member. Identify the speaker and what this character may have really meant. Remember there can be underlining meanings in everything!

_____

_____

_____

_____

_____

_____

_____

_____

_____

_____

_____

_____

_____

_____

_____

_____

_____

_____

Name _____   Student Book Clubs

Literacy Scout.

On this paper, list words (language) you have discovered as unique to the story read. The words can be those unfamiliar or particular to the context language of the stories' setting, characters, or time period. For example, in the novel The Outsiders, the word "greaser" is used to describe a gang of teenagers. What does it mean in the context of the story? Define the word using the context of the reading and how others in your group define it. Describe why you chose the particular word.

_____

_____

_____

_____

_____

_____

_____

_____

_____

_____

_____

_____

_____

_____

_____

_____

_____

_____

Name _____   Student Book Clubs

Questioning the Reader.

On this paper, create quality discussion questions that you might ask to start a discussion among the members of the group. Questions should begin "How did…," "What do you think…," "Why did…," and "Predict what…" All questions must be open-ended, meaning they cannot have yes or no answers. Test your question by asking others for an answer.

_____

_____

_____

_____

_____

_____

_____

_____

_____

_____

_____

_____

_____

_____

_____

_____

Name _____   Student Book Clubs

Summarizer.

On this paper, summarize how you interpret the story you read. Include details about the characters, the setting, and the time period. What are the major events taking place, and how do these events affect the characters? Do events create new ways of thinking or acting? What is the beginning, middle, climax, and resolution? How do you feel the story actually ended? Who changed, and how do you now see the story differently? How did the story affect you or other members of the group?

_____

_____

_____

_____

_____

_____

_____

_____

_____

_____

_____

_____

_____

_____

_____

_____

Name _____   Student Book Clubs

Visual Illustrator.

On this paper, illustrate how you visualize the story you read inside your head. First, write down any and all images you received about characters, setting, and the time period. What do you imagine the characters look like? (Think in color). Does the story give you any clues? How do the characters dress? What do you know about the city where they live? What do you know about the time period? How do the other group members envision the story? Then, on the back or another paper, draw and color your ideas.

_____

_____

_____

_____

_____

_____

_____

_____

_____

_____

_____

_____

_____

_____

_____

_____

_____

_____

Name _____   Student Book Clubs

Questioning the Reader.

On this paper, create quality discussion questions that you might ask to start a discussion among the members of the group. Questions should begin "How did…," "What do you think…," "Why did…," and "Predict what…" All questions must be open-ended, meaning they cannot have yes or no answers. Test your question by asking others for an answer.

_____

_____

_____

_____

_____

_____

_____

_____

_____

_____

_____

_____

_____

_____

Essay Topics for Book Clubs

Rewrite the ending of the story picking up when Johnny runs into the church. Describe in the rewrite what happens to each "main" character. Do not leave any loose ends on any character. This rewrite should be about two pages front and back (500 words), typed, and double-spaced.

Read another novel written by the same author. Make a list of aspects of the stories which are similar, such as young people forced into a position of making mature decisions, tempted by indulgence, or lured into using violence as an answer to problems. This **essay** should be at least 500 words, typed, and double-spaced.

Give a **speech** on the importance of an issue raised by your discussion in your group. The speech should be written to be read to a specific audience. The speech should also be at least 500 words, typed, and double-spaced.

Become a journalist and write a **series of news stories** about the most important events in the story. Choose at least three events to write about. Be sure you include the "how" of new reporting and all the W's: who, what, when, where, and why. Make up the details that are not provided in the story. These should look like newspaper articles with a title and a by line and text written with columns. The number of words should be at least 500.

Write a **biographical sketch** of the author of the novel and the reasons why this author wrote the novel. This **essay** should be at least 500 words, typed, and double-spaced. How does an author get her or his point across through a story? How does the author's life experiences show through the characters' experiences?

Select **poems** which embody ideals that typify characters from your story. Analyze the poems comparing to characters' choices, decisions, actions, and personalities. Choose at the minimum two poems to compare to your reading. This **essay** should also be at least 500 words, typed, and double-spaced.

Write an **extended definition** a concept or context vocabulary word from the reading that adds particular meaning to the story. Give specific examples and cite your examples using lines from the story. (**essay** with 500 words, typed, double-spaced).

Websites

Each website listed here is full of resources for teachers seeking information on student book club ideas. They are easy to use websites with bright and creative art and page directions.

www.webenglishteacher.com
This website is limited to the subject of English as taught in schools. Here teachers may find student book club ideas, literary lessons, resources, etc.

www.ncte.org
This site is the National Council for Teachers of English, where membership may be required to view particular articles. However, this site will keep you abreast of the latest techniques, opinions, and personal experiences of student book clubs.

www.planetbookclub.com
Here teachers may find easy to use ideas for student book clubs, teacher forums, ideas for professional development, and a store.

http://teachers.net
Here teachers may find articles on current trends, chat rooms for teachers to share ideas, teachers' own personal experiences, and other resources.

www.allamericareads.org
Here teachers may find reading strategies, reading theory, discussion ideas, activities, and approaches to book clubs, and lesson plans.

www.eslmag.com
For students of other languages, this website offers real ideas to help students speak about books focusing on the difficulty of using the English language.

www.blocks4reading.com
This web site discusses the differences between student book clubs and literature circles as well as other types of book clubs, professional development ideas, and provides a book store.

www.literaturecircles.com
This site is expressly for ideas promoting Harvey Daniels' literature circles. Teachers can order books, read news and articles, get book recommendations, and research design of the classroom concept.

www.abcsteach.com
Likewise, teachers may find here information on literature circles and resources to use in creating student book clubs.

www.funlessonplans.com
This website was full of various book club ideas for lesson plans, worksheets, and web links to other reading and book clubs.

www.education-world.com
Here teachers can find professional development, lesson plans, ideas on classroom management, and lesson plan ideas.

www.scholastic.com
This is the official Scholastic website where teachers may receive book order forms for student purchases. Teachers receive points toward free books and discounted prices.

Chapter **5**

A Conservative Radical: Finding a Safer Space for Freedom in the High School Classroom

Two students pass in the hallway between classes:
"What do we have to do in English today?"
"Nothing! It was great; we just talked!"

Jennifer Cockrill

I have heard this exchange before between students, stating it as if they have "gotten away" with a scam or tricked the teacher into "just letting them talk" all period. I often thought about what we as teachers have done to students to make them think that in order for an investment of their time to qualify as "real work" it had to be written down, or stressful, or devoid of pleasure. Unfortunately this is a direct result of schooling. The well-schooled students are not always the best learners or the most intellectually curious; they are the ones who know how to "do" school. Very often, they are girls. They know how to study, how to memorize, how to prepare for class, but they lack the skill and motivation to read critically. I would identify myself as one of those "well-schooled" students in high school; I could do the work, but was very dependent on teachers to confirm and validate my ideas. Simply looking for passages in a book and revealing why I connected with them would have frightened me. I was burdened by a need to be sure I picked the passage that was considered one of the "right" ones, in other words, a passage that the teacher had marked in his book.

New Directions

After participating in Mark's book club class and hearing about Holly's initial experiments with student book clubs at her school, I became enthusiastic about introducing the concept to my own students. The book club class opened my eyes to a new way to reconnect students with a love for reading, a way to create a safer environment for them to speak their minds, a way to take the "expert" out of the immediate conversation, a way to give students room to speak about their ideas as they occur during a discussion.

I started using student book clubs in my classroom as a second year teacher at Cavalier High School, a college preparatory private school in suburban Atlanta, after completing a Master's degree in English education at the University of Georgia. The majority of students I taught worked to earn what they felt were acceptable grades. With very few exceptions, I did not have excessive problems with resources or struggles with students in terms of getting them to do their homework or participate in class. All of my students came from upper-middle- and upper-class families and the majority of my students were white. In addition, almost all of my students knew how to "do school," or, in other words, knew how to get the grade without learning or encountering much discomfort.

A tension exists between what I regard as valuable in school, specifically between what is actually taught and learned in an English class and what is prescribed by the curriculum. What the school requires of me as a teacher involves lists of terms and books to cover, but the curriculum says little and reflects little in the way of encouraging young people to love reading. Instead of allowing students to determine their own successes, as teachers we are placed in a position where we are forced to judge the success of our students. I want to invite my students to take a broader view of what can count as academic success and to help them determine what is a valuable use of their time.

The kind of response I am looking for from students avoids the "getting away with just talking" sense they have in regard to discussion. I want them to see a connection between their potential to engage with literature on a personal level and their respect for traditional curricular goals. To negotiate this challenge I find myself returning to a set of essential questions that guided one of my graduate school classes and continues to help me organize my thoughts before beginning a new school year, a new unit, or simply a lesson: Why do I want to teach? What do I want to teach? How will I teach it to best fit the needs of my students? Here I want to discuss these questions in light of my emerging understanding of student book clubs as a powerful tool for helping me reach my goals.

I would say that my overall aim is to encourage a life of reading because I believe reading fosters connections and understanding among humans and allows space for a variety of experiences that have the possibility to enrich lives. In an essay called "Reading Poetry: A Lost Craft," which appears in a collection of essays entitled *The Crafty Reader*, Scholes (2001) writes that a person who truly wants to be an English teacher must offer students a space in which to learn "a craft of reading that connects literature to life." (p. 12) Scholes argues that academic criticism as this is typically defined in high school and college classrooms has the effect of coming between readers and texts. In well-intentioned efforts to teach certain texts, many teachers turn students off to reading. Although Scholes does see teachers as part of the problem, he also recognizes that positive change must begin with attitudes rooted in our collective assumptions about reading, teaching, and learning. (p. 13)

What I want to teach students is to approach reading as a source of pleasure and insight whether they read primarily to escape, to critically analyze and discover the inner workings of the author's craft, to understand the life experiences of others, or some combination of these. Many of my students arrive at my door already having developed an individual reading style but many see no connection between this aspect of their lives and the requirements for academic success. For them, required reading for school serves a different purpose as compared to the reading they do on their own. These are the students who "do school" to satisfy the requirements or what they believe is expected of them and look elsewhere outside of school to enrich their reading lives. One of my aims as a teacher is to disrupt this assumption and help my students build connections between what they perceive as two distinct purposes for reading.

In my daily confrontation with "how" best to achieve my goals as a teacher, I am constantly reminded of ways they conflict with expectations created by the environment at Cavalier High School—teacher-centered, lecture style. The curriculum at Cavalier is designed to cover representative selections from the literary cannon and includes a heavy focus on writing essays. Many of my colleagues would point to the fact that they succeed in preparing students for classroom experiences they will have in colleges around the country. Though this argument has merit, there are several reasons why I choose to reject it with respect to my own teaching, especially when it comes to reading novels in class. For one, it sets me up as the expert on a particular novel rather than creating a space where students contribute to understanding a text. Two, for the well-schooled in my classroom, this design imposes a very dull reading experience in which the student reads a text with the objective of reading to get out of a text what a teacher wants a reader to get out of the text. In other words, my students read as "student" rather than reading as a "reader."

Risk Management:
A New Teacher's Concerns

Despite the eye-opening experience of participating in a book club in an academic setting, I had some reservations about transposing what I experienced as a graduate student participating in a book club into something that would be appropriate for students in my 10th grade American Literature classroom. First of all, I was worried that some of my students might not uphold their responsibilities to their student book clubs, that they would not be motivated to keep up with the nightly reading assignments and would not be willing to share their honest reactions in public. Once in place the student book clubs would exist as a smaller version of our classroom community and thus be vulnerable to some of the same problems; if one person failed to participate, it would affect the progress of the group. The success or failure of groups could influence others outside of the class and can affect the chemistry of a class.

As teachers well know, all it takes is one student's sour attitude and the class balance or attitude is offset and difficult to recover. In my mind, this was one of the most difficult challenges concerning the students. As a graduate student in a course or as a volunteer participant in a book club, I had chosen to be a part of a group and knowingly agreed to uphold my end of the responsibility in hopes it would be an enriching and pleasurable experience. However, in a high school classroom, most are not there by choice (on some level), but rather they are in the room simply because it is where they are supposed to be whether dictated by parents or principal. This is the central challenge in transferring the concept of the book clubs people join for fun or for social reasons into a high school classroom as an academic approach to studying literature.

It was not a book club experience like ones we as adults might choose to join since my students had no real choice in the book or in joining the "club." This weighed heavily on me because I recognized then that I had to take on a bigger responsibility of creating an environment in which the students did have a sense of the choices they were making in joining the community of learners in the classroom. Since no one, to my knowledge, had ever done student book clubs in the classroom with these students before, I had the responsibility to convince them how and why it could work and to show them that they had, in fact, made some choices in being at school and in participating in class that they may not have realized. But student book clubs could offer my students a great deal more than what the curriculum required of me in terms of personal connection to texts and other classmates. It is a space where they can develop social skills and practice their literary language through a common text and with peers who are grappling with the same language; it offers the opportunity for a more powerful experience because of the daily meetings over a long period of time.

In order to prepare them for this new approach using student book clubs, I had to get my students to "buy in" to the idea of student book clubs and to feel their responsibility in the inclusion in a community of learners. This process of building community started early in the school year, long before I implemented a student book club with a novel. It is important to frontload this effort at the very beginning of the year, in order to give students a fair chance at developing that intrinsic motivation for participating. In the end, I learned that nothing would motivate peers like their peers.

The groups became self-governing in the sense that each determined how to handle non-readers either by stating their disappointment outright or by creating more concrete assignments until the non-reader got on track. Individuals in the group worked to accommodate and address challenges within the group without coming to me to impose some sort of consequence for challenges such as a non-reader (someone who simply did not do the group's assignment). They worked to solve these issues with tangible assignments. One group who suspected a non-reader decided that they would share underlined passages and come to class with written discussion questions.

My role was to encourage students to ask questions and to lose that expectation that every question had to be answered. In my experience, I understood that this was a constant pressure for this class—to feel like they could always produce an answer for the questions handed to them. This is why it may be so hard for them to come up with discussion questions. They first hypothesize an answer and then form the question so that they might have an answer to their own questions. Questions that they genuinely did not know the answers to that were then posed to their peers might be interpreted as showing weakness. Upon review of the journals and notes that my students kept, this was not always the case. Some students felt tremendous support in the groups and were grateful to the students that reached out and helped with a general understanding of some thematic concerns of the book. For example, following a discussion of *The Great Gatsby* in her student book club, one student referred in her journal to asking a question about the Valley of Ashes being "in between." *"Ben explained to me that the Valley of Ashes is an area that is surrounded by success, wealth, beauty (the American Dream) and is trapped in its poverty stricken, secluded area." (Katie)* The student who wrote this happened to be a very academically competitive student. The person she credits for her understanding of what the Valley of Ashes might represent in the book is a quiet young man, who is very bright, certainly her academic equal, but who rarely speaks up in class.

Community Building on a Level Field: Laying the Groundwork For Student Book Clubs

When planning assignments and exercises to help foster the idea that we (the students and I) were all participants in a learning community, I went back to the experience I had in the book club class and some of Mark's other classes in the hope of finding ideas for implementing the ideas in my own classroom. I revisited notes and assignments from my graduate school classes and re-visited the concept we discuss in Chapter 2: what is a life-long reader, what do they look like, and why is our goal to instill a life-long love for reading in our students? One of the first assignments Mark had us do was one I used in the first week of class. I do it every year now. Mark gave us a homework assignment, I now call it the Book List assignment, where we listed 25 books that changed us in some way, books we loved or hated. The beauty of this Book List assignment was that it started out as a very personal experience that blossomed into a very social experience. I was at home with my pad and paper listing books, reminiscing about the characters and experiences I had while reading them. It was for personal reasons that I would remove one book from the list in order to include another. When I finally felt I had a list that "looked like me" I typed it up and brought it to class. Mark had us read selections aloud and as each person read titles from the list, the class responded with a burst of emotion. With each title, bonds were formed, connections were made between fellow life-long readers. It is a visual demonstration of the way reading is both private and social.

Using the Book List exercise (which may be found in the Appendix at the end of this chapter) in high school serves two purposes: it allows student to connect and recognize the social aspect of reading, and it reminds them of a time in their lives when they loved to read before someone imposed reading requirements on them. Every year, I look forward to this class period where students remember parents reading to them at night, or the book they read during puberty that made them feel "normal." Experiencing this as a teacher is wonderful because I was able to actually hear the students connect. At first, students were reluctant to start their lists and share. But after a few titles were read and students revealed, "That is on my list, too" and "I loved that book" the room became lively with shared memories and experiences. Students would actually try to name books that others forgot to add to their list. It almost became a competition to remember the book that would make the most people respond.

I also have copies of the standard children's books that make the list so that they can flip through them and remember that reading was fun at one time in their lives; books such as *Where the Wild Things Are, Goosbumps, Dr. Seuss, Amelia Bedelia, Clifford,* and Judy Blume books seem to make lists frequently. I try to bring in newer children's books like *Tar Beach* to introduce more recent children's literature. In giving the original assignment, I invite student to bring in their copies of the books that they list to share, but most tend to wait until the day after to bring in books. I believe this is evidence of their renewed interest after revisiting those old emotions surrounding reading. The discussion of the list and the approval and connections with their peers makes it "okay" to like reading and bring in the old copies of books.

In addition to this community building activity, on parent's night I like to expand the community to include the parents by asking them to write their favorite book title and name on a piece of colorful paper that I have pre-cut. I have to set it up as a quick activity because of the litany of items teachers are asked to cover on parent's night, but it is well worth it. At the end of the night I post them on the bulletin board in my classroom and it creates an interesting collage of titles and colors. I let students discover it the next day. They first search for what their parent(s) wrote and then look for what their friends' parents listed. Some sons and daughters are struck by the fact that they did not know a parent read that particular book—reinforcing a personal aspect of reading made public by the bulletin board. If it is a book the student has never read, without fail it peaks interest in the book (especially if I note in certain cases that it was actually a banned or challenged book in a school system). This turned out to be a great way to connect parents as part of our learning community and a way for students to see parents modeling reading habits. It also creates an opening to follow up with a letter home about the student book club style that will be used in the English classroom. I will write more in the section entitled "A Safe Social Space?' about the importance of parent communication when implementing student book clubs in a classroom.

In recognizing the social aspect of reading by using the book list exercise, students connected in ways that eliminated some social hierarchy in the classroom at least around books—making literature a different space that is somewhat separate from the social settings and dangers sometimes present in hallways and classrooms. Whether a student was very popular or considered an outsider, many of them shared memories of childhood books. It was a beautiful scene to watch these students call out books across the room, reminding others of forgotten stories. It put all of the students on a "level field" by taking them back to a common time in their lives, before they knew one another, and before the lines in the social structure of a high school class were drawn. Make no mistake that I feel this removal of hierarchy was temporary and existed only in this discussion. I do believe though that is creates the possibility to designate literature as a place where we can find commonalities. Though I feel it is nearly impossible to create a safe place for adolescents in high schools, it does set the tone around literature that it is a safer and unique place where we can talk about issues of concern and interest.

A Safer Social Space?

But we weren't to the novel yet. I needed to find a way to break this range of students up into groups that would work. I did not want to just let the students choose, though some teachers may disagree with my method. I have read books that present the idea of literature circles and book clubs as a safe space for students to share ideas. On some levels I agree in that a student feels less risk in presenting an idea to three or four other students struggling with the same ideas rather than presenting it to the person they see as the expert standing in the front of the room with an audience of 20 students watching. However, in the high school classroom I think it is a mistake to overlook the social hierarchy at work and present even in small groups. My classroom was rich with cliques and I know that sometimes allowing students to choose their own groups can be terrifying for those on the fringes of social life in a high school. If I were not careful, I could have paired the polar opposites in conflicting social groups setting them up for personal conflict or, worse, I could be silencing the socially "weaker" of the two by isolating him or her in a group of four people.

In a perfect world, the student book club would be a place where the two students on opposite ends of the high school social hierarchy could come to terms and find understanding and commonality through literature despite social codes. I think many students can handle it and are forced to on days when we have mini-groups for single assignment. And while I feel that has some value in terms of teaching students that sometimes the world calls them to work with people they normally wouldn't associate with, I wasn't willing to take that risk for weeks of a novel unit by randomly assigning the groups. This is not to say that I did not mix social groups up—I certainly did; but I was careful to do so based on tolerance I had seen demonstrated within classroom discussions and I was careful to speak to members of groups to see me privately if any conflict was hindering progress in the individual student book clubs.

So how then does a teacher approach group assignments? To form groups in the context of his book club class, Mark gave us surveys, ones that called for a great deal of self-awareness as students and participants in discussions. I doubted that my students possessed that requisite degree of self-awareness and confidence to make this approach work so I adopted a different strategy that eased my students into the idea of forming student book clubs. To begin the process of helping my students articulate what they think needs to happen in a discussion in order for it to have value for them, I distributed copies of six different short stories and asked each student to select one that they would want to read and discuss. I then created small groups comprised of students who had selected the same story.

The stories I passed out were short enough to read in class and corresponded to the unit we were covering at the time. Students read the stories and discussed them in small groups. I had to assure them several times that there was no trick, no pop quiz, and no strings. They simply needed to read the story and share their reactions to it. Since we were focusing on the development of an American style in the early history of American Literature, many students focused on that. Others investigated the characters or worked to uncover a thematic concern. Although they took the task seriously, it became evident to me that I would have to help them ask more probing questions and guide them toward developing more complex responses.

Immediately after this event, I asked students to begin work on a survey that questioned their comfort level with the many directions a literature conversation can take forcing them to think meta-cognitively after their mini-book club experiences with the short stories. [see Appendix] Questions such as "do you think a good discussion about a story must keep the story at the focus or are you comfortable with using the story as a springboard to make different connections?" The survey was designed to make visible student preferences that might have some bearing on their ability to work together in a student book club.

Based on the feedback the surveys provided and my knowledge of each student's needs/requirements for a good discussion and membership in social groups, I began to create group assignments. Going through the group assignment surveys, I paired people based on their answers and their level of participation thus far in the class. For instance Craig was a far more outspoken student than Andre. Craig could hold his own in any group, so I felt comfortable pairing him in a group of other girls who liked a more guided approach rather than Craig's willingness to let the conversation take him where it may. This was a very tough job because I did also feel compelled to consider the cliques that I knew existed in my class—it was a place where my philosophical beliefs conflicted on some levels with my eagerness to please my employers with happy, comfortable students.

During this step, I was reminding myself of Freire's (1970) idea that when one is uncomfortable, she is learning. As an adult, I have come to recognize such moments as times when I can truly learn about myself and open my mind. My desire to make my classroom a safe space does not mean that I did not also desire to help my students raise questions about literature and life. I believe this critical work depends on everyone involved feeling okay with discussing what they think in a tentative way . . . But was this a concept I was ready to present in my classroom, and would they accept the discomfort as willingly as an adult-learner?

At my school, teachers are assigned as advisors to individual students. Our role is to be someone a student can turn to, someone who will be an advocate throughout his or her years at Cavalier. Turning to my colleagues, I was able to acquire information about my students that was helpful in creating small groups that might succeed as student book clubs. For instance, it was useful to learn about various cliques and other social formations operating in the culture of the school that might have a bearing on whether or not students would be able to collaborate. I limited myself to showing the advisor the class list and asking, "whom should I be careful not to pair together?" It was helpful in protecting particularly vulnerable students and made me more comfortable in setting up these student book clubs in my classroom. I realize that not all schools have teachers who are this close to students, but I would suggest meeting with a school counselor or asking other teachers their ideas in case they have witnessed some behavior in their classroom that might be overlooked.

I was honest with my class and discussed Freire's idea of discomfort by asking students to reflect on a time when they were uncomfortable. They wrote these reflections in their journals. Then I asked them to reflect on what that experience had taught them and encouraged them to think hard about what they really learned. Most confessed to learning very powerful lessons and attributed the lesson and directly connected its memorable-ness to the discomfort they experienced. It created a good place to ask that they open themselves up for the possibility of discomfort for the sake of learning. I find that if I do not blindside my students with my approach to teaching and remain open to their suggestions, feedback, and emotional responses that they are more willing to approach the lessons with maturity. They have more patience and they rise to the occasion.

I would like to address the importance of inviting parents on this student book club journey as well. Involving parents and keeping them informed is always an invaluable part of classroom management and effective teaching. It remains an important aspect of the teacher's responsibility when implementing student book clubs. A parent can be a tremendous ally by expanding the reading community for the classroom and students and by supporting a student through any difficulties he or she might encounter in the student book club. As I mentioned before, some parents will see the student book club as a radical approach. The best way to ensure that a teacher's efforts are interpreted correctly is to make sure all of the parents stay informed either through a letter or e-mail. A letter can help remind parents of the school's role in teaching young people how to work with one another and it can help a teacher solicit parental support with students who may encounter any difficult episodes with group members. A sample letter is included in the Appendix.

Novel Ideas

As I mentioned before, one purpose of the book clubs is to help my students learn how to situate academic reading within the total picture of reading in their life. Academic questions pertain to issues that are important in the realm of literary scholarship. Questions having to do with literary history and criticism—what some educators refer to as cultural literacy—are a predominant concern within the school curriculum, and I believe I have a responsibility to make sure my students engage with them at some level. At the same time, however, I did not want to leave them with the impression that such concerns represent the only legitimate way of responding to a book. I wanted to help them value a book for more—as an experience that could be transformative, one though which they can experience many different lives in their one life.

I approach the American Literature class chronologically and am required to introduce students to certain texts each semester. Our dean required all 10th grade classes to cover equal material each year, so there was not much room to stray from the list of required texts or use additional texts, and we had a considerable amount to cover each semester. One of the required novels falling in the middle of the school year was *The Great Gatsby*. I chose to launch student book clubs with this novel for several reasons. First, it was a book I was required to teach and one that I felt comfortable with in terms of my own understandings and interpretations of the book. Second, the book is rich with symbolic possibilities with the green light at the end of Daisy Buchannon's dock, East Egg and West Egg, and The Valley of Ashes, and, of course, Dr. T. J. Eckelburg's eyes. I wanted to believe I could help my students understand these possibilities in the context of their personal engagement with the book. Student book clubs were going to be a tool for connecting this and other literary concepts such as narrative technique, characterization, theme, and imagery in a manner that would be respectful of teenagers reactions and concerns as readers.

Literary history as well as literary criticism is emphasized by the curriculum in place at my school. Therefore, teachers are expected to present *The Great Gatsby* with an eye on the context in which it was written. Background information on concepts such as the literary modernism, the lost generation, and the American dream is an important part of the required curriculum. Before beginning the novel, we discuss various interpretations of the American Dream in its original context (e.g., America is the New Eden with unexplored frontiers and opportunities for the taking, America is a place where hard work is rewarded and everyone has an equal chance at success). *The Great Gatsby* offers a look at the dream through the eyes of the disillusioned. It is a book where students can take their understanding of the components of the American dream in its purest form and early innocence and trace its decay. I have always found *The Great Gatsby* a pleasure to teach because students are able to raise questions about the decaying American dream through the characters.

Before the clubs met we situated the American dream as a rags to riches idea of success in America—that hard work would breed success however one defined it. It did not take long for students to characterize the American dream as a myth, citing that all the hard work in the world cannot always overcome certain evils in the people who make up our society. The decay of the American dream or American myth and *Gatsby's* representation of the corruption of that dream was often a topic covered within the groups.

Using a novel with a linear plot and rich character development, like *The Great Gatsby*, turned out to be a wise decision for me in my first attempt to implement student book clubs in my classroom. I struggled with making sure that I met the requirements of the curriculum and was learning to trust student book clubs as a means of reaching those expectations. Along with my students, I was learning to trust this new technique and learning to view it as legitimate.

Three or four days prior to the first student book club meetings for *The Great Gatsby*, I reviewed two important concepts: questioning and community. To introduce the process of creating a range of student-generated questions, I opted to have the class as a whole write down three questions that they thought would be a good springboard into discussion. Students must work to design these questions since they are often tempted to create questions with a concrete answer that often models what they have encountered on tests.

We developed a couple of strategies for facilitating discussion and forming questions we had as readers. One strategy involved underlining passages in the novel and writing down why a particular quotation struck a student. As I roamed from group to group, I heard students reading a passage from the book, and posing a simple "What do you think that means?" In the early chapters of the novel, one student circled how often Gatsby used the phrase "Old Sport" finding it both an odd expression and one that might be revealing about Gatsby. "Is he trying to be British?" which coupled with the student's tone suggested he felt Gatsby might be putting on airs or trying to act more sophisticated than he actually was. The quotation could then be analyzed by paying attention to concepts such as character development, plot development, or thematic concerns. Once students had generated some questions, I helped them pay attention to their language.

Students volunteered their questions and we worked through them on the board to expand them to allow room for broader interpretations and discussions. Students questioned Gatsby's motives—was it for love or for revenge that he made his fortune? And they grappled with the choices a woman had in high society and the decisions Daisy made when faced with her options in life—love or money. For example, a student question such as "Why does Daisy say she married Tom?" might be suggested. From there we worked to expand the questions to allow space for a conversation about choices and the choices a woman had. Then the one question would split into several such as "Does Daisy have choice in whom she marries?" and "What does the character of Daisy Buchannon reveal about the other characters/society/role of women in *The Great Gatsby*?"

We had to work together to take a question that is somewhat concrete to move it to a space where the goal is to foster discussion and not to determine who completed a close reading. Another important aspect of this process is to help students understand that although the question makes room for an opinion and interpretation, textual evidence can be used to clarify, explain, and support those opinions and interpretation. Teaching questioning lends itself well to guiding students to pay attention to their reactions and make decisions about what seems to demand closer attention as they go through a process of developing coherent responses. Some of these lend themselves to being formulated like traditional "thesis statements" others were less definitive, more open ended in tone.

To address the second concept, community, I drew on their experience of the short story group discussions we had created just a few days prior and I emphasize the importance of the learning community. If we were going to do student book clubs and do them well, everyone had to show respect to the groups by holding up their end of the conversation. Beyond reading for homework, students had to commit to come prepared for class in terms of creating questions or topics for discussion. They all seemed to buy-in to the idea, eager to use class time to reflect on their own ideas instead of take notes or absorb lectures.

We also spent some time discussing what these student book clubs would "look like" in the classroom. All of my students could relate to small group work and small discussion groups and how they work. I assured them that they could expect a different feeling and experience in student book clubs.

One difference was the task size. Most small group discussions only ask members to complete a small task or assignment together. With the student book clubs, student would meet with their groups everyday. They would be working together and depending on each other to read and discuss the novel. Another aspect that is different involves the social and private aspects of reading. The student book clubs called for the trust of each member on some level. Since in their readings and questionings they would be producing all of the work, they had to trust one another to put in the effort and they had to trust one another enough to share questions, interpretations, and ideas about the novel and their interaction with the text.

Early on I got the idea that following up on my initial contact with parents in relation to this project might help us all adjust to the new approach. To experiment with this idea I sent a letter to parents inviting them to participate by re-reading the book or by working from memory and asking about their child's response to the book. *Gatsby* is often a familiar book to parents. In my classroom and parent newsletters, I encouraged parents to re-read the book and to have conversations at home about the book. The only feedback I received was a few e-mails stating that it was great to have their child come home and say more than "fine" when asked how school went. I suspect parents had better questions as a result of the information they received. But it did seem to generate a few responses from the class when we turned the discussion to the larger group. It seemed that one student had run a few ideas by his dad before suggesting them in class about the character of Meyer Wolfsheim and fixing the World Series in 1919; this was one of the first times that the word "disillusionment" came up in class.

Once the book clubs were underway they provided space to talk about the range of interpretations of the American dream on their own terms without having a teacher defining it for them. I set the context of the topic within guidelines of the curriculum, but allowed them to take it beyond what a lecture could provide. From the start when students discussed whether or not they thought Nick was a trustworthy character based on how he characterized himself as a narrator and how he behaved in the book, we were already covering some concepts we needed to cover according to the curriculum. In this space, students were able to fold critical terms into conversation—terms like critical view, irony, symbolism, and thematic concerns without having someone, like a teacher, listening in all the time to "correct" or to prevent them from practicing this vocabulary. Here the terms become more meaningful because the students are gaining the confidence to apply them without authoritative approval. Again, they learn to trust their peers as fellow experts within the group. The student book clubs created a space for the academic strand and the personal interpretations of the book as students saw fit to discuss them.

My role in providing space for the student book clubs to read and discuss the novel as groups did not eliminate my presence from the classroom or the groups entirely. Many times, I sat in with groups and eventually they realized that I was not there to judge, just to participate. Early in the experience, I would pull up a desk to a student book club group and could sense their tension. The made attempts to be formal and to sound "academic." Whenever that happened, I would be sure to add a comment about how I connected with a certain character or what a scene reminded me of in my own life experience. This helped send a message that I did not expect them to produce a dissertation at the end of the novel. I expected them to make connections with one another and with the book, be it good or bad. I allowed my own comments to go "off topic" (a term students created that I will address later) with theirs, demonstrating my approval and understanding that sometimes a book takes us in unusual directions.

The boundaries of going "off topic" and slipping into casual conversation is an important consideration for each teacher who may decide to use student book clubs in his or her classroom. There is a tendency to follow a stream of discussion away from the immediate relevance of a book discussion or a novel. When students begin to discuss a book's relevance in their own lives, there is a possibility that the conversation will shift beyond the scope of a book club discussion. The lines are hard to determine for anyone and harder to explain to students. In my case, I found it helpful to not limit them at first since my class struggled with allowing themselves to loosen up a little and express their ideas.

Still, it was clear at the conclusion of each class that students were suffering discomfort surrounding their concern with covering what was deemed "right." It wasn't enough to tell them that I trusted all of their conversations were the "right" ones. In order to help them allay that fear, I gave a "quiz" occasionally, straight from a popular teaching guide, but didn't count it in the grade book. Almost all earned an "A" on the quiz, which in turn encouraged them; when I returned the quizzes, there almost seemed to be a collective release of tension, but I worked to remind students that they were making far more meaningful connections beyond that of what a quiz could measure.

It was important, more important than I realized, to give them a "standard" or "traditional" reading quiz (one that was focused on recall abilities) as a way to connect this new approach to their concept of academics or what an academic classroom should be. It was pleasing to see that the students felt discomfort since I felt that meant they were learning something new, but also felt it was my duty to use that as a means of building confidence in their interpretations of the literature. After giving the quiz, I reminded students that the quiz-makers shouldn't always dictate what was important and that my purpose in giving them the quiz, which was essentially what they wanted, was only to assure them that they were covering or addressing the questions commonly posed by literary critics and the concerns traditionally raised within academic readings of *The Great Gatsby*. I asked them to consider how much more they covered and learned about one another in the journey and through their conversations.

Here I meet my tensions again. I see my role as helping my students to recognize that they accomplished far more than simply reading and talking about a book. They learned about each other, about ways to balance a conversation with many different ideas, interpretations, and value systems present in the members of the groups. They learned to honor each member's reading of a text through their life context. When one considers all they accomplished in this light, a teacher might almost be surprised at how limiting these academic concerns were compared to what the students were able to address within their book clubs.

During the third week of club meetings I did a quick survey to check on what the class needed from me and how they felt concerning their ability to read and discuss the text. From that survey, I found that some groups struggled with the new and different structure, students who I identified as the schooled ones, and wanted questions to help them "dig deeper." They were prepared and working, but they needed a jumping off point, and I believe they wanted some cues from me that they were doing the "right" things. The next day, I came in with some lists of what I called "Ideas to Consider" which were simple words, phrases, or character names that were so broad that students surely would have covered despite the list (see example in the Appendix at the end of this chapter). It was a list of items or incidents from the texts that might help a discussion when it came to a halt; it was also my way of giving very similar questions as the ones they were developing on their own. This served as a visual support of their need for a cue from me, and as a way to validate what they were doing independently.

The danger here again is not to let anyone or any group of quiz-makers determine what were the most valuable aspects of a text or the most important. The students determine what is valuable to them as readers. In a survey, one student captured a sentiment that was expressed by several others as well when she wrote, "I like the [student book clubs] because my group members catch things that I sometimes miss, and they contribute ideas that I would not have thought of. This makes for a more thorough understanding of the book." Another student noted, ". . . People in my group bring a different, yet useful, perspective of the book to [discussions]."

There were groups who had a tendency to want to run through the list of ideas/topics and call it a day, feeling that they had covered what the teacher wanted. (The ideas were nothing elaborate, and at times they may have just been a character's name, but they served as a support system for students who needed more direction and structure. I also learned that they depended on those quizzes to validate the student book clubs. One student wrote in her follow-up survey that ". . . they [the book clubs] must be working because I got a 100 on the quiz." This points to the students' recognition that the quiz is the standard to meet and surpass—the quiz is the goal. By making the quiz inconsequential in my class, I lend it less power as a tool for validating. In other words, I situated the quiz as something meaningless to me as their teacher. I took a very "uninterested" tone when I passed it out, demonstrating my confidence that there was no need to "prove their learning" to me with some silly quiz, and that I knew they would pass with ease.

I also always maintained that the final project worthy of their thoughts and attention was the essay they would write. The assignment was a thesis/argument driven paper concerning *The Great Gatsby* and the American dream. The student book clubs offered students a place to talk through the argument they would explain in their papers. It provided a place where they could ask their peers to play devil's advocate and offer counter-arguments to their points.

While I cannot claim that they all wrote brilliant essays, I can claim that most of my students expressed verbally or through their writing that they were more comfortable throughout the writing process because of their familiarity with the material, or, I would argue, their confidence in expressing their opinions as a result of practicing these conversations with their groups. Students who normally struggled with being specific in their examples or in supporting their points with textual evidence showed marked improvement by citing specific quotations as evidence for their beliefs. I recently asked a former student who participated in this experience about the American dream and her thoughts on it now: "To tell the truth, I haven't thought much about the American dream since Gatsby—since it illustrated the Dream so satisfyingly back in 10th grade. Back then, I thought of the disillusionment and vain attempts of Gatsby throughout the book as a sad, yet truthful view of the American Dream. Lately we have been studying dreams of independence and happiness in books about female awakenings by Chopin and Hardy's *Tess of the d'Ubervilles*. This could be a parallel topic since the women, like Americans, try over and over again to grasp a little piece of fantasy or a dream that they never really would be able to attain without fantastic literary circumstances. It always ends sadly because people never feel resolution with an impossible outcome."

The "Right" Stuff: Who Is the Expert?

> *"There are now so many other people who know of and*
> *understand my poems a good deal better than I do that I'm*
> *rather diffident about giving any sort of explanation, be-*
> *cause they appear sometimes to mean so much more, and*
> *such different things, than anything I ever thought."*
>
> —*T. S. Eliot*

As a community, the students and I worked hard to overcome the idea that there was a "right" interpretation. Of course my students felt that the "right" passages to mark were the ones I had marked. T.S. Eliot's words in the quotations at the beginning of this section served as my guide in leading my students through the student book club experience since it helped me to convince them that their experiences as readers could count for something in my class and that there is not necessarily one correct interpretation of a literary work. Not even a great author like T.S. Eliot can claim to have anticipated all the possible readings of his poems.

Assigning a paper as the culminating assessment for this unit worked beautifully with the efforts I made to assure students that if they could account for their interpretations with textual evidence that they were "right" or could demonstrate some expertise. The concept mirrored that of an argumentative essay or paper in which students developed and explained a point that they wanted to make about the novel. In terms of meeting the expectations of "covering" *The Great Gatsby* as required by the curriculum through student book clubs, the experience was a success. Students wrote papers reflecting confidence in the material through their specific examples supporting their claims about the novel. But my students recognize that reading isn't limited to those kinds of questions? I received a range of responses from students.

In my first experience with using student book clubs in the classroom, I had one student who completely rejected the experience. This student was a very anxious young man, who often became obsessed with succeeding at school. Darryl never got comfortable looking to his peers to work to make meaning of a text. He would have much preferred that a teacher, whom he would readily accept as the expert, stand in the front of the room for 55 minutes and tell him what he needed to know about a book. He made his discomfort and disapproval of this approach very clear to me in his behavior in class and in the surveys he answered. I knew it would be a challenge for Darryl and I had conversations with him. He resisted acknowledging any benefit in the groups and I suppose that the only times he made an effort in his group were for my benefit, rather than in an effort to truly open his mind. He was not willing to see his peers as some of the many voices in a text, nor would he acknowledge that there was more than one "right" interpretation. The "right" one was the opinion that the teacher held and the one he hoped to be tested on.

I never pressed Darryl to accept the approach because I knew it was fruitless. It was enough for him to even participate. I did press him to continue to participate in the discussions since he would spoil the chemistry of his group. He was pleased with the assessment assignment—a paper—something he felt comfortable doing. After a conversation during which I assured him there would be no test beyond the paper, he agreed to participate with less visible anxiety and disapproval. I made it a point to check in on his group often. His group was made up of students who were incredibly accepting of Darryl and his approach to school. Ultimately, I think this situation turned out to be an excellent example of what students learn to deal with on a social level in book clubs. Darryl had to learn to work within a situation that made him uncomfortable but was required of him and his group members had to learn to be encouraging and to work with a member who was somewhat disgruntled. This is probably one of the truer reflections of what happens in our own lives.

Many students struggled until the end to overcome the fear that there was some evil multiple-choice test looming in the future that they wouldn't pass since they weren't receiving a lecture each day. What they did not recognize until they had some assessment and documentation to prove it was that they covered all they needed to know for any objective test and more . . . and, to their surprise, they enjoyed the process. I truly believe that they felt because it was somewhat pleasurable or enjoyable that they couldn't possibly be learning or valuable, and, it is my hope, that their participation in a student book club changed that. They had a very hard time feeling confident that they had the power to unlock information and make meaning of the book themselves without a teacher dictating what was important in the book or necessary to know to survive in college someday.

What Did My Students Think About This Approach?

At the conclusion of the *Gatsby* Book Club, I asked students to fill out a survey that allowed plenty of space for anonymous feedback. The survey asked for general responses and thoughts about the effectiveness of the student book clubs, positive feedback, and problems the group encountered, ideas on improving the student book clubs (solving the problems), and any additional comments. In reading the responses I was able to categorize most responses in terms of *schooling, guidelines,* and *effort.*

One striking result of the survey revealed that most students seemed to describe themselves the way I saw myself as a student—needing reassurance in their opinions or interpretations of the novel. More than half of the class voiced concerns similar to Heather's "I feel we aren't getting as in depth as you want us to . . ." She then goes on to suggest that we have an occasional class lecture as a means of checking-in on a weekly basis. I take some blame in not reassuring my students enough that they were on the right track, yet I do not regret standing out of the center of the class and letting them feel their way through the novel and surrounding discussions on their own.

Others enjoyed what they termed "freedom" in the student book club meetings, with their only concerns being limited time to talk "a little off topic." My understanding of "off-topic" as described by my students would be a situation in which a group is talking about more personal experiences that relate to one of the themes or situations in the novel they are discussing. They made up this term on their own and governed their own groups when it happened, though I never explicitly expressed it as a concern. This was probably the most challenging aspect of encouraging students and an area where I improved with each student book club classroom experience.

Again, because I would not allow myself to participate too often in student discussions, I missed chances to encourage students on their connections that were thoughtful and connected to the issues brought up in the book. While I would often make broad announcements about the good work I heard in the student book club meetings at the end of the class, I feel now that I should have invested more time in the beginning of the meetings to specifically reassure students that their individual stories mattered and if the book took them there, then it has value. Since this experience with *The Great Gatsby*, I have learned how to "front-load" this kind of work and experienced better results in terms of the comfort level of my students. They are still good about self-governing their discussions and getting back on track when they all feel they have strayed, but I see that they are more comfortable to move slightly off topic when I am around since I made an effort in the beginning to value their stories and responses.

Most students requested the list of general topics that I listed on the board at the start of our student book clubs. I resisted putting topics up every meeting since I felt it infringed on their "freedom" in discussion and set up my presence in each group (i.e., "this is what Ms. Cockrill wants us to discuss . . ."). But students argued that with the topic lists, they felt they were better able of maintain a focus on the book and not get "off-track." This is a tricky aspect because I do feel that posting questions forces a focus, an order, and it doesn't help those "schooled" students to trust their own instincts and interpretations. In fact, for some groups, it became limiting. They would stop at the completion of the coverage of each question or topic. I feel a good compromise is to list very broad topics specific to a series of chapters or events. For example, I might list "Jordan—character development" on the board as a way to help a group discuss what happened not only in last night's reading but in previous chapters. It allows for as little or as in-depth coverage as a student book club deems necessary for their group.

The Teacher as Learner

It took a good deal of courage for me to try book clubs in my classroom. Admittedly I am still working to move out of habits I fall into as a result of my own schooling. As I mentioned before, student book clubs seemed radical to me. It meant that I did not have control over what was discussed or covered. I did not miss the "control" of the class—I did not miss that at all—but I did like having the ability to report to anyone who asked that a particular topic was covered on a particular date. I am learning that this had more to do with a need to perform well in my first years of teaching, and that I cared far too much for how those outside of my classroom judged me. As I receive feedback from students after their student book club experiences, I am heartened. They remember the classes fondly and can recall not only the books and their thoughts, but also encounters with other students. When I send e-mails or see students and ask about school, they tell me they miss the student book clubs or share ideas for books to read in such a setting. All of this serves not only as a reminder that the student book clubs are valuable and successful, but it also assures me that my purpose, my true purpose, is being served. These students have fond memories of reading in an academic setting and continue to consider the possibilities of reading in their lives.

I often consider how the experience might look different for me each time I implement book clubs in the classroom. Will I be more aggressive about exposing the tension I feel and opening up the space even more? As I gain more experience with teaching, I gain more confidence in standing up for what I understand as my students' needs. I gain more confidence in my philosophy of teaching and learning. I work harder to let go of requirements on paper and hold on to the real purpose of school—to foster young minds that will spend the rest of their lives learning, and hopefully, they will see that reading provides the means for learning.

Appendix to Chapter 5

Invitation to Parents
Join Our Community of Learners

Dear Parent(s)/Guardian:

Welcome to Parents night! Your first assignment is to think of one of your all time favorite books. Please write it neatly on the construction paper along with the author's name. Please add your name at the bottom. By completing this assignment, you are taking the first step in joining our learning community. Your book title and name will be posted on the bulletin board in my classroom for your child and his or her friends to see. These titles will create a collage of diverse reading selections that may inspire our young readers to not only select new titles based on your recommendation, but also encourage reading to become a more social activity.

This year students in my classes will participate in student book clubs. The class will read the same texts, but their discussions will take place in small groups within the classroom, much like the book club settings many of you have experienced outside of school. Student book clubs in the classroom create a hybrid space where both the private use of books and the goals of academic reading are valued in the classroom. Students learn to trust their own opinions as they learn to trust in their group members, and they learn valuable social skills in managing this responsibility.

Using a book club approach suits my goals as a teacher, which is to foster a life-long love of reading in my students, which covers a breadth of other important life-skills. In order to best achieve this goal, I used student book clubs in my classroom to model how people use literature outside of the classroom. After reading research about how students who loved to read up until their middle school years lose their enthusiasm when they are told what and how to read and analyze literature, a book club approach felt right to me as a teacher. It offered a way for me to help students sustain their personal connection with reading while at the same time respecting the college preparatory curriculum I needed to cover.

Before groups are set, students will have some practice within small groups and will learn some tools and techniques necessary for becoming a good participant in a discussion, such as asking questions and reflecting in preparation for discussion. They will also fill out a survey about themselves as readers and discussion participants.

If you have any questions or concerns feel free to contact me at _____. I am looking forward to a successful school year with your student!

Sincerely,

Name:_____

Book Club Reading/Discussion Style Survey
Check the statements that apply to you.

1. Are you more likely to:

    _____initiate conversation

    _____participate once someone has started the conversation

2. Which of the following most interests you?

    _____discussing overarching themes

    _____discussing symbolism and the intentions of the author

    _____analyzing quotations in depth

    _____connecting literature to modern day themes/ideas

    _____relating the current novel to other novels/movies/stories

3. Are you likely to:

    _____interrupt to add to the conversation if you are in a talkative group

    _____wait to be asked for your opinion

    _____uphold your end of the conversation but have patience not to interrupt

4. Are you likely to:

    _____write down ideas for discussion topics for homework

    _____keep up with the reading

    _____get behind and catch up later

    _____be impatient with those who do not keep up with reading

5. My strength is:

    _____uncovering themes in a novel

    _____picking up on symbolism in a book

    _____analyzing characterization in a novel

Conversation Notes   **Date:**_____

Use this handout as a graphic organizer for note taking during your book club discussions. Fill in the member blanks with names of members from your group and use the space below to make note of interesting comments or observations. Use the space at the bottom of the page to list topics you would like to cover next session.

Novel/Chapter/Topic:

Member: _____   **Member:** _____

Member: _____   **Member:** _____

Topics to cover:

Adapted from Jim Burke's Conversational Roundtable in Tools for Thought at www.englishcompanion.com.

Student Book Club Survey   **Date:_____**
General Feedback

1. What are your thoughts on the student book clubs so far?

2. What are some positive comments you have to make about the student book clubs?

3. What are some problems you are encountering in your group? Do you foresee any problems ahead for your group?

4. Do you have ideas on ways to improve the student book clubs? Any suggestions?

5. Do you have any other comments to add?

Chapter 6

Retracing the Map: A New Approach to Literature Instruction In the High School English Class

Holly Isserstedt

My decision to implement student book clubs grew out of an internal struggle I was having about whether or not the study of literature was useful in high school English classes. This sounds like an absurd dilemma for someone who has been teaching little else for the past six years. But what began as a career steeped in my love of reading had gradually become a job that no longer mirrored its motivation. It had fallen into a kind of monotony where the aim of what I was doing was no longer clear. I have always believed that literature is a means to knowledge, not because when I read I am necessarily enlightened, but because it challenges, expands, or confirms what I already know. And as such, something new is formed from something that already exists. However, I did not see this kind of transformation taking place in my classroom with the literature we read. I did not see my students connecting their reading to their own social reality. Instead, I saw them tolerating these books as a necessary evil to pass my class, a means to an end, a body of works to be dissected and mastered. But most troubling was that my students seemed to view reading in the classroom as an isolated event that in no way paralleled the reading they did outside the classroom.

I suspected the problem was not the literature because these were the same books that ignited the fire within me years ago that led to my career in English

Education. Instead, I was convinced that the problem was the instruction of these texts. I realized that the way in which literature was being taught in my high school did nothing to celebrate the joy of reading but rather suffocated it until students' desire to read was nearly extinguished. Literature instruction in my high school was designed like a one-way road map with a predetermined destination. Students were not allowed to detour or explore the terrain. There were no scenic routes or opportunities for exploration and discovery. If they got lost or could not follow the map, the consequences were severe. This method runs contrary to everything I know of books and reading.

I wanted my students to be their own cartographers and decide for themselves the direction they would travel as readers. I wanted them to see books as a location of possibility in which they were their own navigator. I wanted a strategy for teaching literature that would honor public and private reading without communicating that reading was something to be compartmentalized. I needed my students to understand that reading, both inside and outside the classroom is a continuum. Everything we read connects, intersects, and overlaps to become an ongoing event without conclusion. In effect, it is a journey without destination. I knew that student book clubs would not be the easy answer to questions I was having about the value of literature in the English classroom, but if done correctly, they might be the catalyst for reimagining how books can be taught in school.

I first learned of student books clubs in graduate school where my inquiry into reading theories first began. My return to school was, in part, a series of steps to address my questions surrounding the purpose of literature in high school English classes. I spent some time with theorists like Rosenblatt, Fish, and Iser, listened to their ideas and took copious notes. As a graduate student, I became increasingly more perplexed as to why the models of reading instruction in high school were not grounded in these theories. Even more significant was that the reading experiences I created in my classroom had no resemblance to my own life as a reader. The processes were all wrong and lacked those important aesthetic qualities that have made me a life-long reader. I needed to put these theories to practice. For any real change to occur, the traditional models of literature instruction had to be disrupted. Student book clubs seemed like a good place to start.

Initially the reason student books clubs appealed to me was because they offered a departure from the pedagogies to which I could no longer prescribe that overlooked or completely dismissed a student's response to literature. In addition, I wanted student book clubs to be more than just a small group sitting around reacting to a book. I was unwilling to abandon the importance of literary engagement in favor of a chance happening. I do not believe that one must be sacrificed for the other to occur. I wanted the book clubs to produce something meaningful, a space for response—analysis and synthesis—where spontaneity and structure meet and combine.

In this chapter, I discuss three of my experiences with student book clubs in my classes across varying academic levels that I feel represent a cross section of the different ways I have implemented this method. These illustrations are not intended to be exhaustive or prescriptive, but are a way of situating my claims about student book clubs within the context of my own classroom practice. These examples support my contention that student book clubs, unlike literature circles or small group activities, are more than supplementary activities to literature instruction. They are integrated part of an existing curriculum that add new dimensions to work already in progress. Thus, book clubs offer new ways of looking at a familiar landscape.

Forging a New Trail

My first experience with student books clubs was with a class comprised of 11th grade vocational students who I knew to be overwhelmingly reluctant and low-level readers with very little intrinsic motivation for academics. They historically chose the path of least resistance. For example, they frequently used mass-marketed novel guides, "borrowed" essays already written, "shared" homework answers, "forgot" assignments, and the like. This group typically did only the amount of work required to pass and found few reasons to advance beyond the minimum unless the assignment was particularly entertaining or appealed to their individual interests.

This group was distrustful of authority and accepted nothing at face value. If I wanted them on board, I had to legitimize each assignment in the hope that they would see its value. I quickly learned that the best way to engage them was to appeal to their collective sense of powerlessness by inviting their input whenever possible. I was more successful with them when they thought what they were doing was of their own choosing, not just another directive from me. If they felt excluded from the decision making process, they were less likely to participate. With this knowledge, I constantly searched for ways to promote democratic approaches to learning without yielding to their ambivalence, even with book clubs.

First, I devised a way to learn more about the experiences and events that shaped their literacy. In the month before I introduced book clubs, I had my students complete a *Reader's Autobiography* in which I asked them to provide an inventory of their reading experiences both past and present (see Appendix at the end of this chapter); simply tell me the stories of their lives as readers. This proved a useful tool in helping me understand the kinds of reading experiences in which they were previously and currently engaged and how those experiences might influence what they would accomplish later in the book clubs. It also gave me some insight as to how and what they read, their attitudes toward reading and their levels of motivation. But most importantly, when the autobiographies were complete, the student had documented confirmation that they are readers—in their words, not mine.

The autobiographies revealed that even students, who denied any current involvement with books, had a history of reading. This assignment was a way to help them glimpse a childhood pastime lost, but not forgotten, in the drudgery of school. I deduced from their autobiographies that their love of reading was one of the many things they discarded in their blatant acts of defiance toward a system that repeatedly fails them. I felt that student book clubs might help them to reclaim some of their interest in reading and show them that reading in school can be more than a process of call and response, more than another location for failure. It can be all that they remembered from their early years as readers and more.

Since their autobiographies reported that an overwhelming number of them now avoided reading whenever possible, one of my objectives of using book clubs with these students was to help them rediscover the simple pleasure of reading. I began by allowing the students to choose their own book for the assignment. The more interested the students are in the text, the greater the chance of engaged reading.

I believe that choice is a vital, yet often overlooked component in literature instruction. Even when the curriculum does not allow for book choice, there are countless ways to provide space for student contribution. Eliminating choice from literature instruction is just one more example of how literature teachers reinforce the fallacy that school and home reading are separate practices. Students invariably work harder when their opinions are counted.

In this particular class, my students and I agreed that they would have four days to decide on and obtain a book they wanted to read or reread that contained no material inappropriate for school. I emphasized that rereading can be just as significant as a new read, very much like traveling somewhere you have already been and discovering a wealth of things you missed on your first passage. I knew that several students in the class had named favorite books in their autobiographies and I wanted to leave open the possibility of revisiting a familiar text. Several of my students responded positively to the option of rereading.

For those choosing new books, I wanted to offer some guidance, as well. Because many of my students had not read a book outside of school for many years and did not know how to begin the selection process, I spent a few days offering suggestions and familiarizing them with new fiction. Based on the data I collected from their autobiographies, I created a list of several young adult book titles on their reading level, which included plot summaries that I thought might appeal to them. In conjunction with the distribution of this list, I also read three of the books from the list and spent one day doing "book talks" in class to both captivate the students' interest and demonstrate my own enthusiasm for reading. From my own experience, I know that sometimes the singular act of seeing another reader's passion for reading can have a profound and lasting impact. In addition, I scheduled a day for my students to browse the media center in case they did not have the resources to purchase their own book. I made arrangements in advance for the media specialist to pull and reserve the books on my list so they would be readily accessible to my students.

The following week, I chose a day that my students were to bring their books to class. I scheduled four days of silent reading in class, and four days of book clubs to discuss the readings. This helped the students choose a book that they could finish in the allotted time. On the day before the students were to bring their selections to class, I divided them into groups of four. I selected students for each group with varied interests as indicated in their autobiographies. My hope was that multiple interests might increase the richness of the experience for the members of the group and allow each member to have a sense of uncontested authority on their chosen genre and text.

On the day the students brought their books to class, I was surprised by the books I saw sitting on the desks. I was not anticipating the range of books my students chose. Of course the irony is that the very thing I hoped to create within the book clubs had occurred before we even began. No matter how articulately I thought I was communicating my expectations for book selection, my students had their own interpretation of my instructions. Hence, I prepared for book clubs with discussions of everything from racecar manuals to *Green Eggs and Ham.*

The immediate consideration, of course, was the varying lengths of each book—some that would take several days to read while other would take only one. I could have required the students who chose the "easy reads" to choose another book appropriate for their reading level. But if I did, the students might perceive that I valued only specific kinds of reading experiences—clearly not the message I wanted to send. Furthermore, I was beginning to see a small spark of interest in our assignment and to now try to change or invalidate their book choices might turn them off to the assignment. I decided instead that students with shorter books must bring other reading material to class on the reading days to supplement the time, but could use their chosen book during the discussions. I did not compromise the required reading time, but still honored their choices.

While students were still in the process of deciding on a book, I spent an afternoon after school reconfiguring my room as a way of creating a physical space that looked more like the desirable reading locations my students described in their autobiographies. I found some inexpensive beanbags to scatter around the sides of the room and brought in a couple of old chairs I had in my basement. I placed a few lamps sporadically around the room and moved the desks around for more floor seating. I also decided to allow my students to bring in pillows on their reading days. When my students saw their new classroom, they were both delighted and concerned. They worried that I might "get in trouble" because it no longer "looked like school." Their reaction confirmed that they were beginning to notice my attempts to integrate their social and academic worlds.

On the reading days, I was sure to bring in my own book so that they could observe me engaged in my own reading. It was important that I participate in this reading community that I was building. We spent four consecutive days reading for an entire class period. My students dispersed throughout the room, locating comfortable places to do their reading. I brought in several books, newspapers, and magazines each day for students with short reads, just in case. What I discovered during our silent reading days was that the students actually looked forward to class. There were several times when I looked up from my reading and saw a room of students engrossed in their books.

When the students met in their groups for discussion, I worried that without my direction, they would find it difficult to sustain earnest, engaging conversations for an entire period. Instead, my students were eager to exchange knowledge of their subject matter and their reading. For many, this was the first time I had seen them demonstrating confidence, participating without uncertainty. They were making authentic connections and generating a powerful learning experience—all self-directed. They were no longer "remedial" students but experts on a piece of literature about which they spoke with authority. They were readers with a story to share, a voice being heard, a contributing member of something larger. They were using the text to share aspects of their own expertise and life experiences. It was not the stuff of advanced scholarship and would never impress a college entrance board, but for high-risk students with deflated confidence and years of academic failure, this mattered.

What amazed me the most was that my students challenged my own ideas about what constitutes valuable reading. I admit that I was apprehensive at the beginning. I worried that if the books were "too simple" then my students would never make meaningful connections. I also worried that their reading and discussion lacked the kind of critical thinking that made book clubs different from other group reading strategies. I was wrong. My students, although not advanced readers or experts at literary analysis, were discovering the equivocal connection between life and text on their own terms.

One of the most exciting conversations I heard was in a group where a student was discussing his reading of a Dr. Seuss book. As I listened to him talk, I heard him quoting lines from the book and commenting to his group members that the story was "just like" an experience in his own adolescent life. He used the story of *Green Eggs and Ham* to explain how he had been avoiding a friendship with someone in his biology class because this student "just seemed too different." He continued to detail the list of reasons why he thought they would not "have much in common." He finished his story by describing how the teacher paired them as lab partners for a particular assignment. As a result, the two were forced to work together to complete the lab assignment and to my student's surprise, became fast friends. My student said, "Just like in this book I really disliked this kid for no good reason. As it turns out, we like a lot of the same things." Knowing that this student had chosen a children's book as an easy way out of the assignment, I was delighted when he said, "At first I thought kids books were just for kids, but there is a whole lot of stuff in here that's not just for kids."

The rules of reading that schooling conditioned them to abide, were suddenly dissolving. Students were seeing their own lives on the pages of those books, across all genres and texts of various reading levels. The books gave them a language to share their thoughts and tell their stories within the book club. In addition, students were coming to their own understanding that an experience with a text changes depending on the time and place it is read. No reading experience can be fixed; each encounter with a book is unique.

At the end of the unit, I assessed my students an "essay" which I called a "reflection paper" in which they were asked to describe what occurred in their groups. When they finished their reflections, I paired them with the autobiographies and returned them so that they were able to see how what they once did with books as children could be something they could do again as young adults. And though the real difficulty lies in how to keep them reading, their attitudes of resistance had softened from this experience.

I have thought about this class a great deal over the years. The Reader's Autobiography completed by my students at the start of that year reported only two of twenty-eight had read more than one book while in high school, and ninety percent of the students did not name themselves as readers. These are not at all atypical responses from students I teach. Most students will admit that reading is the lowest common denominator in their lives. I believe that schooling and the instruction of high school literature does much to squelch student's love of reading. Book clubs do more than invite students to become active readers, listeners, and speakers. It reshapes attitudes toward reading.

When I am asked to justify the use of book clubs with reluctant learners who "require more structure," I always refer back to these autobiographies, which support my decision to use this method of reading instruction. I have yet to see any evidence that student book clubs conflict or compromise my curriculum. In fact, I would argue that book clubs require more from my students because there are no free rides. Each student must be a participant in order for book clubs to function. Students learn quickly that the more they put in, the more they take away. But more importantly, book clubs bridge the imaginary gap that students believe exists between academic and pleasure reading, illustrating that the two can and do exist in tandem.

I do not consider myself overly idealistic about the literacy achievement of high school students and not all my book club trials are success stories, but I see more and more evidence that when students are trusted to make meaningful connections with a piece of literature without rules defining what that connection should look like, they begin to take responsibility for their own learning. They often discover that reading is a valuable, worthwhile endeavor. When this happens, their chance of developing a life-long relationship with books has improved tremendously.

The Wayward Travelers

Every year I teach at least one class of students my school labels "moderate achievers." These are the students who exist on the margins—not high enough test scores to place them in a gifted, honors, or college prep category, and not low enough scores to land them in special education or vocational programs. The challenge of this group is that are often more social and require different kinds of classroom management to stay on task. I sometimes believe it is because students who fall in the medium, ironically the largest percentage of our students, have to work harder to be noticed than those at the higher and lower academic ends. Being in the middle often means being overlooked. Many faculty members in our school label them "average." I would call them anything but. They are students who possess many extraordinary gifts that rarely receive recognition. It is often a balancing act to meet these students where they are while challenging them to learn material above their level of comfort because they have grown accustomed to their invisibility—often used as a license to coast. The first time I tried book clubs with one of these classes, it was not surprising that I ran into obstacles I had not experienced with other classes.

When I first introduced the concept of book clubs to this class, their responses indicated they thought this would be an "easy" assignment, which translates as "we won't have to do any work." My job as facilitator is to correct this common misconception. I like to make clear from the beginning of student book clubs that being enjoyable is not necessarily to lack rigor. I use the example once given by my seventh grade music teacher. She said that our class could all attend a concert and have an individual, if not profound response to that experience. But in the absence of knowledge of the masters, varies forms of composition, instrumental and vocal theory, reactions from others in attendance, and our own experiences with music, the event would be shallow and limited. It is only with the work that comes from taking that single event and finding its connectedness to our lived and unlived experiences do we fully construct something worthwhile; something that resonates long after it ends. I want my students to learn how to do this with books.

In this particular class, we were reading *The Crucible* in preparation for the state-mandated test required for graduation. Since this was my first trial with book clubs in this class and I knew that self-selected groups might result in socialization that detracted from my objective. Therefore, I created four groups of six randomly selected students. The students would spend an entire semester with their book groups, completing four reading units, *The Crucible* being the first. One important aspect of book clubs is giving students opportunities to learn how to develop a truly collaborative context that fosters a sense of trust and agency shared among the other group members. Students often take greater risks when the other members are not students with whom they already share close personal relationships.

Once the groups were assigned, I distributed a reading/discussion schedule. I anticipated that the lesson would take about three weeks. Each group would read the play aloud by parts I assigned each day. At the end of each of the four Acts, they would discuss their reading within the group, alternating days respectively. Each group was given an audiocassette recorder and tape to record their discussions that followed their reading as a method of assessment. The students were informed that on the reading days, I would take a participation grade for reading assigned parts of the play that was intended to improve attendance. In addition, each group was given a specific location where they could gather apart from the other groups. Some stayed in my classroom, some met in the media center, and others worked in the hall. I spent the hour moving from group to group to ensure that they were completing the assignment.

The reading was completed for Act I with much prompting and reprimanding on my part, but when the discussions began, the groups were a mass of noise and confusion. The space they occupied was so loud, that nothing productive was happening. When I listened to the tapes that afternoon, there were so many students talking at once, that it was difficult to discern one speaker from the next. I had to devise a new strategy and have my students complete a discussion of Act I again. I needed to establish a more equitable system for discussion. There were other problems as well.

An Important Detour

While listening to the first recordings of Act I, I had an important epiphany. I was suddenly struck by the social dynamics that emerged during their conversations. Some students did not talk at all. Some students talked constantly while others were trying to over talk the most dominant voice. Also, their language was loaded with biases and assumptions and there appeared to be enormous power struggles among the members. A crucial intervention was needed.

During my first attempts with book clubs, I did not spend much time examining the power dynamics or social inequality in the groups. I was concerned mostly with the quality of engagement between student and text and their textual interaction. It was not until I was immersed in the audiotapes of this group, listening to their discussion of *The Crucible,* that I became painfully aware of my oversight in not paying more attention to the underlying power structures operating within the groups. Although I have always tried to promote a tolerant learning environment where, as a class, we talk and write freely about difference and diversity. However, I had neglected this component in book clubs. As I was listening to the tape, I was suddenly struck by the words and phrases being used, judgments being made, and the aggressive way some voices were clearly silencing others.

At this point, I was unsure how to breach this topic with my students. I did not want to further marginalize students in my class with my approach. But, neither could I let it slide. This was an opportunity to show my students the ways in which language is used to privilege and oppress, even in the classroom. I want to also show that even the text is not innocent. Critique of text and talk can be a significant component of transactional reading which further illustrates for students the plurality of meaning.

I spent several days discussing with my students the power of language. Using several examples from film, newspaper, music, and books, we talked about how language (historically and in contemporary culture) is used in destructive ways. Over the course of that week, we examined race, class, gender, and the language of oppression. This was my chance to connect the micro to the macro. I gave my students several assignments where they used actual pieces of text in order to identify areas where the language seemed racist, classist, homophobic, or sexist. I asked them to consider how their own language might reflect some of the discriminatory attitudes.

I put the students back in their book club groups and gave them a transcribed section of their earlier discussion of the novel. I asked them to work together to list some examples from the transcript that illustrated the power differences within their groups. Then, I asked them to make suggestions for how their conversations might be improved. This was an eye-opening assignment for many of my students whose responses ranged from defensive to apologetic. The students were forced to take ownership of their words and acknowledge the emotions those words might evoke.

I also asked them to think about how their language was culturally informed. Through this conversation analysis, the students were able to reevaluate how they use language and communicate with others. In addition, they were able to see how the power shifted depending on the members of the group and the topic being discussed. I recognize that this particular novel, with its complex themes of gender, sexuality, and religion was the perfect piece for this discussion, power relations exist within any group. I now believe that to use book clubs without including this important component would be not only a disservice to my students, but socially and culturally irresponsible.

Once I felt my students were ready to proceed with a renewed sense of awareness of how they constructed the language of book talk, I still had to determine a new discussion management technique. I decided to regulate the book club discussions by giving each group members five pennies. The students were instructed that they were responsible for making one comment, asking one question, or providing one redirect for each of the five pennies. They were required to use all five pennies and once the pennies were gone, they could not contribute until the other group members had exhausted their pennies as well. When I listened to the tapes after implementing this new method, the discussions were more orderly with fewer interruptions. Because each student was limited to only five inputs, it seemed they were more thoughtful with their responses. The pennies worked wonders for organizing the group and keeping the members on task during their 50-minute class period. The students' "penny" contribution/participation was graded on a rubric, which I categorized into three types of responses (Surface, Intermediate, and Comprehensive) and assigned a point value to each (see Appendix at the end of this chapter).

Structuring the book club in this way served two ends. First, the reading method gave the student creative license to create the characters as they envisioned them. The students did a great deal of experimenting during the reading such as using a variety of voices, inflections and mannerism as they read their character. The play was a meaningful application to the drama unit that preceded the book clubs where they learned about staging, diction, dialogue, monologue, and other elements of theatre. In addition, the students were connecting their American History lessons (on McCarthyism, The Red Scare, and Communism), which ran in parallel to our reading of the play without any prompting from me. Through their discussions, connections with the text were surfacing across multiple social and academic contexts.

Second, the discussions had no predetermined objectives so the groups were free to explore the topics of the book at their discretion. This meant that they could talk candidly about the motifs of the play. Their discussions were passionate and risky, including a range of topics such as adultery, religion, and sexism. The students used their new critical pedagogies to examine and critique the exclusionary language and discriminatory metaphors they located in the text, turning their knowledge they gained from the conversation analysis back onto the text.

At the end of the year, their final exam reflected an overwhelming recall of this reading assignment. I don't know if it was the play itself, the book club or a combination of both. I like to think it was the latter. But in all, I believe the students began to see reading as something that goes well beyond the surface of the text. Even they were surprised by how the personal connections they made helped them to access the details of this book months after the reading.

By the end of the first book club meetings, I felt as if students were developing a sense of identity within the groups. There were no longer traces of the awkwardness of their first meetings. They had negotiated their own rules of organization and had an establish protocol for operation. They demonstrated found respect for other group members and appeared to be forming a cohesive unit strengthened by the risks they took together. They had established a unique rhythm.

Uncharted Territory

One of the most rewarding experiences as an English teacher is to teach a class of students who already love literature and have been engaged readers for most of their life. There is nothing like sharing the experience of reading with students for whom reading is a pleasure. These students are generally avid reader both inside and outside of school and will take on almost any book with enthusiasm. Book club seemed tailor made for these students. But in fact, this group of 12th grade honor students, who I assumed would respond favorably to book clubs because they typically relish independence in the classroom, proved my most difficult audience to convince.

These students were grade-driven, intrinsically motivated, and experts at "doing school." They thrived in authoritative classrooms and enjoyed fierce academic competition among their peers. They excelled individually and collaboratively and could easily adapt to change in instructional methods. They completed assignments on time and regularly did more work than was required. But, they had very definite ideas about what kinds of assignment were academic. Usually, these students thought "good teaching" was synonymous with a lesson that invited frustration and confusion. The more difficult the lesson to complete, the more scholarly merit it held.

My introduction of book clubs with this group was immediately met with resistance. The assignment tested their fear of ambiguity. Books were something they did well and book clubs went against every kind of literature instruction they had ever had in school. Therefore, it could not possibly be intellectual. In their minds, there was a definite divide between reading for pleasure and reading for school. Their ideas about reading had been hardwired into them from their early years of schooling. I knew that it would take some time before they began to make the web of connections that emerged in book clubs effortlessly with many of my other classes.

Their skepticism led me to rethink the way I had previously constructed book clubs. In order to gain their confidence, I needed a strategy that would validate the assignment and clearly communicate its purpose. I began by creating "roles" for each student in the group, which was inspired by a seminar model used in one of my graduate courses where everyone is responsible for a specific leadership assignment. I divided my students into six groups of five and assigned the following roles within each group: (1) The Discussion Leader (2) The Summarizer, (3) The Context Enricher, (4) The Word Finder and (5) The Sustenance Provider (the latter because it was spring semester and we were able to have our meeting outside on the picnic benches in the Courtyard). The students understood each role to carry with it the following responsibilities:

- *Discussion Leader* served as the member responsible for initiating the conversation within the group and monitoring the flow of the discussion by posing questions, presenting topics for discussion based on the text, or pulling notable quotations/selections from the book worthy of discussion. This role also kept the group on task.

- *The Summarizer* provided a typed summary of the reading assignment to distribute to the members of the group that later served as chapter review for the text.

- *The Content Enricher* brought an "addition" to the discussion that was related to, but not directly from the text. This served to expand the discussion by drawing parallels between "real life" and the themes of the text. For example, anything that might enrich the discussion by adding a new dimension such as a film clip, a poem, another piece of text, an artifact of pop culture, a current event, or a piece of art.

- *The Word Finder* was responsible for finding five unfamiliar words and creating a definition sheet and explaining the context in which the word is used in the text.

- *The Sustenance Provider* brought snacks for the group that related in some way to the themes of the text. This role was meant to encourage socialization within the group, but also to give them an opportunity to think creatively about what they were reading. Even though this was much more rigid a structure than I had used previously with book clubs, it was a way of blending their ideas of reading instruction with mine as I eased them into a new way of thinking about books and reading.

The groups were reading *One Flew Over the Cuckoo's Nest* in a series of novels that might appear on the advanced placement tests. The novel is divided into four "sections" rather than individual chapters. The groups read independently for four days and then met on the fifth day of every week to discuss their reading and fulfill their leadership roles. This allowed for sixteen independent reading days and four book club meetings. On the reading days, students completed individual assignments that corresponded with the text such as reflection journal entries (see Appendix at the end of this chapter) and vocabulary assignments. which became part of their unit grade. In the book clubs, each person fulfilled each role one time in rotation. For every one of the roles, the students were provided a "role sheet" (see Appendix at the end of this chapter), which was a one-page typed explanation/description of their contribution for the meeting. The Discussion Leader for the meeting was also the time keeper, making sure each person was given ample time to present his or her contribution. These handouts were collected during each week and assembled into the students' notebook. By the end of the unit, the students had a substantial accumulation of information pertaining to the text and beyond.

I also required that the groups audiotape each of their discussions. Each group was assigned an audiocassette recorder and an audiotape. At the end of each discussion, the students were asked to turn in their tapes. One of my concerns was that the students would be so aware of the recording they would plan their responses, losing the natural ebb and flow of conversation that occurs when speakers are involved in engaged discussions. However, this group needed to feel that I was holding them accountable for what they did in these groups, which the audiotapes accomplished. Even though audiotapes are useful with student book clubs, I use them knowing they sometimes compromise the authenticity of textual responses, particularly with gifted and overachieving students who are experts at performance.

Using roles as part of book clubs has been a tremendously successful technique in my experience, particularly for classes that respond better to traditional, structured methods of instruction. Because the use of roles requires that students within each group assume a leadership position, students are more likely to come to class prepared and they have subsequently done a more extensive read of the material. The students did amazing things with their roles. Even the Sustenance Provider role was useful. For example, one of the students brought Little Debbie "Nutty Bars" and wrote an interesting commentary spinning off one of the powerful themes in the novel of how "labels" are used in our society and the dangers of being labeled "crazy" or "nutty." It is these kinds of powerful conversations and connections that might never occur were it not for the book club.

When the book clubs in this class completed their final meeting, they began asking me about the "test." I had not planned on giving a formal assessment, but instead intended to assess their portfolio and leadership contributions. It became apparent to me that these students needed the closure that testing provides and reassurance they were still "doing literature" as they always had however unconventional the method of instruction. I was nervous about testing them on the material with a standardized novel test, which seldom if ever gives consideration to the individual reading and interpretation of the text. However, I knew there would be dissension among my students if I did not "prove" to them that they had learned something.

I pulled a teaching manual for the novel we were reading that had a premade study guide and test. Apprehensively, I administered the test without any advance review of the material. I admit that I anticipated low grades since I had done no teaching of the topics covered on this text in advance. To my surprise, the students scored exceedingly high on this test. Perplexed by the exceedingly high test results, I went back and reviewed some of my notes from the taped discussion from the groups. What I discovered was that students were using all of their critical literacies to read this text. In part, they were reading the material using traditional methods of literary analysis, which they had been conditioned to do in other English classes. Within the discussions was talk of imagery, metaphor, allusions, character development, plot structures, motifs, and other devices. But in addition, the students were bringing their lives into the text and using the text to talk about their lives. The students combined both their individual literacies and those literacies they had been taught in school to make their own connections with the text. The only difference was that they were using these literacies to make sense of these elements in their own way within the whole of the experience—not as fragmented pieces severed from the text. They combined their old and new strategies for reading canonical texts, which produced a more comprehensive, encounter with the text than if they had used any of the strategies alone.

Once the tests were handed back, I think my students were surprised that they could perform well on an objective test with an integrated approach such as book clubs. I think they their personal investment in literature did not have to be superceded by instruction that isolated literary knowledge and skills. The book clubs were one way of showing them how to deconstruct traditional reading instruction without eliminating or devaluing those methods. In effect, I could show them that the more ways we know how to read a text; the more the experience will yield. Further, book clubs illustrated that the life they live and the books they read, inside and outside the class, are inextricably linked. Reading is a component of living and living is a component of reading.

The Territory Ahead

In each of my three classes highlighted in this chapter, book clubs were integrated into structures and curriculums already in place. Though the expectations of what each class could accomplish differed from group to group, book clubs did nothing to lower the bar or compromise what I required of my students academically. In the vocational class, book clubs were used as a way to motivate reluctant readers without giving them an easy out, while in the other two classes, book clubs took required reading and demanded that the students produce more than correct answers on a test. In every instance, book clubs held students accountable for their own learning. Substantive interaction and collaboration are the cornerstones of this methodology, which pushes students to be actively engaged. Students learn to use their linguistic ability, lived experience, cultural awareness, reading and response skills, and individual expertise to make meaning from text in ways that many approaches to teaching literature neglect. Student book clubs can reach beyond the boundaries of traditional literature instruction and the limits that schooling has imposed on books because of their ability to present students with interrelated wholes rather than divided parts.

Book clubs challenge students to find new ways of seeing, interpreting, and understanding books, themselves, and each other. Each class described here used the book clubs to do different things. With my reluctant learners, book clubs helped to restore some of their interest in reading and teach them how to use texts to articulate their own "real life" experiences. They were able respond to their reading in a space that honored their individual and collective voice. With the intermediate students, book clubs showed them how to frame their reading using their social and academic experiences to situate the text within a context that was both historical and immediate. They used their text to look across other disciplines of study as well as to pull stories about their own worlds from the events taking place in the book. Book clubs helped the advanced students to mesh their different reading lives into one by disrupting the notion that academic and pleasure reading are monolithic. They were able to combine their literacies to produce a greater range of interpretations and create deeper connectivity.

Perhaps the most compelling aspect of book clubs is that each one is its own creation that cannot be duplicated. There is no magic formula. No standardized approach. This method of teaching literature cannot be drafted into a workbook or novel guide. Rather, book clubs are grounded in the assumption that reading is an intensely personal experience, a point that cannot simply be dismissed because students are reading in school. Book clubs must be incorporated into the curriculum without discarding the essential role of the reader. Book clubs acknowledge that reading and response is too complex a process to be reduced to a one size fits all model. Book clubs are as individual as the reader.

The hope is that book clubs will give students the opportunity to see the value of living a life that includes reading. I want to show them the profound power of reading and its importance in my own life. I want them to imagine reading as a life-long journey with endless possibilities. I believe it can be done. Students can learn to chart their own direction by determining individually and collectively what they will explore. It is simply a matter of teaching them how to retrace the map.

Appendix to Chapter 6

Book Club Participation Rubric

A six student will:

- be a prompt and regular attendant;
- contribute to group and class dynamics by eliciting feedback from others and helping to keep group on task;
- participate actively and regularly in group work by offering ideas and asking questions;
- listen respectfully when others talk, both in groups and in class;
- offer thoughtful comments in draft workshops and on critique sheets, and articulate constructive criticism as needed;
- participate actively and regularly in class discussion;
- always ask insightful questions that reflect thoughtfulness and connectivity

A five student will:

- be a prompt and regular attendant;
- participate actively and regularly in group work by offering ideas and asking questions;
- listen when others talk, both in groups and in class;
- offer thoughtful comments in draft workshops and on critique sheets, and is able to articulate constructive criticism as needed;
- participate actively and regularly in class discussion;
- often ask insightful questions that reflect thoughtfulness and shows connectivity

A four student will:

- be a prompt and regular attendant;
- generally participate in group work by offering ideas and asking questions;
- listen when others talk, both in groups and in class;
- offer thoughtful comments in draft workshops and on critique sheets, and makes an effort to articulate constructive criticism as needed;
- participate regularly in class discussion;
- occasionally ask insightful questions that reflect thoughtfulness and show connectivity

A three student will:

- be irregular in attendance and show a pattern of (unexcused) tardiness;
- rarely participate in group work by offering ideas and asking questions;
- not listen when others talk, both in groups and in class;
- disrupt the class with private conversations;
- offer minimal comments in draft workshops and on critique sheets, and makes little effort to articulate constructive criticism;
- not participate regularly in class discussion;
- never ask insightful questions that reflect thoughtfulness and shows connectivity

A two student will:

- be irregular in attendance and show a pattern of (unexcused) tardiness;
- only offer a comment when directly asked by fellow group members or instructor;
- not listen when others talk, both in groups and in class;
- sabotage group and class dynamics through clowning, pouting, or other distracting behaviors;

- disrupt the class with private conversations;
- offer minimal comments in draft workshops and on critique sheets; what criticism is offered may be rude or inappropriate;
- not participate regularly in class discussion;
- ask no questions and makes few comments

A one student will:

- display all of the above (2) behavior and refuse to change when confronted.

IDEA BANK FOR BOOK CLUBS
Book Club 101

Before You Read
- **Anticipation guide**: take a theme or multiple themes and create some thought-provoking questions to get your students interested in the book.
- **Reading survey**: find out a little about how your students read and what they remember about their reading experiences.
- **Book selection**: decide what book you will read, or let your students decide as a class (you can also have groups read different books!)
- **Book club format**: decide how often the book clubs will meet, communicate your objectives, decide the format of the discussions (will there be snacks, can they bring pillows for floor discussions, what do they need to do to prepare for the meetings?)

Book Club Meetings
- **Tape Recorded Conversations**: this is a good method for student accountability and helps you assess how the conversations are going.
- **Assigned Roles**: some suggestions are *discussion leader* (the person who keep the conversation going and has an outline to keep the group on track), *content summarizer* (the person who provides some summary information from the book), *contextual enricher* (a person who provides outside materials that enrich the book topics or conversation—this is subject to interpretation such as info on other books and movies, newspaper articles, etc.), and other roles that you add yourself (for example, I have a *sustenance provider*!) The roles should change each week.
- **Student Journals**: often I will have students keep a reader response journal. This is another effective way to assess their writing.
- **Essential Question:** sometimes it is helpful to have students bring one question written on a note card that they have formulated during their reading that they would like to discuss with the group. This makes for interesting dialogue and it can also be used for assessment. (I will often have them bring in 4 questions: a character question, a plot question, a theme question, a personal reflection question.)

Assessment
- **Reflection Paper**: this is a writing assignment that gives students an opportunity to reflect on the book and can be designed to meet your objectives. It is also a good opportunity to use with the response journals.
- **Inquiry Project**: this is where students use one of their "essential questions" and create a project in which they explore the question further. This is a good way to have them use different sources, material from their journal, and reflections on the book club dialogue. I love to do this as a multi-genre project such as incorporating things like (creating a soundtrack for this book, rewriting the ending, found poems, etc.—be creative!)
- **Traditional Assessment**: my experience with book club has proved to me that students can successfully complete any traditional test using this method. Sometimes, I will begin the project by telling them that we are using an "alternative assessment" and then at the end give them a traditional test that is not for a grade. They are always shocked at how well they know the material! They always assume that in order to get pass a test, there must be teacher-led discussions.

Book Club Consent Form
(For self-selected titles)

OBJECTIVE: This project is designed to help readers and non-readers engage in the literature of their choice. Through this project, they will have an opportunity to express orally and in a written format their personal views of a piece of literature. While completing the project, the student should have ample opportunity to embrace the work they are reading and examine it from various perspectives. They will also begin to practice effective time management skills in the completion of the project. Ideally, students should complete one section of the project per week once the reading is completed. However, this will not be policed; students will have the freedom to manage their time in their own way, but the full assignment will have a specified due date.

Students should select a book that is appropriate for their grade level and meets the approval of a parent or guardian. A proposal should be submitted to the instructor for approval prior reading and authorized by the parent in writing.

Book Proposal (Minimum 200 pages):

Title: _____   Author _____

Genre: _____   Publication Date _____

Description/Synopsis:

****Please note that **Amazon.com** has a wide selection of books for teens and provides reviews that have been submitted by readers. This is a good resource when making your decision.

I understand that my child is participating in an independent reading project and has been given the freedom to choose his/her own book. I further understand that any title other than those on our approved school reading list can not be endorsed or required reading {Teacher}, {School} or {County/State school board}. In addition, there are many Board approved titles and are available at your request.

I give my permission for my child to read the following selection.

Book Title _____ Author _____

Student's Name (please print) _____

Parent Signature _____ Date _____

Book Club Portfolio   Name: _____

Rubric for grading your portfolio

Periodically, I will check the progress of your journal. These will be random checks, so make sure your portfolio is updated at all times (do your make-up work immediately if you are absent). I will take 10 daily grades from this project this semester. Keep this sheet IN THE FRONT of your notebook at all times! I will also take a project grade at the end (which counts for 10%) of your test average. Points translate to our regular grading scale as follows: 5=25 pts, 4=20 pts, 3= 15 pts, 2= 10 pts, 1= 5 pts.

Organization: Is the material neat and in order?
Completeness: Are all assignments included and complete?
Thoughtfulness: Are the assignments completed as instructed?
Originality: Does the work reflect individuality?

	Date	Organization	Completeness	Thoughtfulness	Originality	Total
1.						
2.						
3.						
4.						
5.						
6.						
7.						
8.						
9.						
10.						

Book Club
Role Sheets for Meeting Date: _____   Name: _____

Role: _____   Book Club Number: _____

Explanation/Description:

Further Questions:

Additional Comments:

*Make one copy for each group member. All five role sheets should be included in your portfolio with all materials from each book club meeting. Be sure to keep sheets in order by date.

Essay Grading Standards   Student Name _____

Grade_____

Content	Organization	Sentence Construction and Style
It has a significant thesis, clearly defined and supported with substantial and relevant information. The essay includes a wealth of details, examples, or imagery. The essay contains strong analysis of the film is well grounded in the literature.	It is planned logically and progresses in clearly ordered and necessary steps. It is developed with originality and attention to proportion and emphasis. The paragraphs are logically and effectively developed. The transitions between paragraphs are effective.	The sentences are skillfully constructed, effective, and varied. Words used are vivid, accurate, and original. The writing is without serious flaws in grammar or mechanics. A personal style is evident.
10 Pts.	5 Pts.	5 Pts.
Thesis is apparent but perhaps too general or commonplace. It is supported with some proof, but it may be sketchy or occasionally irrelevant. The content may be thin, although some generalizations may be supported with examples from the film. The essay is moderately grounded in the literature.	The plan of development is apparent but not consistently followed. The writing lacks clarity or is repetitious. The paragraphs are generally effective, but transitions may be weak or mechanical.	The sentences are correctly constructed but lack distinction, creativity, or style. Words are generally used correctly, and the vocabulary is adequate. There may be some lapses in usage, grammar, punctuation, or spelling.
8 Pts.	3 Pts.	3 Pts.
The thesis is lacking or is only implied, confused, or not supported with appropriate detail. The writing is thin, with few concrete examples or illustrations to support the generalizations from the film. The essay is not well grounded in the literature.	The plan and purpose of the essay are not apparent. It is not developed or is developed with some irrelevancy or redundancy. The paragraphs are incoherent or undeveloped. Transitions are weak or lacking.	Often, sentences are not grammatically correct. The vocabulary is elementary, not college level. Words are used incorrectly. There are persistent usage, spelling, or punctuation problems.
5 Pts.	1 Pt.	1 Pt.

Additional Comments

"In Thought and Language, Vygotsky presents a sophisticated argument demonstrating that language, the very means by which reflection and elaboration of experience takes place, is a highly personal and at the same time profoundly social human process" (pp. 126)

Lion

Sheep

Cow

Monkey

1. _____

2. _____

3. _____

Horse

4. _____

5. _____

Vygotsky, L.S. (1978). *Mind in Society*. Cambridge, MA: Harvard University Press.

Personality Test

What to leave first…

You are in a desert. You have with you the following animals: a **Lion**, a **Cow**, a **Horse**, a **Sheep**, and a **Monkey**. To escape the desert, you are going to have to get rid of one of your animals. Which one do you drop? (You can use whatever logic you like. List the animal you discarded on line number 1.)

You have 4 animals left

The desert is burning up! It goes on for miles. Sand is everywhere.

You realize that in order to get out, you are going to have to drop another animal.

Which one do you drop? Write that animal in line 2.

Walk, walk, walk…Hot, hot, hot! You are so tired you can hardly stand.

Disaster! The oasis you have been searching for is dried up! You have no choice but to drop another animal. Please write your animal in line 3.

You have 2 animals left.

Ok, it's a long hot walk. You can see the edge of the desert on the horizon. Unfortunately, you can only leave the desert with one animal. Which one do you drop and which one do you keep? Write your discarded animal in line number 4.

Please write your remaining animal in line number 5.

The answers are based on Japanese Archetypes. The desert represents a hardship and the animals represent:

Lion=Your pride

Monkey= Your children

Sheep= Your friends

Cow= Your basic needs

Horse= Your passion

So, in the face of hardship, you will sacrifice each of these things in turn. Your last animal represents the thing you would cling to at the expense of all others.

Personality Test Guide Sheet

Think about….

What animal did you discard and why?

What logic did you use to make your decisions?

Were you worried that there was a "correct" answer?

Why this activity?

All of you had the same paper, the same instructions, heard the same story. However, your interpretation of each animal, its value to you, and significance to the story varied. Each of you drew from your own lived experience to make sense of the activity. Reading is very much the same way. I can give all of you the same book, and chances are each of you will have a different reading of that book. And, even your own reading could vary depending on when you read it, what is going on in your life while you are reading it, and numerous other factors that determine how you make meaning from text.

Book clubs give your students an opportunity to explore the different ways they read books by creating a space in which to engage with other students in meaningful dialog about that reading. Because this method of teaching literature allows for inclusion of different perspectives that are socially and culturally constructed, it expands the learning experience and the available perspectives therein.

Book clubs are an effective way to encourage students to take responsibility for their own learning because they are peer-led and are typically an emergent event. In other words, the outcome of the experience has not been predetermined by you (the teacher). It also allows each participant a "voice" in the discussion and a space for that voice to be validated.

So what about assessment?

Book clubs do not follow the traditional teacher-led literature discussion model, but they can still be assessed. However, you must first determine what it is you want your students to gain from the experience. From there, it is easy to create a rubric or other assessment method that measures achievement of your objectives.

Reader's Autobiography

Questionnaire Questions: Please complete the following information.

1. Age: _____

2. Do you consider yourself a social reader?

☐   Yes
☐   No
☐   Uncertain

3. Were you read to as a child?

☐   Often
☐   Occasionally
☐   Never

4. Did you enjoy reading as a child?

☐   Always
☐   Often
☐   Occasionally
☐   Never

5. Do you enjoy reading in school?

☐   Always
☐   Often
☐   Occasionally
☐   Never

6. Do you feel that you comprehend what you read?

☐   Always
☐   Often
☐   Occasionally
☐   Never

7. Are you more likely to read if you can choose your reading material?

☐   Yes
☐   No
☐   Uncertain

8. Have you ever participated in a social reading group?

☐   Yes
☐   No
☐   Uncertain

9.   Have you ever had a discussion about a book with a friend or parent?

☐   Yes
☐   No
☐   Uncertain

10. Do you consider yourself to be social around your peers?

☐   Always
☐   Often
☐   Occasionally
☐   Never

11. How often do you read for pleasure?

☐   Never
☐   Occasionally
☐   Often

13. Have you ever kept a reading log or written about your reading?

☐   Yes
☐   No
☐   Uncertain

Please tell me a few specific details about your life as a reader.

14. Describe your earliest memory as a reader? Who were you with? What did
     you read? What do you remember about this experience?
15. Is there anyone in particular that influenced you as a reader? If so,
     what do you remember about that person?
16. If you read socially, or even if you don't, what kinds of books do
     you/would you choose? What reading do you most enjoy (magazines,
     newspaper, fiction, nonfiction, short stories, comic books, etc.)
17. How would you describe yourself as a reader?
18. What, if any, are your goals for yourself as a reader.
19. Describe your best reading experience.
20. Describe your worst reading experience.
21. Describe your ideal reading environment. Be sure to include the
     location, furniture, time of day/night, and any other essential details
     that come to mind.

Part **3**

Readers/Teachers as Learners

*"The purpose of art is to lay bare the questions
that have been hidden by the answers."*

—James Baldwin

"To Carve and Paint the Very Atmosphere and Medium Through Which We Look": Student Book Clubs and Literary Theory

"It is something to be able to paint a particular picture, or to carve a statue, and so make a few objects beautiful; but it is far more glorious to carve and paint the very atmosphere and medium through which we look, which morally we can do. To affect the quality of the day, that is the highest of the arts."

—*H. D. Thoreau,* Walden

Part 3 situates our descriptions of student book clubs from the standpoint of literary theory, in particular three key theorists whose work informs our understanding of literary reading as a more or less open-ended, exploratory process. As we have been saying all along, our purpose is to enhance not replace middle and secondary school literature curricula. At the same time, we acknowledge that the classroom practices described in Part 2 of this book imply a theoretical stance toward literary reading that disrupts mainstream assumptions about what constitutes a sound, academic approach to literature instruction. We turn now to scholarship that supports our call for a less comprehensive treatment of literary criticism and history in order to make time for shared reading experiences directed toward the goal of helping people grow into lifelong readers.

For those who are interested, this chapter points as well to the theory behind what we said in the "Teachers as Readers" section of this book about the value of amateur reading as an activity that, ideally, combines influences derived from a variety of sources including but not limited to school. We want to emphasize, however, that our foray into the realm of literary theory in this chapter is intended to be neither summative nor definitive. Our aim is to point to theoretical work that might help others as it has helped us to account for our choices as teachers and as readers in search of experiences that enable us to make connections between literature and life.

We begin with a brief look at the history of reader-response theory as this pertains to our understanding of reading as an open-ended process evolving in and over time. A central figure in that history is Louise Rosenblatt (1938/1995, 1978/1994). Although variously interpreted over the years, we think her transactional theory of the literary work still stands as a useful reference point for teachers who are attracted to the idea of a response-oriented approach to literature instruction. In addition, Rosenblatt's idea of "literature as exploration" resonates with our stance as teachers who also see themselves as learners.

Following our overview of reader response theory, we move on to a discussion of work by Mikhail Bakhtin (1968/84, 1981, 1986), the Russian philosopher and linguist, whose career in some respects parallels that of Rosenblatt. Writing in the 1930s, both theorists challenged the norms governing literary discourse at that time and did so in ways that are only now beginning to be fully appreciated. It is from Bakhtin that we derive our notion of *hybridity* (mentioned in Chapter 2) as it applies to our definition of amateur readers and reading. Another of Bakhtin's concepts, which he calls "carnival spirit," also helps us to theorize what becomes possible in academic contexts through the use of student book clubs.

Finally, we turn to that most imposing figure among contemporary literary theorists, Jaques Derrida (1976, 1982, 1992) specifically, his controversial approach to reading—and living—that goes by the name *deconstruction*. Although claiming mastery is not part of our game, especially with respect to the high theory practiced by philosophers like Derrida, we will try to explain why we like the word, "deconstruction." For us, it provides an alternative to thinking in either/or terms about our engagements with literature, that is, as if these are necessarily private or public, personal or critical, amateur or academic. We have learned to value the way a deconstructive reading disrupts our desire for certainty at the same time as it opens up new possibilities for thinking about how to read and why.

As adults, we have come to believe that learning how to read is a life-long endeavor to connect with other human voices. As teachers, we believe that this learning process should require us to engage with ideas and feelings different from our own. Experience has taught us that trying to help students sustain or move toward an image of themselves as life-long readers produces challenges that are not addressed very well by literature instruction that emphasizes critical thinking at the expense of personal engagement. By the same token, we also have learned that promoting personal engagement without inviting critical reflection also fails to model the kind of reading that makes such a profound difference in our own lives as adult, amateur readers. Now that we have described *how* we use student book clubs as a tool for connecting personal engagement with critical reflection, this chapter explains *why* we think our approach is not only desirable but also theoretically sound.

Louise Rosenblatt and Reader Response Theory

Years ago in the 1920s, I. A. Richards, a powerful advocate for the professionalization of literary study, challenged a group of his students at Oxford University in England to read and respond in writing to poems without first telling them when and by whom the poems were written. Richards later published what he believed were the dismal results of his "research" in a book entitled *Practical Criticism* (1929). This book, a kind of highbrow expose, features Richards' detailed analysis of the students' responses in support of his conclusion that even the best and the brightest college students of the day were woefully incapable of applying their extensive, but abstract, knowledge of literary history and criticism to the task of actually reading poetry. It is interesting to read the book today because the students' responses do not seem nearly as outrageous and incompetent as Richards makes them out to be. In hindsight, it is easy to see that Richards' students were caught between conflicting purposes for reading that produced a condition, so to speak, of being neither here nor there. Not having fully mastered the critical discourse espoused by Richards and his colleagues, they had learned nonetheless to devalue their spontaneous impulses connected with years of reading experience outside the walls of the academy.

At about the time Richards was conducting his famous "experiment," a young, student at Barnard College on the other side of the Atlantic was beginning to formulate a very different point of view that one day would play an important role in the emergence of a new field of literary study, known today as reader-response theory. Where scholars like I.A Richards sought to efface the unpredictable effects of amateur reading practices with a more or less scientific approach to literary interpretation, Louise Rosenblatt envisioned a different approach based on her conviction that academic reading should not necessarily require the rejection of personal, private responses. Her most famous book, *Literature as Exploration*, published in 1938 (and recently reissued in a fifth edition) makes a case for understanding literary reading as a process whereby personal responses are continually transformed to create an ever widening net of relations connecting individual readers with the world at large. Following her reading of John Dewey's philosophical writings, especially his famous essay on aesthetic theory entitled *Art as Experience* (1934), Rosenblatt developed her "transactional theory of the literary work of art," which, despite certain limitations, still stands as a major contribution to debates over the aims of literary reading and teaching.

For decades, however, Rosenblatt labored in relative obscurity, as there was little interest in her suspiciously feminine emphasis on the "lived-through experiences" of readers. An approach to literary reading developed during the 1920s by a cadre of literary scholars (including, not surprisingly, I.A. Richards) and commonly referred to as the New Criticism so overwhelmed competing points of view that by 1940 it had become difficult for anyone to imagine another way to have a serious conversation about literature (Graf, 1987). The New Criticism revolves around the conviction that a literary text exists "in-itself" and as such needs to be studied in a manner analogous to the way a scientist studies natural phenomena. This approach is summed up (more or less admirably) in a famous book by Cleanth Brooks and Robert Penn Warren called *Understanding Poetry*, that ironically was published in the same year, 1938, as Rosenblatt's *Literature as Exploration*. Few paid any attention to the latter while Brooks and Warren went on to contribute mightily to the widespread professionalization of literary study in the United States, a turn of events epitomized by the success of the Great Books Movement in the 1950s. As previously noted in our introduction, the heyday of what amounted to a monolithic definition of academic reading informed by the New Criticism would be short-lived.

Among the many consequences stemming from the cultural upheavals of the 1960s was an erosion of faith in teaching practices aligned with New Criticism and its portrayal of literary texts as timeless, disembodied containers of exclusively "literary" meanings. Maverick scholars, notably Stanley Fish (1972) and William Slatoff (1970), began to ask unfamiliar and troubling questions about the role of the reader in the production of literary meanings and out of this questioning reader-response theory was born. Well, sort of. The fact is that by the time the phrase, reader-response, had become commonplace, Louise Rosenblatt had been writing for years and was well positioned to become something of a celebrity when her second book, *The Reader, The Text, The*

Poem was published in 1978. For better and for worse, her work soon became for many educators the most visible if not the most carefully studied example of a radically new approach to literary reading and teaching.

For our purposes the origins of reader-response theory are less important than what has become of the concept over the years leading up to the present time. (Those interested in learning more about the various possibilities opened up by the "first wave" of reader-response theory during the 1970s and 80s are referred to Richard Beach's (1993) *A Teacher's Introduction to Reader-Response Theories*.) Looking back, we see a huge problem in the fact that reader-response theory initially was framed almost exclusively in opposition to New Criticism but in a way that left much of the New Critical legacy, including many questionable assumptions about textuality, interpretation, and literary meaning, intact. Scholars and schoolteachers alike, who, in the 1970s, were drawn to the idea of paying attention to the experience of reading, found themselves unable to let go of the basic idea that literary texts must exist as (timeless) art objects that must be (properly) interpreted by readers (see Clifford, 1979). Perhaps inevitably this situation produced seemingly endless—and we would argue misguided— debates about the relative validity of so-called personal, idiosyncratic (i.e., subjective) responses versus the academic, argumentative (i.e., objective) responses generated through using the tools of New Critical analysis.

Ultimately, the inability of its proponents to effectively counter the charge that reader-response theory encouraged subjective, impressionistic, and thus irresponsible approaches to literary reading/teaching meant that a promising theoretical stance, one that appeared to offer a radical redefinition of academic reading, would be relegated by the mid-1990s to a lowly corner of the literary establishment. To some extent, this banishment was justified as is made abundantly clear by recent critics of the way Rosenblatt's work typically has been appropriated by teachers (Appleman, 2000; Dressman, 2001; Pirie, 1997). On the other hand, we would point to possibilities, including the possibility of revaluing Rosenblatt's contribution (Clifford, 1990; Faust, 2000), that have been opened up recently through the emergence of more complex, more supple versions of reader-response theory that address questions about the role of readers and reading from an interdisciplinary standpoint (Beach, 2000; Carey-Webb, 2002; Enciso, 1998; Iser, 2000; Morgan & Misson, in press; Shusterman, 2000; Sumara, 1996, 2000).

It is this "second wave" of reader-response theory that interests us and informs our theoretical stance with respect to our stance as amateur readers and as teachers interested in using student book clubs to help teenagers connect with reading. We take this body of scholarship as an invitation to move our thinking beyond the unnecessary and ultimately self-defeating argument that there is no value in so-called "personal" responses to literature unless these are superceded by some form of "critical" thinking. We need to be careful here lest we open ourselves to the charge leveled at early proponents of reader-response theory that our stance must entail a belief that "anything goes," that there is no legitimate basis for discriminating among responses and among literary texts themselves for that matter. The key to disarming this charge, we have come to believe, lies in paying attention to what actually happens when people become readers through engaging with texts. This is precisely what recent advocates of reader-response theory are doing and their scholarship has guided us toward an understanding of literary reading as a process that folds *both* personal *and* critical aspects together to produce useful insights. In other words, becoming critical should not necessarily require the relinquishing of one's personal investment in a reading event.

Dennis Sumara (2002) argues that "literature still matters" because it is created by and for "people who make it their business to interrupt the familiarity of their own perception and interpretations of the way the world 'really is.'" (p. 157) If there is any validity to this claim, and we think there is, then the act of becoming critical is actually dependent upon a person's ability and motivation to foreground their own perceptions and interpretations of the world. Learning how to read (and write) is a life-long commitment, according to Sumara, who calls this a process of "learning how to create insight." (p. 17) In a recent article, Sumara (2000) links reader-response with an emerging field called complexity theory. This work joins a growing number of multidisciplinary studies that wed reader-response theory to other perspectives such as feminist theory (Ensico, 1998), activity theory (Beach, 2000), and cultural studies (Carey-Webb, 2001) to offer teachers (and others) new possibilities for using their experiences with reading as a source of insights about themselves, others, and the world.

Two related points need to be made in conjunction with the claim that, far from being mutually exclusive, the terms personal and critical actually presuppose one another. In the first place, we need to let go of the New Critical dogma which asserts that literary texts "say what they mean and mean what they say" all-at-once and for all time. The history of literary theory and criticism itself argues against this claim insofar as it is easy to demonstrate that even the most sacrosanct texts (*Hamlet* or *Paradise Lost* for example) now mean much more and many different things than they possibly could have meant for their original audiences and even for the authors themselves. In the second place, we need to acknowledge that it is impositional and potentially dangerous to decide in advance what will count as a "critical" response. Such responses will be meaningless if they are not situated in relation to particular perceptions and interpretations, which by definition are precisely what is supposed to be called into question by critical thinking.

We have come to believe that the great divide between professional (i.e., scholarly) reading practices and amateur (i.e., unscholarly) reading practices is an artificial and unnecessary construct that harks back to an earlier time when the very idea of making English an academic subject was debatable. We heartily agree with those who argue that by now the professionalization of literary study has gone too far and that a correction is necessary if there is to be any future for literary study as an academic subject (Scholes, 1998, 2001; Sell, 2001). Richard Shusterman (2000) likewise questions the social value of what he calls "an institutionalized priestly class of professional appreciators" who look down on "mere lay readers" (p. 105).

> Though I'm not clear how reading pleasure should be measured, my (professional and non-professional) experience suggests that trying to crank out academic papers with novel interpretations is not always more satisfying than simply reading a literary work as an amateur focused on its more common understanding (p. 105).

Moreover, Shusterman argues, when we place too great a premium on scholarly reading, we run the risk of making "the best become the enemy of the good by rejecting the value of ordinary readings because of the greater thrill of extraordinary ones" (p. 105).

We turn now to Rosenblatt's transactional theory which can be and we think must be read with a new accent in light of the continuing evolution of reader response theory. Rosenblatt clearly allows for the existence of extraordinary readings in the sense implied by Shusterman above, namely that such readings introduce radically new possibilities for interpreting a work of literature but in ways that nonetheless seem plausible to a broad audience of other readers. The beauty of transactional theory, however, is that it also accounts for the fact that even—and especially—the most extraordinary readings do not arise out of nowhere. Far from being the product of some sort of inspiration, extraordinary readings result when someone—usually but not always a specialist in literary study—has learned how to make texts speak in highly unexpected, provocative, and yet persuasive ways. At the same time, Rosenblatt asserts that an extraordinary reading, like any other, is always situated with respect to a variety of factors, such as time, place, and audience. For example, what might count as an extraordinary reading made by a fifteen year old among his or her peers might not seem so coming from a fifty-year-old professor addressing a community of scholars.

A third and for us most vital aspect of transactional theory is that it gives readers and teachers permission to see value even in a reading that does not stand out from the crowd, so to speak, a reading that amounts to what

Shusterman refers to above as a "common understanding" of a literary work. Ultimately, we will argue as does Rosenblatt that this latter point represents a more significant concern for classroom teachers than the actually much less subtle matter of defining what counts as an extraordinary reading. As potentially valuable and exciting as innovative, scholarly readings can be, we also want to be able to see value in our experiences with literature that are more ephemeral, that is, tied to more immediate needs and concerns than those of the community of professional readers. We aim to help ourselves and our students see value in the process whereby we "carve and paint the very atmosphere and medium through which we look" (Thoreau) whether or not what we achieve rises to the level of scholarly interpretation.

Rosenblatt's transactional theory turns on her crucial and oft cited distinction between "efferent" and "aesthetic" reading. "Literature," she writes, "offers not merely information but experiences." (1995, p. 236; this and all citations of Rosenblatt in this chapter refer to the fifth edition of *Literature as Exploration*) Although it is possible to read *efferently*, that is, solely for the purpose of extracting information—people do it all the time—it is also possible to read for the sheer enjoyment of the experience. People do this all the time as well and when they do, Rosenblatt would say they are at least moving in the general direction of reading *aesthetically*.

This distinction between efferent and aesthetic needs to be qualified in two ways. First, the terms, as Rosenblatt uses them, describe what readers do with texts rather than the opposite. In other words, while it may seem logical to expect that a certain type of text will be read efferently, a science textbook for example, and another type, such as a novel, will be read aesthetically, there is no guarantee that this will be the case for an actual reader. If a novel were read for no other purpose than the pleasure of using the information provided in order to determine "who did what to whom," the balance between efferent and aesthetic impulses would definitely be skewed toward the former. By the same token, it should not be difficult to imagine someone with a passion for astronomy deriving a great deal of aesthetic enjoyment through reading to learn about a topic of interest in that field. This observation points to the second way we believe Rosenblatt qualifies her distinction between efferent and aesthetic reading.

Although it is possible to imagine an efferent reading completely devoid of any aesthetic feeling whatsoever, as would probably be the case if someone were reading for information in an emergency situation or studying for a test, the reverse cannot be said regarding the aesthetic side of the equation. Though it clearly precludes gathering of information for its own sake, aesthetic reading does not denote a complete absence of regard for information. The term, aesthetic, refers to reading with an eye on the way new information is contributing to an evolving experience. An aesthetic reading, according to Rosenblatt, is

> a special kind of intense and ordered experience—sensuous, intellectual, emotional—out of which social insights may arise . . . From a mixture of sensations, feelings, images, and ideas is structured the experience that constitutes the story or poem or play. (pp. 31, 33)

Or, we would add, the biography, the newspaper; in fact, any type of text at all provided the reader is able and willing to "live through what is being created during the reading." (33)

What exactly is this special kind of intense and ordered experience that becomes a creative force during a reading event? To shed some light on this question, we turn to a second, less well-known distinction Rosenblatt makes between *evocation* and *response*. We believe that the terms efferent and aesthetic make little sense apart from this additional distinction and that both are equally crucial to an adequate appreciation of Rosenblatt's transactional theory.

"Reading," argues Rosenblatt throughout her published work, "is a constructive, selective process over time in a particular context." (26) We think it is worth noting that this argument applies to reading in general, that is, whether one is using information obtained from reading for predominantly efferent or for aesthetic purposes. Here we want to focus on the latter purpose since that is what we aim to promote as teachers of literary reading. Rosenblatt uses the term, aesthetic, to describe what becomes possible when a reader, even an amateur reader, begins to understand the connection between language and experience. In other words, the language a person uses is connected with the way that person recognizes his or her own experience as potentially "intense" and "ordered."

In Chapter 2 we discussed at length our practice as amateur readers in terms of Csikszentmihalyi's concept of "flow." There we connected the basic factors leading to a "flow experience" with four aspects of our own practice as readers. Following Atwell, we called these choice, response, time, and community. We pointed out how each aspect of our reading practice is connected with a sense of agency, that is, a sense that we play an active role in deciding not only what books we read but how we choose to read those books. For us and for other amateur readers we know, sustaining a flow experience requires more than being able simply to decode written language and react to what we think the words are saying. It is only when we engage with our own and others' reactions so as to formulate insights that are connected with real concerns we have, as readers of our own lives, that we experience anything like a flow experience.

Rosenblatt writes, "the peculiar power of the literary work of art resides in its influence on an emotional level, analogous to the kind of influence exerted by people and situations in life." (181) Reading the word and the world are for her two sides of the same coin. Her use of the word, evocation, refers to the moment when a text begins to speak, that is when a reader begins to hear the voice of a speaker or narrator and envision a particular situation involving that speaker and other persons or characters. No two evocations even of the same text (and even by the same person at different times) will ever be identical and, for Rosenblatt, the subtle qualitative differences in reading experience are potentially significant. They constitute the stuff out of which meaningful responses or interpretations are made. "Every time a reader experiences a work of art, it is in a sense created anew . . . not even an author's statement of his aims can be considered definitive." (107–8) If this is true, one might ask, how do we know when it becomes appropriate to say that a reader has "experienced" a work of art? How does Rosenblatt avoid the criticism mentioned above that was leveled at early proponents of reader response theory, namely that this theory endorses an irresponsible "anything goes" approach to understanding literary reading?

The answer to this question obviously depends upon what one means by experience. In English, the word experience has two meanings and Rosenblatt's transactional theory requires us to distinguish between them. Most commonly, the word experience is understood as synonymous with merely having some degree of conscious awareness that one is alive. But we also use the word to denote events that stand out from the stream of everyday experiences. In this sense, an experience becomes memorable for being "intense" and "ordered" in ways that distinguish it within the whole of our conscious lives. When Rosenblatt talks about experiencing a work of art, she clearly has the latter definition in mind and this points to the connection she sees between literary reading and the transformation of mundane, everyday experience into an event.

"Literature," Rosenblatt writes, "is not a photographic mirroring of life but the result of a particular socially patterned personality employing particular socially fostered modes of communication." (239) In this way, she understands literary response as a process that is *both* individual *and* social. By holding the words, response (and interpretation), in reserve, so to speak, and using them only to name what happens when readers deliberately attend to their own and others' ongoing evocations of a text, Rosenblatt asserts that a reading experience will be "intense" and "ordered" only to the extent that an individual reader is motivated and capable of making it so. Equally important is her recognition that reading experience, like all experience, is embedded in social contexts that inevitably play a role in determining what it will be possible for an individual to see and understand.

Aesthetic reading does not just happen spontaneously but becomes possible only when readers attend to what they are doing thus catching themselves in the act so to speak and setting up a rhythm between their own or others' reactions and a range of possible responses. Generally speaking (but not always), adult readers are more knowledgeable and "experienced" than adolescents. They have more to draw on than their younger counterparts when it comes to envisioning possible ways of responding. Nonetheless, the underlying process described by Rosenblatt in terms of evocation and response is the same for all readers regardless of their age or degree of maturity.

A fifteen-year-old reader who accounts for nearly every detail in Robert Frost's poem, "Stopping by Woods on a Snowy Evening" by envisioning the speaking voice as a medieval knight en route to a final confrontation he knows will end in his own death has produced an "intense" and "ordered" experience that deserves to be heard even though it would not likely pass muster from a scholarly perspective. We do not construe Rosenblatt's claim that teachers of literature ought to "convey the spirit of scrupulous inquiry" (136) as a platform from which to judge and censure particular responses such as the one just mentioned. Given our take on transactional theory, we would want to help that student situate his response to Frost's poem in relation to others, that is, acknowledge that others have envisioned the poem differently, but at the same time we would want to show respect for the process that resulted in a unique and interesting experience. We are much more interested in helping students understand *how* particular responses or interpretations are generated than we are in judging the degree to which their readings approximate those proffered by literary critics.

Due to the fact that Rosenblatt's rise to fame in the 1970s is tied to the emergence of reader-response theory, it is easy to overlook the equally significant fact that her best work antedates that theory by several decades. We bring this up in order to disengage transactional theory from other approaches that fail to allow for the importance of critical thinking in literary reading and teaching. Rosenblatt does indeed assert that young readers "must be free to grapple with their own reactions" (63) but not in order to stop there but because ignoring student reactions "would destroy the very basis on which any greater literary sensitivity could be built" (225). "Literature is something [that must be] lived through, something to which the student reacts on a variety of emotional and intellectual planes. Therein lie its many educational potentialities" (228). According to Rosenblatt, a literary education should consist of experiences that have the potential to make a difference in an individual's life. It should not consist of a lot of information about literary history and criticism memorized in isolation from any connection with actual experiences with reading. Neither should it consist of pre-scripted interpretations determined in advance without regard for the context in which students currently are living their lives.

Does this mean, however, as some have claimed, that teachers are free to ignore the legacy provided by several centuries of literary history and criticism in the interest of respecting a student's "personal space"? Not necessarily! The question presupposes two extremes neither of which has any role to play in teaching informed by transactional theory. "When literary training is viewed as primarily the refinement of the student's power to enter into literary experiences and to interpret them, there will be little danger of excessive emphasis on one or another approach." (51) Aesthetic reading literally depends upon critical thinking but not to the extent that one's personal investment in an emerging experience is lost "Language," Rosenblatt is at pains to emphasize, "is socially evolved, but it is always constituted by individuals, with their particular histories. [Therefore] the uniqueness of the transaction between reader and text is not inconsistent with the fact that both elements in this relation have social origins and social effects." (25)

Reading with a "spirit of scrupulous inquiry" (136) means something different to us now than it once did when the New Criticism reigned supreme. Critical thinking can now be seen as an integral aspect of reading for purposes of aesthetic enjoyment but not in any sense that would deny the importance of the personal. Letting go of the fantasy that a literary text somehow exists in a timeless, universal realm apart from the conditions in which it is read does not mean, as the New Critics once argued, that it "ceases to exist as an object of study." (Wimsatt & Beardsley, 1948) Rosenblatt counters this claim in no uncertain terms when she writes:

> Terms such as the reader, the student, the literary work . . . are misleading, though convenient fictions. There is no such thing as a generic reader or a generic literary work; there are only the potential millions of individual readers of the potential millions of individual literary works. A novel or poem or play remains merely inkspots on paper until a reader transforms them into a set of meaningful symbols. The literary work exists in the live circuit set up between reader and text . . . a more or less organized imaginative experience. (LE 24)

Reading for aesthetic purposes places one squarely in the midst of a socially situated event. Of course, one can choose to ignore the fact but doing so severely limits the range of insight, the potential "enlargement of experience" (189) that becomes possible through questioning the social origins and effects of one's personal reactions and responses.

Rosenblatt goes so far as to say that "the ability to listen with understanding to what others have to say and to respond in relevant terms" (68) is one of the most valuable outcomes of literature instruction informed by transactional theory. A perusal of the chapters we wrote for Part 2 will produce numerous instances of this abstract idea in action. Individual differences notwithstanding each of us has found ways to experiment with student book clubs so as to foreground reading as a socially situated event that yet has profound implications on an individual level.

We take Rosenblatt's transactional theory as continuing to offer a useful point of reference, especially for teachers seeking an introduction to response theory. We embrace her claim that the ultimate value of aesthetic reading—for all readers not just literary specialists—lies in its potential to generate insights that increase self-awareness in the process of acknowledging other points of view. The implicit tension here between self-awareness and other awareness is one that Rosenblatt chooses to leave unresolved and we see that as a major strength of her theory of aesthetic reading. Hardly anything in our lives feels as personal as the connection we have with certain books yet we understand that these experiences are profoundly "social in their origins and in their effects." Ignoring this tension from either side of the equation—personal or social—leaves a person trapped in their accustomed ways of thinking about things. On the other hand, engaging with the tension between self and other without seeking to make the tension go away is connected with the power of the aesthetic to make a profound difference in an individual's life.

Rosenblatt's theory of aesthetic reading underlies our belief that student book clubs open up a space where all students not just the "best and brightest" can begin to think differently about the role of reading in their lives. Next we want to talk about two other champions of reading as an open-ended process leading to important insights that might be described as *both personal and critical*. In different ways, our reading of Bakhtin and Derrida complements our assessment of Rosenblatt's transactional theory. Each has played a major role in helping us develop an alternative to thinking in either/or terms about our engagements with literature, that is, as necessarily either private or public, personal or critical, amateur or academic. We see unresolved tensions rather than an impulse toward consensus and/or closure as one of the hallmarks of aesthetic reading.

Carnival Consciousness: Mikhail Bakhtin on Language and Learning

The trajectory of Bakhtin's life and career coincides with that of Louise Rosenblatt in several interesting ways. Both were born around the turn of the last century and reached maturity during the years following World War I. To a great extent their respective ideas about reading and literature were shaped by the intellectual and political climate of the 1930s when literary modernism had reached its zenith and the threat of totalitarian governments swept across Europe. Both Rosenblatt and Bakhtin produced what is arguably their best work during this time yet neither reached a wide audience until the 1970s when literary theorists began to entertain new possibilities for thinking about what happens during the course of a reading event. Without overstating the matter, we want to suggest that Rosenblatt and Bakhtin offer complementary points of view on literary reading as an open ended, exploratory process.

In Chapter 2 we highlighted some of the unresolved tensions that are evident in our own reading practices, in particular, the tension between our academic training as teachers and various impulses stemming from our personal lives. We alluded to the terms "hybridity" and "hybrid construction" as a way of accounting for our ability, connected with our position as teachers who are also readers, to transform an awareness of tensions—personal and academic, reader and text, self and other—into a positive force shaping the flow of a reading event. Our use of those terms is derived from our reading of Bakhtin whose work for us extends and amplifies key elements of Rosenblatt's transactional theory.

Bakhtin's theory of dialogue informs every aspect of his many and diverse writings on subjects ranging from linguistics to philosophy, literary criticism, and social history. For our purposes we have elected to approach his overall perspective on language and learning as "dialogic" through a focus on the specific and related concepts of "carnival consciousness" and "hybridity" We think this approach makes sense because it allows us to connect two of Bakhtin's most influential ideas with the immediate concerns of this book.

Like Rosenblatt, Bakhtin believed that language is social in its origins and its effects. Both saw unresolved tensions standing at the heart of human experience, especially the experience of reading, and both resisted the impulse toward closure, that is the resolution of tensions that, in their view, are better left unresolved. If anything, Bakhtin goes further than Rosenblatt toward embracing a view of language as inherently unstable and productive of new possibilities for meaning. Nonetheless, the generative tension we discuss above between phases of reading Rosenblatt calls "evocation" and "response" bears comparison with what Bakhtin has to say on the subject of "speech genres."

Bakhtin uses the term "speech genres" to name what humans do to counteract the effects of "heteroglossia," that is, the potentially infinite play of language in any particular situation. For this to make any sense, one needs to understand that, according to Bakhtin, language does not consist of knowledge or skills that an individual simply possesses. Rather, language is a kind of tool, if you will, that people learn how to use for the purpose of navigating through their relations with other people and the natural world. Life can seem so complicated at times because that tool, namely the language(s) we speak, only exists *between* people and thus is constantly evolving as individuals try to control its effects in a given situation. It is a truism that we don't really know what we think until we have to put our thoughts into words. Bakhtin takes this one step further in arguing that we need an audience; we need others to respond to the thoughts we are able to express and help us understand ourselves.

Language, Bakhtin argues, is inherently dialogic in the sense that it presupposes the co-existence of multiple selves struggling to make sense of the inevitable tensions that arise when a communal space is fashioned out of many individual points of view. What keeps this struggle from always spiraling out of control to a point where language would cease to function as a tool for communication are the many speech genres human beings have invented to interject pattern and consistency into relations that otherwise would tend towards anarchy. Put simply, we all have mastered a variety of generic and habitual ways of speaking that help us get through the day without having to constantly reinvent ourselves in every situation. Speech genres range in scope from the everyday patterns that, for instance, help two people sustain a marriage, to the far-reaching and pervasive patterns that structure the behavior of soldiers, students, and diplomats, not to mention many others including politicians.

Bakhtin would be the first to admit that speech genres are vitally important to the continued existence of human society. At the same time, he was deeply suspicious of the human tendency to gravitate towards what he called a state of monologism in which the dialogic potential of language is completely suppressed and no thought occurs outside the limits of a particular dominant discourse or speech genre. Although the threat of that possibility is ever-present and was particularly so during Bakhtin's lifetime when the Soviet Union was ravaged by Stalinism, it is difficult to imagine a totally monologic culture. Our saving grace, so to speak, is the equally ever-present tension between what Bakhtin referred to as the "centrifugal" force of heteroglossia and the "centripetal" force of various dominant speech genres. This concept of an ultimately unresolvable and thus productive tension or dialogism marks, for us, a point of contact between Bakhtin's theory of language and Rosenblatt's transactional theory, in particular, the unresolvable tension she maps out using the terms "evocation" and "response."

Among Bakhtin's most influential books is a study that traces various ways the sixteenth-century French novelist, Rabelais, has been interpreted by successive generations of readers. A brilliant blend of literary scholarship and social commentary, *Rabelais and His World*, introduces Bakhtin's notion of "carnival consciousness" and sets the stage for later work in which Bakhtin develops, among other important ideas, the one most relevant to our argument, namely, the idea that language evolves both personally and socially as a "hybrid construction." We find both ideas—carnival consciousness and hybridity—helpful in naming what happens in the context created by student book clubs. In addition, these concepts help us establish a connection between student book clubs and claims we want to make concerning the pleasure and value of amateur reading.

Bakhtin's book on Rabelais is ostensibly about carnival consciousness as manifested in the Middle Ages literally in the way people at that time in Europe celebrated specific holidays and festivals. Nonetheless, Bahktin continually points to broader implications stemming from his discussion and invites readers to take what he says about Rablelais and his world as a specific instance of a more general trend in human history. Carnival consciousness is nothing less than Bakhtin's name for the human potential to withstand and sometimes openly resist the effects of tyranny and oppression. Bakhtin situates this potential in light of his theory of language and celebrates it as the source of growth and change both in individuals and in society at large. Although our work with student book clubs in schools may seem like small potatoes in comparison with the broad canvas of Bakhtin's thought, we want to claim that the work we are describing in this book represents a tiny but not insignificant example of carnival consciousness in action.

In the first place, carnival consciousness is about laughter, about the capacity to avoid taking oneself too seriously. Bakhtin makes much of the distinction between mocking, satirical laughter that targets someone other than oneself for abuse and comic laughter that makes light of human foibles in a spirit of inclusiveness. As many of us have explained to our children, there is an important difference between laughing *at* someone and laughing *with* them. Our experience with book clubs including student book clubs is that they allow conversation to become playful and serious at the same time. We agree with Bakhtin that comic laughter opens the heart and mind to different ways of thinking within and about a given situation.

Related to this is the way carnival consciousness makes possible a special type of communication between people, one less bound by routines dictated by dominant speech genres be they institutional (e.g., school, workplace, etc.), social (e.g., cliques, jocks, nerds, etc.), or cultural (e.g., differences connected with identity markers such as race, class, and gender). A comment we hear consistently from students and teachers alike after they participate in student book clubs expresses surprise at the way they were able to connect with others who might otherwise have remained total strangers. Of course, neither Bakhtin nor we are suggesting for a moment that one can ever escape the effects of dominant discourses but it is possible to resist their force and we have found that student book clubs constitute an environment conducive to a different quality of conversation in which adolescents make small but important steps toward listening to others.

Third, we have found that participation in student book clubs provides students with opportunities to negotiate the inevitable tension between reading for their own purposes and reading for academic purposes. We have found that when confronted with the multiple points of view that come into play through student book clubs, students become more likely to question all claims to authority including that of their teachers. And this is good! At the same time, they begin to see that different points of view are not random but products of particular ways of seeing. Bakhtin (1968) offers another way of putting this when he refers to the blending of official and unofficial discourse in carnival consciousness. "[O]ne might say that carnival celebrated temporary liberation from the prevailing truth and from the established order." (34) Places where official and unofficial discourses meet create the potential for liberation "from the prevailing point of view of the world, from conventions and established truths, from cliches, from all that is hum drum and universally accepted. Carnival spirit offers the chance to have a new outlook on the world." (34)

In our view, the purpose of the literature curriculum and, for that matter, of academic discourse in general, should be to broaden and otherwise enhance not to supplant ways of seeing students have already developed during the course of their lives. Unless basic concepts such as plot and setting, as well as more complex ideas connected with terms such as character development and irony become part and parcel with how students talk about their experiences with literature, what then is the point of a literary education? We find Bakhtin's concept of "hybridity" useful in addressing all the delicate issues raised when the legitimacy of literature instruction is called into question as we think it ought to be.

When Bakhtin celebrates carnival consciousness as the blending of official and unofficial discourses he is suggesting that language evolves gradually for individuals as well as for society as a whole through countless interactions between people engaged in conversations requiring them to hear and respond to different points of view. In school contexts where literary reading is concerned this phenomenon is focused, ideally, on a blending of personal (unofficial) and academic (official) ways of responding to literature. What would make such blending a "hybrid construction," according to Bakhtin, is the potential for something new to be created whenever this phenomenon occurs. When the variety and energy of personal experience is allowed to breathe life into the abstract terminology of literary history and criticism, those academic categories, in turn, offer a tool kit for organizing and developing responses that otherwise would remain vague and idiosyncratic.

As we have been saying in different ways throughout this book, our interest in the idea of student book clubs evolved as a direct consequence of our frustration with what usually passes for "class discussion" in school contexts, including our own classrooms. What brought us together to work on this project was a common realization that each of us had been searching for ways to help our students slow down as readers and pay closer attention to what they are doing but without sacrificing the pleasure of reading. We all embraced the New Critical legacy favoring "close reading" but at the same time we wanted to disrupt authoritarian versions of that practice so as to help our students use literature not just to pass our exams but also to make a difference in their lives. In retrospect we find that Bakhtin's concepts of carnival consciousness and hybridity help us to account in theory for the positive effects of the student book clubs we described in Chapters 3 through 6.

Thus far in this chapter we have set key ideas derived from our reading of Rosenblatt and Bakhtin side by side to indicate how each has helped us to theorize our work with student book clubs. Admittedly, we have situated them using broad strokes that do no more than gesture toward the full potential of either to account for the social origins and effects of literature instruction in schools. Nonetheless, we hope we have said enough to convey some idea of the strong theoretical support that exists for our commitment to the particular classroom practices we have described. These practices are based on a vision of literary reading as a lived-through experience that is best understood as open-ended and exploratory rather than as a search for definitive answers. As teachers, we are advocates for the idea that literary reading makes a difference in our lives only to the extent that it helps us perceive differences that cut across our interactions with others and within our own individual ways of seeing and doing.

After a good deal of deliberation, we decided to extend our discussion of student book clubs in theory to include a reference to Jaques Derrida's controversial concept of "deconstruction" as we think it pertains to our work. As noted above, we do not claim to have mastered this concept any more than we can be said to have mastered those we have quoted from Rosenblatt and Bakhtin. Our modest goal is to invite others into a conversation that is ongoing from our standpoint as teachers who see themselves as learners. Having said that, we believe our take on Derrida can stand beside others that have been developed by and for teachers in ways that warrant mentioning for the most part because they complement Rosenblatt and Bakhtin in supporting our broadly populist notion of aesthetic reading.

Demystifying Deconstruction: Jaques Derrida on the Work of Reading

"Reading is not about assignable destinations, but about possibilities; reading is a destiny without a destination."

—Jaques Derrida

Derrida's current status as one of the world's foremost philosophers is largely due to the way his work has been picked up by literary theorists since the publication (in English) of his first major work, *Of Grammatology*, in 1976. Since then, it has become increasingly difficult to ignore Derrida's controversial theories about language, writing, and reading. His constantly evolving ideas have exerted an enormous influence on a broad spectrum of scholarly work, including the theory and practice of literary criticism, and this, despite his renown as a writer of prose some have described as unreadable. We would certainly agree that his writing makes great demands on us as readers. Nonetheless, it has been our experience that, with a little help (e.g., Crowley, 1989; Linn, 1996; Sumara 1996) the experience of reading Derrida is a worthwhile challenge.

Our attraction to Derrida's work and our reason for venturing to include a discussion of it in this chapter centers on his much discussed, much maligned, concept called *deconstruction*. We want to show that, as we understand it, this concept connects our various descriptions of student book clubs with a powerful theory of critical reading. In the first place, deconstruction names what we have been describing as the practice of laying bare unresolved tensions submerged in everyday discourse. Second, deconstruction supports the basic premise of this book, which is that literary reading need not and indeed should not be disconnected from the aesthetic potential of ordinary experience.

Any attempt at demystifying the concept of deconstruction must begin with a preliminary glance at Derrida's radical critique of common sense notions about how language works. Thus, our discussion opens with an—admittedly oversimplified but hopefully not simplistic—overview of Derrida's theory of language. To a greater degree even than Bakhtin's theory of language as dialogue, Derrida's work disrupts the idea that words stand opposed to reality the way a mirror represents objects in view. After developing this idea a bit, we go on to situate our take on deconstruction with respect to various ways that others have appropriated the term, especially as it pertains to literature instruction in schools. Ultimately, our goal in this section is to explain why we think deconstruction can be a useful concept for teachers attracted to the claim that student book clubs might play a role in improving the quality of literature instruction in middle and secondary schools.

Above all, Derrida calls into question the effects of what he calls "logocentrism," or the tendency to assume that things exist in a one-to-one correspondence with the words we use to name them. For example, our language points to a clear, some might argue an absolutely clear, distinction between "man" and "woman." These words, it is said, name basic categories of identity such that it is impossible not to be one or the other. Thus, many people want to believe in the existence of essential attributes associated with being masculine and opposite, but equally essential, attributes associated with being feminine. Derrida points to the fact that our language is saturated with distinctions such as this—he calls them binary oppositions—whereby people organize what they take to be reality into innumerable and inviolable identity categories: good/evil, self/other, young/old, rich/poor, white/black, able-bodied/disabled, to name a just a few in addition to those we have already fore grounded (e.g., academic/amateur, critical/personal, text/reader).

Derrida does not deny that these categories exist. Quite the opposite. He insists that it is impossible not to think in terms of binary oppositions like male/female. Moreover, he insists on recognizing that the way these oppositions are deployed produces very real material effects in the life of every individual on the planet. How a person is positioned from birth by seemingly inflexible identity categories will exert a profound effect on what that person's life will be like. Of course there is nothing controversial about this assertion. Everyone knows it is true. Derrida begins to cause trouble, however, when he observes that the binary oppositions people use to categorize the real always depend on one side being privileged over the other, such as in western cultures, those who are born male and white are certain to enjoy status and privileges that with very few exceptions are going to be unavailable to those born female and black. Even more controversial is Derrida's assertion that the categories whereby people name what is real are neither as absolute nor as inviolable as they appear to be in everyday discourse.

For Derrida, language is less like a mirror of reality and more like a tool people use to realize some possibilities while suppressing others. Returning for a moment to the binary opposition between male and female, geneticists, psychologists, and historians all tell us that the distinction is more complex than many people would like to believe. In fact, it has been demonstrated that each of us is marked by unresolved tensions between masculine and feminine qualities both mentally and physically (mind/body is yet another binary opposition that is open to question). When cross-cultural differences as well as historical considerations are thrown into the mix, it becomes abundantly clear that gender is a highly complex and malleable construction.

Of course, this argument does not make the categories "man" and "woman" disappear but it does introduce a degree of "play" into how these categories are constructed in relation to one another. And this leads to another of Derrida's insights. Far from naming preexisting realities, the words "male" and "female" are co-determinate, that is, neither term could exist without the other. Thus, the historical privileging of "maleness" in patriarchal societies depends on a commensurate definition of "femaleness" as deserving of second-class status. Both terms name sociocultural categories that have little if anything at all to do with so-called objective reality. In every respect, what we take to be real appears to us as mediated by language. To say this is not to claim that language and reality are identical, but it certainly does mean that language is always and everywhere tied to particular ways of seeing that are often used to legitimize inequitable if not oppressive relations between people.

Derrida's basic insight is that it is literally impossible to say where reality ends and language begins and to seek that point of difference is to misapprehend something fundamental about how language works. Words do not point to what is "out there." What is "out there" comes into being as a possibility realized by virtue of the fact that people are able to give it a name. Again, this is not to say that reality is merely a figment of human imagination. Rather, it is to account for the sense we all share that reality ultimately exceeds our ability to represent it in words. Derrida has named this phenomenon using the word "differ*a*nce," which, roughly speaking combines the English words, to differ and to defer. As such it points to the fact that there is no end game with respect to the task of naming ourselves as individuals or more broadly in terms of human societies.

Once one begins to question the status of fundamental categories like "man" and "woman," there is no turning back. At that point it becomes impossible to escape the consequences that follow from knowing that reality, however this is conceived, is always and everywhere mediated by language. Once acknowledged, this insight leads directly to the idea that one's current ways of seeing are always subject to deconstruction.

Our discussion has brought us to that word, deconstruction, and we turn now to ways it has been taken up by scholars who share our desire to improve literature instruction in school contexts. First of all, it needs to be said that the English translation of the French word for deconstruction suggests a tone of negativity that is absent from Derrida's use of the term. Throughout his work, deconstruction refers to neither more nor less than the practice of paying attention to language so as to generate hitherto unrecognized possibilities for meaning. By raising questions about how, for example, gender roles are being constructed in a particular situation, deconstructive practice produces at least the possibility of thinking differently about how men and women might relate to each other in that situation. Deconstruction names a practice of opening up conversations about matters normally taken for granted in our everyday interactions with each other.

Over the past two decades, deconstruction has been interpreted in two distinct ways. The first is derived from a brand of literary criticism made famous by scholars at Yale University (led by Paul de Man and J. Hillis Miller) during the 1970s and 1980s. They developed an approach to reading that enabled them to point to discontinuity in virtually any text. From this perspective, deconstruction names a practice of turning an author's language against itself, so to speak, so as to render visible unintended and/or contradictory meanings running against the grain of mainstream interpretations of well-known literary works. Although not intentionally negative or nihilistic, the Yale Critics did in fact contribute to the common perception that, by foregrounding the instability of language, deconstruction heralds the ultimate failure of language as a means of communication between people.

In the wake of the Yale Critics controversial claims, scholars working in the field of education began to add deconstruction to their repertoire of "critical lenses" for interpreting literary texts. Deborah Appleman's (2000) book, *Critical Encounters in High School English: Teaching Literary Theory to Adolescents* exemplifies this approach and Appleman does a good job of disengaging the word, deconstruction, from its potentially negative connotations. Arguing that "a literary work is usually self-contradictory" (100) in at least one respect, she vividly illustrates how performing deconstructive readings can prompt high school students to resist taking words and phrases at their face value. In doing so, she observes, young readers begin to understand why it is never safe to assume that words simply say what they mean and mean what they say.

In Appleman's hands, deconstruction is made to stand beside other types of literary criticism informed by reader-response theory, feminism, Marxism, and postmodernism. Without denying the potential value in framing deconstruction the way Appleman does as one among many critical lenses for interpreting literature, we prefer to align our own work with scholars who take a broader view of deconstruction as connected with Derrida's overall theory of language. Anna Soter's (1997) *Young Adult Literature and the New Literary Theories* offers a good example of this alternate take on the word deconstruction. At first glance and primarily because she limits her discussion of deconstruction to a single chapter in her book, Soter appears to take the same stance as

Appleman and others. A closer look at what she says, however, quickly dispels this notion.

Soter describes deconstructive reading in terms that resonate with our own view, which is to say she positions deconstruction, not as a particular critical lens, but as an inescapable effect of the way language operates in human culture.

> We are all (writers and readers) perceived as engaged in the construction of meaning, and so meaning becomes dependent on *who* is engaged in that construction and *when* and *how* that construction is being carried out. In effect, our constructions are always contextualized in terms of who we are and all the circumstances that surround us at the time of those constructions—hence the essential indeterminacy of meaning. (74)

Is Soter trying to suggest that we give up trying to communicate with each other through writing? Not at all. Far from being a source of despair over the ultimate failure of language, this "essential indeterminacy" is, for Soter, something to celebrate. If the meaning potential of a text is always in play, so to speak, then re-reading is always a possibility as is the possibility that it may be apprehended differently in different contexts of reading. We believe this insight leads to important consequences for anyone who is willing to acknowledge it.

Dennis Sumara (1996) acknowledges the essential indeterminacy of meaning and his work more than any other has helped us connect Derrida's ideas with our own. Like Soter and, of course, Rosenblatt, Sumara argues, "Meaning only occurs when a reader becomes purposefully engaged with a text." (1996, p. 32). But he goes on to align his work with Derrida in making even more explicit claims about the potential for reading to be productive of meaning. "For Derrida, the reader does not exist before the work, but is invented by the work through her or his engagement with the work." (p. 33) In other words, the work of reading evolves as a process whereby an author's words become reinscribed in a new context. Ultimately, readers must bear full responsibility for determining what a writer's words will mean at a particular place and time.

Does it follow then that reading is a completely boundless, unregulated activity, that "anything goes" as some critics have argued is the logical conclusion one must draw from Derrida's position? We think this argument fails to acknowledge Derrida's basic point that people use language not to mirror reality but as a tool for engaging with each other and the world at large. We think it is true that readers must take full responsibility for their responses, which is to say, we do not believe any reader can claim that their response simply mirrors what an author intended or what a text "really means." At the same time, we think it is crucial to add that reading is not a process of making something out of nothing. An author's words always stand as a point of reference that may not determine but will certainly limit the possibilities available to readers attempting to make something of them.

Following Derrida, Sumara puts it this way: "Literary fiction does not contain a transcendent core of meaning but rather has a repeatable singularity that depends on a structural openness to new contexts." (p. 31) As readers of *The Great Gatsby*, for instance, we always return to the same words (repeatable singularity) but they never mean quite the same thing from one reading to the next or across the experiences of more than one reader (structural openness to new contexts). Paying close attention to what one is doing as a reader of this novel makes it possible to better understand and account for one's responses but this never seems to erase completely the possibility that one's next encounter with Fitzgerald's words might produce something altogether unexpected.

Where scholars like Appleman tend to argue that a deconstructive reading exposes multiple and contradictory meanings contained in a given text, we would go further and argue that every reading event is a unique event and that similarities/differences across readings cannot be accounted for with reference to texts independently of the circumstances in which the readings take place. Derrida develops a concept he calls "dissemination" that bears comparison with Bakhtin's concept of "heteroglossia" because both advance the idea that it is impossible to suppress the play of language, that is, its capacity to mean different things in different contexts. Both Derrida and Bakhtin claim that it is literally impossible to use the same word twice and mean exactly the same thing both times. Another way of putting this would be to say that what any word means is always to a greater or lesser extent conditioned by the way it is used in particular situations.

Our understanding of deconstruction as a form of critical reading foregrounds what, by and large, other approaches to critical reading seek to overcome, namely, the inescapable play of language and the impossibility of at arriving at determinate meaning. Because we find Derrida's arguments persuasive and attractive, does it follow that we believe there is no point in drawing conclusions and trying to account for our responses as readers? Far from it. Our view is that Derrida's theory of language and reading positively demands that we never stop attempting to do this work and that as much as possible we try to read with other people whose different points of view might enhance our ability to make something useful out of our experiences with literature.

What makes an experience with literature useful as well as pleasurable? We think the answer to this question has something to do with the power of literary reading to produce surprise. Italo Calvino (1986), the great Italian novelist, once remarked, "I expect readers to find things in my books that I didn't know but I can only expect this from those who wish to read something they didn't know." What this suggests to us is the fact that reading opens up a space where no one, not even the author, can ever be sure what is going to happen next. A character in one of Calvino's (1979) novels says, "Reading is going toward something that is about to be, and no one yet knows what it will be." We read literature to find out what is going to happen next. Whether this means searching for answers about a narrative situation, that is who, what, when, and where, or stepping back to ask questions about why that situation appears to us and others as it does, reading challenges us to figure out where we think we are. Engaged with a literary text, we necessarily give ourselves over to a situation that to a greater or lesser extent remains unfamiliar territory.

Derrida argues that we only begin to read at that point where we cease to be sure that we understand where we are. Thus, deconstruction names a practice of critical reading focused on looking for trouble, that is, making a deliberate effort to question one's perceptions so as to keep open the possibility that there might be other ways of thinking about a given situation. Here again, we cite Sumara (2002) on "why reading literature in school still matters" because what he says addresses an obvious question. Why would someone choose to subject his or her reading to deconstruction?

> [W]riters provide readers with an opportunity to notice that life is not an achievement, but instead in an ongoing interpretive process . . . [W]riters write because they are interested in what the practice of writing helps them to learn . . . Literature is a product that is created by people who make it their business to interrupt the familiarity of their own perceptions and interpretations of the way the world 'really is.' (154, 155, 157).

Learning how to read is a life-long endeavor because we can never arrive at definitive answers to the questions that are most important to us and even when we think that we have achieved a degree of certainty, new questions come along to trouble our established ways of thinking. Reading literature teaches us, as Rilke (2001) noted, "to be patient toward all that is unsolved in our hearts" and "to love the questions themselves like locked rooms and like books that are written in a very foreign tongue." (p. 35).

How then, you may be asking, is all this connected with student book clubs? Our response would be to cite Derrida's argument that his brand of critical thinking called deconstruction presupposes a particular context of reading. Apart from anyone's ongoing lived-through experience with a text there would be nothing to deconstruct. Even the highly text-based work of the Yale critics mentioned above focused on deconstructing particular ways that others either had or might have read canonical literature. From our standpoint as classroom teachers of literature it becomes crucial to provide students with opportunities to engage with assigned texts so as to generate a context of reading that reflects what they are able to see and understand. Teaching students to read critically requires us to help them pay attention to what they are doing in order to identify questions that are relevant to the situation they have, in part, produced through their reading.

Student book clubs provide space for young readers to generate perceptions that can become the basis for considering other possibilities. In addition, student book clubs initiate shared reading experiences through which young readers are inevitably impressed by the fact that different people see and understand what they read differently. Often, students disrupt each other's assumptions providing fertile ground for teachers to intervene to help them see that what they are doing is synonymous with the work of reading. In the chapters they wrote for Part 2, Cheryl, Jenny, and Holly variously describe what this process looks like in their different classrooms. All three use versions of deconstructive practice to guide their students and themselves toward more complex understandings connected with their reading of literature. Each is committed to the idea of curriculum development as a work-in-progress based on a revised understanding of what it might mean to perform a critical reading in classroom contexts and beyond. In the final chapter, we offer an overview, albeit a tentative overview, of what follows from adopting such a stance toward literature instruction in schools.

Chapter **8**

Unresolved Tensions: Reconsidering Critical Reading In Classroom Contexts

In the first two parts of this book, we describe crosscurrents connecting our identities as life-long readers of literature and as classroom teachers of the language arts. Here in the third and final part, we situate ourselves as learners by trying to make explicit connections between what we do as readers/teachers and theoretical claims advanced by, among others, Rosenblatt, Bakhtin, and Derrida. In doing so we have tried to make a case for our view of what it might mean to perform critical readings in classroom contexts. Overall we would characterize our approach as founded on a narrative of humility rather than of mastery when it comes to helping our students develop an appreciation for literary reading. By that, we mean to suggest that critical reading might well be thought of as a deliberate effort to keep questions open by acknowledging differences and avoiding ultimate conclusions and final answers.

We are indebted to Louise Rosenblatt and reader-response theory in general for helping us begin to question how we had been taught to think about literary reading. Being introduced to the metaphor of literature as exploration gave us strength to resist a deeply ingrained predisposition to situate ourselves (and our students) as passive receivers of meaning that is contained like buried treasure in literary masterworks. We took to heart Rosenblatt's now famous assertion that one "cannot look at the text and predict the poem." Her notion of a persistent and ultimately unresolvable tension between what a text says and what it might mean to a particular reader at a particular time and place so powerfully summed up in terms of a back and forth motion between "evocation" and "response" changed forever how we think about readers and reading.

Reader-response theory opened our eyes to the possibility that the end point of reading does not necessarily have to be conceived in terms of definitive answers and meaning statements. Just as important in retrospect was the way Rosenblatt and others led us to think differently about the language we were using to characterize the experience of reading for our students and ourselves. Our enhanced appreciation for the complexity of language eventually made us receptive to theorists like Bakhtin and Derrida whose work added new dimensions to our own by helping us realize the good effects that follow from a persistent critique of the unresolved tensions in our lives. Among the most important of these effects has been our success in the classroom as defined by our students' increased levels of engagement with literary reading.

We teach in schools where illiteracy is less of a concern than aliteracy, that is to say, where many if not most students are headed for lives that include the ability but not the desire to write and read except for the most mundane purposes. These are students for whom traditional approaches to literature instruction have simply failed to ignite any passion for what literary reading has to offer. As we amply demonstrate in Part 2, our approach to literature instruction based on the use of student book clubs, while not a panacea, leaves no doubt that it has made a huge difference, especially for students caught in the middle, academically and socially. In their chapters, Cheryl, Jenny, and Holly repeatedly allude to students learning how to listen to each other more productively in contexts created by their student book clubs in which they have the freedom and the responsibility to think for themselves.

Admittedly, our direct experience as teachers has not been with students across the spectrum of ability, namely, those labeled "gifted" and enrolled in advanced classes or those who have reached their teenage years still struggling (or perhaps having given up the struggle) to master basic literacy skills. Implementing student book clubs with these populations of students would present a somewhat different set of challenges than those we have described in this book but we do not see this as a serious limitation of the concept. In our opinion, it is not difficult to imagine advanced students seizing the opportunities for independent thinking opened up by student book clubs. Neither is it hard to envision struggling students making great strides through the use of student book clubs to open up a safe space where they would be invited to make those crucial first steps toward engaging with literary texts. Cheryl comes closest to addressing this scenario in Chapter 4.

We do not recommend a prescriptive blueprint or recipe that eliminates choices about how to use student book clubs in particular contexts preferring instead to think of the term, student book club, as a flexible concept based primarily on a theory of reading rather than on a particular set of pedagogical strategies. And this brings us back around to our reasons for writing this book. Our various experiences with book clubs have helped us learn how to think differently about ourselves as readers and as teachers. We have described in detail how student book clubs can be used to foreground immediate reactions as the basis for developing more thoughtful, critical responses. At the same time we highlight our newfound recognition of the potential value that lies in uncritical reactions and responses. We talk about the power of re-reading practices that go without saying in our work as teachers of literature but rarely if ever are included in the curriculum manuals intended to guide our teaching. Throughout, we have tried to stay focused on connecting the concept of student book clubs with our broader concerns as readers and as teachers.

> *"The real voyage of discovery consists not in seeking new landscapes but in seeing with new eyes."*
>
> —Marcel Proust

The experience of participating in various types of book clubs with other adults compelled each of us to reevaluate our beliefs about reading as a solitary activity. At the same time we found ourselves beginning to envision a different way of thinking about the relationship between personal and academic purposes for reading. This book is one outcome of that line of thinking that has transformed and reinvigorated our individual approaches to reading and to teaching. Here in this concluding chapter, we want to share some final thoughts concerning what we have learned about ourselves as readers, why we continue to choose lives that include reading, and how we see this choice as connected with ways we approach literature instruction in our teaching, especially as this involves helping our students adopt a questioning stance as readers of literature, that is to say, we want them to be able to question both what they are reading and how they are reading.

Following Louise Rosenblatt (1938/1995) we use student book clubs as a means for placing great emphasis on seeing "literature as exploration." Our commitment to putting academic purposes for reading into perspective with respect to what we believe about life-long reading means that we have learned to let go of an image of books as mysterious icons containing hidden meanings. Gone is the image of teachers as high priests of literature whose arcane practices serve purposes remote from anything connected with actual life. Cheryl's "gradual approach" to implementing student book clubs (described in Chapter 4) as well as Jenny's approach to "building a community of readers" in her classroom (described in Chapter 5) exemplify ways to connect with students as readers to create a context within which literary terms and concepts might be introduced as subject matter. Even then, we remain committed to the idea that critical thinking has little or no meaning apart from a respect for student interests and concerns.

We have learned to embrace the idea that a book might be approached as the embodied voice of another human being like ourselves and that the meaning even of a literary classic might be variable, that is to say not timeless as if books exist as some form of fossil record of past meaning making. What makes a book "classic" in our view is its susceptibility to being read productively and thus reinterpreted over time. Our goal is to close the gap between academic and personal purposes for reading literature through acknowledging rather than erasing evidence of change and difference. Student book clubs advance an agenda whose ultimate aim is to put students in places where they like to be and also where they might begin to understand that reading can serve a purpose in their lives—as a form of exploration—above and beyond the mere enjoyment of a story line. Holly's image of "retracing the map" (in Chapter 6) perfectly expresses our goal of helping students to "see with new eyes."

When we say that reading can put students in places they like to be, we do not mean to suggest that reading transports people into a fictional, secondary or virtual world. Without disputing the fact that there is a long tradition in western culture of thinking about literature in this way or arguing that this tradition is wholly without value, we are merely stating a preference for thinking differently about the potential value in literary reading. At its best, the experience of reading literature leads one to resituate oneself in a complex world. Each chapter in Part 2 refers to students becoming so intensely engaged with reading that the experience becomes folded in with their overall life-world and the two become almost indistinguishable. Almost, but not quite.

Once again echoing Louise Rosenblatt, what we call "aesthetic reading" describes a stance in which one remains aware that the whole experience is contingent on the fact that one is reading someone else's words and making them one's own. This process requires readers not only to see the words but also to hear the words. By seeing we mean both visualizing a situation and following an idea—as in the phrase, "I see what you are saying." And both of these visual aspects of reading exist in tension with the aspect of listening. During an aesthetic reading event an author's voice coexists with one's own to produce an event that is always potentially underway, always subject to the possibility of re-reading. For us the idea of literature as exploration does not suggest trekking through a parallel universe. We prefer to think of it as an opening onto multiple and often-unexpected ways of engaging with the reality of this world, a world in which we all are trying to learn how to live.

"I expect readers to read in my books something I didn't know, but I can expect it only from those who wish to read something they didn't know."

—Italo Calvino

Ideally, one never knows exactly what is going to happen or what exactly to expect from a book, even if it's a book one has already read once or more than once. At this point in our lives what we primarily look for as readers is to engage with voices other than our own, voices that surprise, delight or perhaps disturb in ways we could not have anticipated. Of course there is no denying the fact that any voices we encounter while reading are in part our own invention but the knowledge that we are literally reading someone else's words opens our minds to hitherto unimagined possibilities. The authors we like best—and we are grateful that so many fall into that category!—are those who assist us in evoking a plausible situation at the same time as they challenge us to think about that situation from multiple points of view.

We wonder why particular characters talk and act the way they do, why an author chose certain words to evoke a particular situation, and what about ourselves becomes apparent as we try to make sense of it all. The stance we take, as readers, is open-ended, like attempting to reconstruct an interesting conversation overheard from a distance, but with an important difference. As readers, we know that we are spectators trying to remember or keep in mind a situation first imagined by someone else. Once we take the crucial step of engaging with an author's voice, however, we become participants in the creation of something new, something uniquely our own yet ultimately contingent on the existence of at least one other voice not our own. Student book clubs enhance this experience for young readers by exposing them to multiple ways that an author's words might be heard and taken into consideration. The idea of multiple possibilities for meaning becomes more tangible in settings where collaborative reading is the norm.

One of the worst effects of mainstream approaches to literature instruction in our opinion is the illusion that literary reading is supposed to produce closure, completeness, that is, the illusion of mastery over someone else's words. We find it difficult to read these days without a pen and packet of sticky notes. Marking pages by underlining, making jot notes, and pointing to bits of text with arrows and stars literally makes our copies of cherished books different from all the others providing tangible traces of experiences we may choose to revisit and maybe share with others. Frequently, we will copy passages that speak to us into small notebooks where we can ruminate further on whatever insights we have been able to generate from reading. Our goal is always to keep the experience open and active for ourselves and for our students. None of us is interested anymore in summing up what a book means or in narrowing our responses down to a fine point or points we think an author may be trying to make. Instead, we are interested in keeping our experiences with reading open and moving so that we can focus on what we are currently able to make of an author's words that may help us live more complex, interesting lives.

> *"The purpose of art is to lay bare the questions that have been hidden by the answers."*
>
> —James Baldwin

None of us would claim the authority to say exactly what James Baldwin had in mind as the first reader of his own words. We know nothing of the context that elicited them. In fact, we know very little about Baldwin himself other than that he was African American, an activist, and the author of some famous books we haven't read—yet—other than his wonderful short story called "Sonny's Blues." We're not even sure where we came across this quote but it speaks to us about the power of art to disrupt habitual ways of thinking. We have no idea whether or not Baldwin would endorse our use of his words to claim that the questions laid bare by a particular work of art are likely to be different for different readers or even for the same reader across multiple readings. Perhaps he would try to persuade us to think otherwise. Perhaps not.

Needless to say, the comment quoted above lends itself to a multiplicity of interpretations. What choice does one have other than to explain how and why it speaks to one—or not—while acknowledging that others may make something different in the context of their lived experience, something that could potentially alter one's own understanding of them? When it comes to literary reading, there is no end game in our view. It's about movement and energy and always arriving where we started and knowing the place again for the first time. Even the word, rereading, strikes us as a misnomer at least with respect to the reading of literature insofar as it implies that such reading is comprised of self-contained events that are clearly demarcated from each other and from the rest of one's lived experience.

When he was 80 years old, Goethe, a man considered by many scholars to be a literary genius of the first order, described himself as still trying to learn how to read. What he said was this: "Ordinary people don't know how much time and effort it takes to learn how to read. I've spent eighty years at it, and I still can't say that I've reached my goal." While making no claim to be geniuses, literary or otherwise, we can relate to what Goethe was talking about. Throughout our lives reading to learn has been synonymous with learning to read and our best hope is to instill this attitude in our students so that they too might embrace the idea of reading as an open-ended, exploratory process that can be used to confront whatever issues and questions are paramount in their lives.

Our concept of a student book club offers classroom teachers a way to respect the unique possibilities as well as the limitations that arise when teenagers encounter challenging literary texts for the first time. Our flexible approach constructs the student book club as a multipurpose tool teachers can use to situate first reading experiences in light of the potential value of re-reading and/or revisiting ideas generated through a first reading. In short, we draw on a revitalized version of reader-response theory to disrupt the sharp distinctions that hitherto have separated critical from personal responses, academic from non-academic reading practices, schooling from life-long reading. Our purpose, throughout, has been to share what we have learned thus far about how to use reading for a variety of purposes in one's own life in conjunction with being a teacher whose best hopes may revolve around inviting young readers to experience for themselves what it means to live a life that includes reading.

References

Applebee, A. (1996). *Curriculum as conversation: Transforming traditions of teaching and learning*. Chicago. IL: University of Chicago Press.

Applebee, A. (1999). Building a foundation for effective teaching and learning of English: A personal perspective on thirty years of research. *Research in the Teaching of English*, 33 (4), 352–366.

Appleman, D. (2000). *Critical encounters: Teaching literary theory in secondary schools*. New York: Teachers College Press.

Appleyard, J.A. (1990). *Becoming a reader: The experience of fiction from childhood to adulthood*. Cambridge, UK: Cambridge University Press.

Atwell, N. (1987) *In the Middle*. Portsmouth, NH: Heineman.

Atwell-Vasey, W. (1998). *Nourishing words: Bridging private reading and public teaching*. Albany, NY: State University of New York Press.

Bateson, M. C. (2000). *Full circles, overlapping lives*. New York: Ballantine.

Beach, R. (1993). *A teachers introduction to reader-response theories*. Urbana, IL: National Council of Teachers of English.

Bhabha, H. (1985). The third space: Interview with Homi Bhabha. (Jonathan Rutherford,Interviewer). In Jonathan Rutherford (Ed.) *Identity: Community, culture, difference* (pp. 207–221). London: Wishart.

Bakhtin. M. (1968/84). *Rabelais and his world*. Bloomington, IN: Indiana University Press.

Bakhtin, M. (1981). *The dialogic imagination*. Austin, TX: University of Texas Press.

Bakhtin, M. (1984). *Problems of Dostoyevsky's poetics*. Minneapolis, MN: University of Minnesota Press.

Bakhtin, M. (1986). *Speech genres and other late essays*. Austin, TX: University of Texas Press.

Barnes, D. & Todd, F. (1995). *Communication and learning revisited: Making meaning through talk*. Portsmouth, NH: Boynton /Cook.

Beach, R. (1993*)*. *A teacher's introduction to reader-response theories*. Urbana, IL: National Council of Teachers of English.

Beach R. & Meyers, J. (2001). *Inquiry-based English instruction: Engaging students in life and literature*. New York: Teachers College Press.

Berleant, A. (1991). *Art and engagement*. Philadelphia: Temple University Press.

Berry, W. (2000). *Life is a miracle: An essay against modern superstition*. Washington, DC: Counterpoint.

Birkirts, S. (1994). *The guttenberg elegies: The fate of reading in an electronic age*. New York: Fawcett.

Brandt, D. (1990). *Literacy as involvement: The acts of writers, readers, and texts*. Carbondale: Southern Illinois University Press.

Brooks, C. and Warren, R. (1938/1976). *Understanding poetry*, fourth edition. New York: International Thomson Publishing.

Burke, J. (2002). *Tools for thought: Helping all students read, write, speak, and think*. Portsmouth, NH: Heineman.

Burke, K. (1937). *Attitudes to history*. Berkely: University of California Press.

Calvino, I (1979). *If on a winters night a traveler*. New York: Harcourt Brace.

Calvino, I. (1986). *The uses of literature*. New York: Harcourt Brace.

Carey-Webb, A. (2001). *Literature and lives: A response-based, cultural studies approach to teaching English*. Urbana, IL: National Council of Teachers of English.

Chandler, K. (1997). The beach book club: Literacy in the "lazy days of summer." *Journal of Adolescent and Adult Literacy*, 41(2), 104–115.

Clifford, J. (1979). Transactional teaching and the literary experience. *English Journal*, 68(9), 36–39.

Clifford, J. (1990). *The experience of reading: Louise Rosenblatt and reader-response theory*. Portsmouth, NH: Boynton/Cook.

Creegan, M. (1997). Reading groups are bridging academic and popular culture. *The Chronicle of Higher Education*, Dec 19, B4–5,

Coles, R. (1989). *The call of stories: Teaching and the moral imagination*. Boston: Houghton Mifflin.

Csikszentmihalyi, M. (1990). *Flow: The psychology of optimal experience*. New York: Harper.

Csikszentmihalyi, M. & Larson, R. (1984). *Being adolescent: Conflict and growth in the teenage years*. New York: Basic Books.

Dale, G. (1999). Practical strategies: Reading and responding in authentic ways to reading—reading club groups. *Literacy Learning: Secondary Thoughts*, 7(2), i–viii.

Daniels, H. (2002). *Literature circles: Voice and choice in book clubs and reading groups*, second edition. Portland, ME: Stenhouse.

Delpit, L. (1998). The Silenced Dialogue: Power and Pedagogy in Educating Other People's Children. *Harvard Educational Review*, 58 (3): 280–298.

Derrida, J. (1976). *Of grammatology*. Tr. Gayatri Spivak. Baltimore: The Johns Hopkins University Press.

Derrida, J. (1982). *Margins of philosophy*. Tr. Alan Bass. Chicago: University of Chicago Press.

Derrida, J. (1992). *Acts of Literature*. Ed. Derrick Attridge. New York: Routledge.

Dewey, J. (1934). *Art as experience*. New York: Berkeley.

Dressman, M. (2001). Retracing Rosenblatt: A textual archaeology. *Research in the Teaching of English*, 36(1), 110–145.

Echlin, H. (2001). How Yale strangles literature. *Hudson Review*, 53, 4, 534-541.

Enciso, P. (1998). Good girls/Bad girls read together: Pre-adolescent girls' co-authorship of feminine subject positions during a shared reading event. *English Education*, 30, 1, 45–62.

Faust, M. (2000). Reconstructing familiar metaphors: John Dewey and Louise Rosenblatt on the literary work of art as experience. *Research in the Teaching of English*, 35(1), 9–34.

Finders, M. J. (1997). *Just Girls: Hidden Literacies and Life in Junior High*. New York: Teachers College Press and Urbana, IL: National Council of Teachers of English.

Fish, S. (1980). *Is there a text in this class*. Cambridge, MA: Harvard University Press.

Flecha, R. (2000). *Sharing words*: Theory and practice of dialogic learning. Lanham, MD: Rowman and Littlefield Publishers.

Flint, A. (1999). *Literature circles*. Westminster, CA: Teacher Created Materials

Freire. P. (1970). *Pedagogy of the oppressed*. New York: Herder and Herder.

Gardner, H. (1983). *Frames of Mind: The Theory of Multiple Intelligences*. New York: BasicBooks.

Gere, A. (1997). *Intimate practices: The cultural work of women's clubs, 1880–1920*. Urbana, IL: University of Illinois Press.

Goldberg, S. & Pesko, E. (2000). The teacher book club. *Educational Leadership*, 57(8), 39–41.

Graf, G. (1987). *Professing literature: An institutional history*. Chicago: University of Chicago Press.

Green, D. (2001). Opinion: Abandoning the ruins. *College English*, 63, 3, 273–286.

Gutierrez, K., Baquedano-Lopez, P. & Tejeda, C. (1999). Rethinking diversity: Hybridity and hybrid language practices in the third space. *Mind, Culture, and Activity*, 6(4), 286–303.

Hartley, J. (2001). *Reading groups: A survey conducted in association with Sarah Turvey.* Oxford, UK: Oxford University Press.

Heath, S. B. (1983). *ways with words: language, life, and work in communities and classrooms.* Cambridge: Cambridge University Press.

Hill, B.; Johnson, N. & Schick-Noe, K. (Eds.) (1995). *Literature circles and response.* Norwood, MA: Christopher Gordon.

Hunt, R. & Vipond, D. (1992). First, catch the rabbit: Methodological imperative and the dramatization of dialogic reading. In R. Beach, J. Green, M. Kamil, & T. Shanahan (Eds.). *Multidisciplinary perspectives on literaracy research* (pp. 69–89). Urbana, IL: National Council of Teachers of English.

Iser, W. (2000). *The range of interpretation.* New York: Columbia University Press.

Langer, J. (1995). *Envisioning literature: Literary understanding and literature instruction.* New York: Teachers College Press.

Laskin, D. & Hughes, H. (1995). *The reading group book.* New York: Penguin Books.

Lesser, W. (1999). *The amateur: An independent life of letters.* New York: Pantheon Books.

Lesser, W. (2002). *Nothing remains: Rereading and memory.* Boston: Houghton Mifflin.

Lewis, C. (2000). Limits of identification: The personal, pleasurable, and critical in reader response. *Journal of Literacy Research*, 32, 2, 253–266.

Kohn, A. (1999). *Punished by Rewards: The Trouble with Gold Stars, Incentive Plans, A's, Praise, and Other Bribes.* New York: Houghton Mifflin.

Kutz, Eleanor, and Hephzibah Roskelly. (1991). *An Unquiet Pedagogy.* Portsmouth: Boynton/Cook.

Long, E. (1992). Textual interpretation as collective action. In J. Boyarin (Ed.), *The ethnography of reading* (pp. 180-211). Berkeley, CA: University of California Press.

Long, E. (2003). *Book Clubs: Women and the uses of reading in everyday life.* Chicago: University of Chicago Press.

Manguel, A. (1996). *A history of reading.* New York: Penguin.

Marshall, G. (2001). *Teachers learning together: Faculty book clubs as professional development in an urban middle school.* Paper presented at the annual meeting of the American Educational Research Association, Seattle, WA.

McGinley, W., Conley, K., and White, J. (2000). Pedagogy for the few: Book club guides and the modern book industry as literature teacher. *Journal of Adolescent and Adult Literacy*, 44(3), 204–214.

Morgan, W. & Misson, R. (in press). The suspicion of pleasure and beauty: Towards a socially critical aesthetic in English teaching.

National Council of Teachers of English. (2002*). Teachers as readers: Forming book groups for professionals*. Urbana, IL: NCTE.

Noll, E. (1994). Social issues and literature circles with adolescents. *Journal of Reading*, 38(2), 88–93.

Nystrand, M. & Heck, M. J. (1993). Using small groups for response to and thinking about literature. *English Journal*, 82(1), 14–22.

O'Brien, G. (2000). *The browser's ecstasy: A meditation on reading*. Washington, DC: Counterpoint.

Pearce, L. (1997). *Feminism and the politics of reading*. London: Arnold.

Pirie, B. (1997). *Reshaping high school English*. Urbana, IL: National Council of Teachers of English.

Popham. (October 1997). What's Wrong—and What's Right—with Rubrics. *Educational Leadership* 55, 2: 72–75.

Richards, I. A. (1929). Practical criticism: A study of literary judgment. New York: Harcourt Brace Jovanovich.

Rilke, R. (2001). *Letters to a young poet*, Reissue Edition. (Tr. M.D. Herder Norton). New York: W.W. Norton & Co.

Romano, T. (1998). Relationships with literature. *English Education*, 30(1), 5–18.

Rorty, R. (1989). *Contingency, irony, solidarity*. Cambridge,UK: Cambridge University Press.

Rosenblatt, L. (1938/1995). *Literature as exploration*. New York: Modern Language Association.

Rosenblatt, L. (1978/1994). *The reader, the text, the poem*. Carbondale, IL: Southern Illinois University Press.

Rummel, M.K. & Quintero, E. (1997). *Teachers' reading/Teachers' lives*. Albany: State University of New York Press.

Scholes, R. (1998). *The rise and fall of English*. New Haven, CT: Yale University Press.

Scholes, R. (2001). *The crafty reader*. New Haven, CT: Yale University Press.

Schwartz, L. S. (1996). *Ruined by reading: A life in books*. Boston: Beacon Press.

Sell, R. (2001). *Mediating criticism: Literary education humanized*. Amsterdam: John Benjamins Publishing Company.

Shusterman, R. (2002). *Pragmatist aesthetics: Living beauty, rethinking art*, 2nd edition. Lanham, MD: Rowman & Littlefield.

Slatoff, W. (1970). *With respect to readers: Dimensions of literary response*. Ithica, NY: Cornell University Press.

Smith, F. (1997). *Reading without nonsense*, third edition. New York: Teachers College Press.

Smith, F. (2002). *Unspeakable acts, unnatural practices: Flaws and fallacies in "scientific" reading instruction.* Portsmouth, NH: Heineman.

Smith, M. (1996). Conversations about literature outside classrooms: How adults talk about books in their book clubs. *Journal of Adolescent and Adult Literacy*, 40(3), 180–186.

Smit, G. (2001). To infuse new thinking, try book discussions. *School Administrator*, 58(11), 34.

Soter, A. (1999). *Young adult literature & the new literary theories.* New York: Teachers College Press.

Sumara, D. (2002). *Why reading literature in school still matters.* Mahwah, NJ: Lawrence Erlbaum Associates.

Sumara, D. (1996). *Private readings in public: Schooling and the literary imagination.* New York: Peter Lang.

Sumara, D. (2000). Critical issues: Researching complexity. *Journal of Literacy Research*, 32 (2), 267–281.

Sumara, D. (2002). *Why reading literature in school still matters: Imagination, interpretation, insight.* Mahwah, NJ: Lawrence Earlbaum Associates.

Wiggins, G. (May 1992). Creating Tests Worth Taking. *Educational Leadership* 49, 8: 26–33.

Wimsatt, W. K. & Beardsley, M. C. (1949). The affective fallacy. In R. Stallman (Ed.). *Critiques and essays in criticism, 1920–1948* (pp. 401–411). New York: The Ronald Press.

Index